UNIVERSITY OF CALIFORNIA, LOS ANGELES   UCLA

BERKELEY • DAVIS • IRVINE • LOS ANGELES • MERCED • RIVERSIDE • SAN DIEGO • SAN FRANCISCO   SANTA BARBARA • SANTA CRUZ

OFFICE OF THE CHANCELLOR
2147 MURPHY HALL, BOX 951405
LOS ANGELES, CALIFORNIA 90095-1405

Dear New Bruin,

You are about to embark upon one of the most exciting chapters in your life. As a UCLA student, you will have access to the very best of what a university can be—a diverse community of talented people who enrich our society every day through hard work, intellectual exploration and active participation in the community. *The Other Wes Moore*, UCLA's 2012-2013 Common Book, is an early part of this great adventure.

The Common Book program and its associated events are sponsored by the Office of Residential Life and other campus partners and are designed to enhance your student experience during your first year at UCLA. In particular, the Common Book is intended to generate discussion and reflection among students, faculty and staff around local, national and global issues; it should also serve as a springboard to build student community while on campus and contribute to the larger community as a Bruin.

The Other Wes Moore was chosen because it provides a platform to discuss how decisions impact our surroundings and the opportunities available to us - but the conversations are just the beginning! Active engagement at UCLA and within the larger community will contribute to your learning and success as a UCLA student and beyond. There are several avenues for involvement and endless ways to shape your experience while at UCLA.

I encourage you to make the most of every opportunity UCLA offers as you grow into an engaged and influential global citizen.

Welcome to the Bruin family!

Sincerely,

Gene D. Block
Chancellor

Praise for *The Other Wes Moore*

"With its unique spin on the memoir genre, this engaging and insightful book ultimately asks the reader to consider the ways in which we as a nation alternately support and fail American children."

—*Library Journal*

"Two hauntingly similar boys take starkly different paths in this searing tale of the ghetto. . . . Moore writes with subtlety and insight about the plight of ghetto youth, viewing it from inside and out; he probes beneath the pathologies to reveal the pressures—poverty, a lack of prospects, the need to respond to violence with greater violence—that propelled the other Wes to his doom. The result is a moving exploration of roads not taken."

—*Publishers Weekly* (starred review)

"Riveting."

—*The Christian Science Monitor*

" 'It takes a village to raise a child,' goes the African proverb. This book is a cautionary tale of what happens when the village is ill equipped to do so."

—*Time*

"Moore etches a broader picture of the pure gamble of inner-city life."

—*Entertainment Weekly*

SPI
EGE
L&G
RAU

The Other Wes Moore

Wes Moore

SPIEGEL & GRAU TRADE PAPERBACKS • NEW YORK • 2011

The Other

Wes Moore

ONE NAME, TWO FATES

ISBN 978-0-812-98482-8
eBook ISBN 978-1-58836-969-7

Printed in the United States of America

www.spiegelandgrau.com

10 9 8 7 6 5 4 3 2 1

Book design by Caroline Cunningham

For Mama Win, Mommy, Nikki, Shani, and my wife, Dawn
—the women who helped shape my journey to manhood

Contents

Introduction   xi

PART I: FATHERS AND ANGELS

1. Is Daddy Coming with Us?   5

2. In Search of Home   26

3. Foreign Ground   46

PART II: CHOICES AND SECOND CHANCES

4. Marking Territory   69

5. Lost   85

6. Hunted   108

PART III: PATHS TAKEN AND EXPECTATIONS FULFILLED

7. The Land That God Forgot   129

8. Surrounded   146

    Epilogue   173

    Afterword   181

    A Call to Action by Tavis Smiley   185

    Resource Guide   187

    Acknowledgments   235

    A Reader's Guide   241

Introduction

This is the story of two boys living in Baltimore with similar histories and an identical name: Wes Moore. One of us is free and has experienced things that he never even knew to dream about as a kid. The other will spend every day until his death behind bars for an armed robbery that left a police officer and father of five dead. The chilling truth is that his story could have been mine. The tragedy is that my story could have been his. Our stories are obviously specific to our two lives, but I hope they will illuminate the crucial inflection points in every life, the sudden moments of decision where our paths diverge and our fates are sealed. It's unsettling to know how little separates each of us from another life altogether.

In late 2000, the *Baltimore Sun* published a short article with the headline "Local Graduate Named Rhodes Scholar." It was about me. As a senior at Johns Hopkins University, I received one of the most prestigious academic awards for students in the world. That fall I was moving to England to attend Oxford University on a full scholarship.

But that story had less of an impact on me than another series of articles in the *Sun,* about an incident that happened just months before, a precisely planned jewelry store robbery gone terribly wrong. The store's security guard—an off-duty police officer named Bruce Prothero—was shot and killed after he pursued the armed men into the store's parking lot. A massive and highly publicized manhunt for the perpetrators ensued. Twelve days later it ended when the last two suspects were apprehended in a house in Philadelphia by a daunting phalanx of police and federal agents. The articles indicated that the shooter, Richard Antonio Moore, would likely receive the death penalty. The sentence would be similarly severe for his younger brother, who was also arrested and charged. In an eerie coincidence, the younger brother's name was the same as mine.

Two years after I returned from Oxford, I was still thinking about the story. I couldn't let it go. If you'd asked me why, I couldn't have told you exactly. I was struck by the superficial similarities between us, of course: we'd grown up at the same time, on the same streets, with the same name. But so what? I didn't think of myself as a superstitious or conspiratorial person, the kind who'd obsess over a coincidence until it yielded meaning. But there were nights when I'd wake up in the small hours and find myself thinking of the other Wes Moore, conjuring his image as best I could, a man my age lying on a cot in a prison cell, burdened by regret, trying to sleep through another night surrounded by the walls he'd escape only at death. Sometimes in my imaginings, his face was mine.

There's a line at the opening of John Edgar Wideman's brilliant *Brothers and Keepers* about the day he found out his own brother was on the run from the police for an armed robbery: "The distance I'd put between my brother's world and mine suddenly collapsed . . . Wherever he was, running for his life, he carried part of me with him." But I didn't even *know* the other Wes Moore. Why did I feel this connection with him, why did I feel like he "carried part of me with him" in that prison cell? I worried that I was just being melodramatic or narcissistic. But still, I couldn't shake it. Finally, one day, I wrote him a simple letter introducing myself and explaining how I'd come to learn about his story. I struggled to explain the purpose of my letter and posed a series of naïve questions that had been running through my mind: Who are you? Do you see your brother? How do you feel about him? *How did this happen?* As soon as I mailed the letter, the crazy randomness of it all came flooding in on me. I was sure that I'd made a mistake, that I'd been self-indulgent and presumptuous and insulting, and that I'd never hear back from him.

A month later, I was surprised to find an envelope in my mailbox stamped with a postmark from the Jessup Correctional Institution in Maryland. He had written back.

"Greetings, Good Brother," the letter started out:

> I send salutations of peace and prayers and blessings and guidance to you for posing these questions, which I'm going to answer, Inshallah. With that, I will begin with the first question posed . . .

This was the start of our correspondence, which has now gone on for years. At the beginning of our exchange of letters—which was later expanded by face-to-face visits at the prison—I was surprised to find just how much we did have in common, aside from our names, and how much our narratives intersected before they fatefully diverged. Learning the details of his story helped me understand my own life and choices, and I like to think that my story helped him understand his own a little more. But the real discovery was that our two stories together helped me to untangle some of the larger story of our generation of young men, boys who came of age during a historically chaotic and violent time and emerged to succeed and fail in unprecedented ways. After a few visits, without realizing it, I started working on this project in my mind, trying to figure out what lessons our stories could offer to the next wave of young men who found themselves at the same crossroads we'd encountered and unsure which path to follow.

Perhaps the most surprising thing I discovered was that through the stories we volleyed back and forth in letters and over the metal divider of the prison's visiting room, Wes and I had indeed, as Wideman wrote, "collapsed the distance" between our worlds. We definitely have our disagreements—and Wes, it should never be forgotten, is in prison for his participation in a heinous crime. But even the worst decisions we make don't necessarily remove us from the circle of humanity. Wes's desire to participate in this book as a way to help others learn from his story and choose a different way is proof of that.

To write this book, I conducted hundreds of hours of interviews with Wes and his friends and family, as well as my friends and family. The stories you will read are rendered from my own memory and the best memories of those we grew up with, lived with, and learned from. I engaged in extensive historical research and interviewed teachers and drug dealers, police officers and lawyers, to make sure I got the facts—and the feel—right. Some names have been changed to protect people's identities and the quiet lives they now choose to lead. A few characters are composites. But all of the stories are painstakingly real.

The book is broken up into eight chapters, corresponding to eight years that had a decisive impact on our respective lives. The three parts represent the three major phases in our coming of age. Opening each of these parts is a short snippet of conversation between Wes and me in the prison's visitors' room. It was very important to me that we return again and again to that visitors' room, the in-between space where the inside and the outside meet. I don't want readers to ever forget the high stakes of these stories—and of all of our stories: that life and death, freedom and bondage, hang in the balance of every action we take.

The book also features a resource guide listing more than two hundred "Elevate Organizations" that young readers, their caregivers, and anyone who wants to help can use as a tool for creating positive change. One of the true joys of this project has been learning about and creating bonds with some of the organizations that are on the front lines of serving our nation's youth.

It is my sincere hope that this book does not come across as self-congratulatory or self-exculpatory. Most important, it is not meant in any way to provide excuses for the events of the fateful day February 7, 2000. Let me be clear. The only victims that day were Sergeant Bruce Prothero and his family. Rather, this book will use our two lives as a way of thinking about choices and accountability, not just for each of us as individuals but for all of us as a society. This book is meant to show how, for those of us who live in the most precarious places in this country, our destinies can be determined by a single stumble down the wrong path, or a tentative step down the right one.

This is our story.

PART I

Fathers and Angels

PART I

Wes stared back at me after I'd asked my question, letting a moment pass and a smirk flicker across his face before responding.

"I really haven't thought too deeply about his impact on my life because, really, he didn't have one."

Wes leaned back in his seat and threw an even stare at me.

"Come on, man," I pressed on. "You don't think about how things would have been different if he'd been there? If he cared enough to be there?"

"No, I don't." The lower half of his face was shrouded by the long beard that he'd grown, an outward sign of the Islamic faith he'd adopted in prison. His eyes danced with bemusement. He was not moved by my emotional questioning. "Listen," he went on. "Your father wasn't there because he couldn't be, my father wasn't there because he chose not to be. We're going to mourn their absence in different ways."

This was one of our first visits. I had driven a half hour from my Baltimore home into the woody hills of central Maryland to Jessup Correctional Institution to see Wes. Immediately upon entering the building, I was sternly questioned by an armed guard and searched to ensure I wasn't bringing in anything that could be passed on to

Wes. Once I was cleared, another guard escorted me to a large room that reminded me of a public school cafeteria. This was the secured area where prisoners and their visitors came together. Armed guards systematically paced around the room. Long tables with low metal dividers separating the visitors from the visited were the only furnishings. The prisoners were marched in, dressed in orange or blue jumpsuits, or gray sweat suits with "DOC" emblazoned across the chests. The uniforms reinforced the myriad other signals around us: the prisoners were owned by the state. Lucky inmates were allowed to sit across regular tables from loved ones. They could exchange an initial hug and then talk face-to-face. The rest had to talk to their families and friends through bulletproof glass using a telephone, visitor and prisoner connected by receivers they held tight to their ears.

Just as I was about to ask another question, Wes interrupted me.

"Let me ask you a question. You come here and ask me all these questions, but you haven't shared any of yourself up with me. So tell me, what impact did your father not being there have on your childhood?"

"I don't know—" I was about to say more when I realized that I didn't really have more to say.

"Do you miss him?" he asked me.

"Every day. All the time," I replied softly. I was having trouble finding my voice. It always amazed me how I could love so deeply, so intensely, someone I barely knew.

I was taught to remember, but never question. Wes was taught to forget, and never ask why. We learned our lessons well and were showing them off to a tee. We sat there, just a few feet from each other, both silent, pondering an absence.

ONE

Is Daddy Coming with Us?

1982

Nikki and I would play this game: I would sit on the living room chair while Nikki deeply inhaled and then blew directly in my face, eliciting hysterical laughs on both sides. This was our ritual. It always ended with me jabbing playfully at her face. She'd run away and bait me to give chase. Most times before today I never came close to catching her. But today, I caught her and realized, like a dog chasing a car, I had no idea what to do. So, in the spirit of three-year-old boys everywhere who've run out of better ideas, I decided to punch her. Of course my mother walked into the room right as I swung and connected.

The yell startled me, but her eyes are what I remember.

"Get up to your damn room" came my mother's command from the doorway. "I told you, don't you ever put your hands on a woman!"

I looked up, confused, as she quickly closed the distance between us.

My mother had what we called "Thomas hands," a tag derived from her maiden name: hands that hit so hard you had to be hit only once to know you never wanted to be hit again. The nickname began generations ago, but each generation took on the mantle of justifying it. Those hands were now reaching for me. Her eyes told me it was time to get moving.

I darted up the stairs, still unsure about what I'd done so terribly wrong. I headed to the bedroom I shared with my baby sister, Shani. Our room was tiny, barely big enough for my small bed and her crib. There was no place to hide. I was running in circles, frantic to find a way to conceal myself. And still trying to comprehend why I was in so much trouble. I couldn't even figure out the meaning of half the words my mother was using.

In a panic, I kicked the door shut behind me just as her voice reached the second floor. "And don't let me hear you slam that—" *Boom!* I stared for a moment at the closed door, knowing it would soon be flying open again. I sat in the middle of the room, next to my sister's empty crib, awaiting my fate.

Then, deliverance.

"Joy, you can't get on him like that." My father's baritone voice drifted up through the thin floor. "He's only three. He doesn't even understand what he did wrong. Do you really think he knows what a woman beater is?"

My father was in the living room, ten feet from where the incident began. He was a very slender six foot two with a bushy mustache and a neatly shaped afro. It wasn't his style to yell. When he heard my mother's outburst, he rose from his chair, his eyes widening in confusion. My mother slowly reeled herself in. But she wasn't completely mollified.

"Wes, he needs to learn what is acceptable and what is not!" My father agreed, but with a gentle laugh, reminded her that cursing at a young boy wasn't the most effective way of making a point. I was saved, for the moment.

My first name, Westley, is my father's. I have two middle names, a compromise between my parents. My father loved the sound and meaning of *Watende,* a Shona word that means "revenge will not be sought," a concept that aligned with his gentle spirit. My mother objected. Watende sounded too big, too complicated for such a tiny baby. It wasn't until later in life that she understood why it was so important to my father that *Watende* be a part of me. Instead, she lobbied for Omari, which means "the highest." I'm not sure what was easier or less lofty about that name, but I was well into elementary school before I became comfortable spelling either.

My parents' debate continued downstairs, but their words faded. I went to the room's only window and looked out on the world. My older sister, Nikki, and I loved to look through the window as families arrived at the swap market across the street. Our home was on a busy street that sat right on the border of Maryland and Washington, D.C., stuck confusingly between two different municipal jurisdictions, a fact that would become very significant in the near future. I pulled back the thin diaphanous curtain that covered the windows and spotted my friend Ayana outside with her mother. She was half Iranian and half Italian, with long, dark hair and warm eyes that always fascinated me. They were light green, unlike the eyes of anyone else I knew, and they twinkled as if they held stars. I wanted to tap on the window to say hello as she walked past our house to the tenement building next door. But I was afraid of making more trouble for myself, so I just smiled.

On the dresser by the window sat a framed picture of me with Nikki. I sat on her lap with my arm wrapped around her neck, a goofy smile on my face. Nikki is seven years older, so in the picture she was nine and I was barely two. Colorful beads capped the braided tips of her hair, a style she shared with my mother, and large, black-framed eyeglasses covered half of her face.

Nikki's real name was Joy, like my mom's, but everyone called her Nikki. My mother was obsessed with the poet Nikki Giovanni, in love with her unabashed feminine strength and her reconciliation of love and revolution. I spent nearly every waking moment around Nikki, and I loved her dearly. But sibling relationships are often fraught with petty tortures. I hadn't wanted to hurt her. But I had.

At the time, I couldn't understand my mother's anger. I mean this wasn't really a woman I was punching. This was Nikki. She could take it. Years would pass before I understood how that blow connected to my mom's past.

My mother came to the United States at the age of three. She was born in Lowe River in the tiny parish of Trelawny, Jamaica, hours away from the tourist traps that line the coast. Its swaths of deep brush and arable land made it great for farming but less appealing for honeymoons and hedonism. Lowe River was quiet, and remote, and it was home for my mother, her older brother Ralph, and my grandparents. My maternal great-grandfather Mas Fred, as he was known, would plant a coconut tree at his home in Mount Horeb, a neighboring area, for each of his kids and grandkids when they were born. My mom always bragged that hers was the tallest and strongest of the bunch. The land that Mas Fred and his wife, Miss Ros, tended had been cared for by our ancestors for generations. And it was home for my mom until her parents earned enough money to bring the family to the States to fulfill my grandfather's dream of a theology degree from an American university.

When my mom first landed in the Bronx, she was just a small child, but she was a survivor and learned quickly. She studied the other kids at school like an anthropologist, trying desperately to fit in. She started with the way she spoke. She diligently listened to the radio from the time she was old enough to turn it on and mimicked what she heard. She'd always pull back enough in her interactions with her classmates to give herself room to quietly observe them, so that when she got home she could practice imitating their accents, their idiosyncrasies, their style. Words like *irie* became *cool. Constable* became *policeman. Easy-nuh* became *chill out.* The melodic, swooping movement of her Jamaican patois was quickly replaced by the more stable cadences of American English. She jumped into the melting pot with both feet.

Joy Thomas entered American University in Washington, D.C., in 1968, a year when she and her adopted homeland were both experiencing volatile change—Vietnam, a series of assassinations, campus unrest, rioting that tore through the nation's cities, and an American president who no longer wanted the job. Joy herself was caught between loving the country that offered her and her family new opportunities and being frustrated with that country because it still made her feel like a second-class citizen.

At college, Joy quickly fell in with the OASATAU, the very long acronym for a very young group, the Organization of African and African-American Students at the American University. The OASATAU was rallying AU's black students into engagement with the national, international, and campus issues roiling around them. The battling organization elevated her consciousness beyond her assimilationist dreams and sparked a passion for justice and the good fight.

A charismatic AU junior named Bill was the treasurer of OASATAU, and two months after they met early in the exciting whirlwind of her freshman year, Joy was engaged to marry him. Despite the quick engagement, they waited two years to get married, by which time Joy was a junior and Bill a recent graduate looking for work. Marriage brought the sobering realities of life into focus. The truth was, they were both still trying to find their feet as adults and feeling a little in over their heads as a married couple.

As the love haze wore off, Joy began to see that the same qualities that had made Bill so attractive as a college romance—his free and rebellious spirit, his nearly paralyzing contempt for "the Man"—made him a completely unreliable husband. And she discovered that what she had foolishly thought of as his typical low-level recreational drug use was really something much worse. In a time of drug experimentation and excess, Bill was starting to look like a casualty.

As the years passed, Joy kept hoping that Bill's alcohol and drug use would fade. She was caught in a familiar trap for young women and girls—the fantasy that she alone could change her man. So she doubled down on the relationship. They had a child together. She hoped that would motivate Bill to make some changes. But his addiction just got worse, and the physical, mental, and emotional abuse he unleashed became more intense.

One night things came to a head. Bill came home and started to badger Joy about washing the dishes. His yelling threatened to wake up one-year-old Nikki, and Joy tried to shush him. He kept yelling. He moved in on her. The two of them stood face-to-face, him yelling, her pleading with him in hushed tones to lower his voice.

He grabbed her by the shoulders and threw her down. She sprawled on the floor in her white T-shirt and blue AU sweatpants, stunned but not completely surprised by his explosive reaction. He wasn't done. He grabbed her by her T-shirt and hair, and started to drag her toward the kitchen. He hit her in the chest and stomach, trying to get her to move her arms, which were now defensively covering her head. Finally, she snapped. She screamed at him without fear of waking Nikki as he dragged her across the parquet floor. She kicked and scratched at his hands.

Bill was too strong, too determined, too high. Her head slammed against the doorframe as he finally dragged her body onto the kitchen's linoleum floor. He released her hair and her now-ripped T-shirt and once again ordered her to wash the dishes. He stood over her with a contemptuous scowl on his face. It could've been that look. Or it could've been the escalating abuse and the accumulated frustration at the chaotic life he was creating for her and her daughter. But something gave Joy the strength to pull herself up from the floor. On top of the counter was a wooden block that held all of the large, sharp knives in the kitchen. She pulled the biggest knife from its sheath and pointed the blade at his throat. Her voice was collected as she made her promise: "If you try that shit again, I will kill you."

Bill seemed to suddenly regain his sobriety. He backed out of the kitchen slowly, not taking his eyes from his wife's tear-drenched face. Her unrelenting stare. They didn't speak for the rest of the night. One month later, Joy and Nikki were packed up. Together, they left Bill for good.

My mom vowed to never let another man put his hands on her. She wouldn't tolerate it in others either.

My parents finished their conversation, and it was obvious that one of them was heading up to speak to me. I turned from the window and stood in the middle of the room, mentally running through my non-existent options for escape.

Soon I could tell by the sound of the steps it was my father. His walk was slower, heavier, more deliberate. My mother tended to move up the stairs in a sprint. He lightly knocked on the door and slowly turned the knob. The door opened slightly, and he peeked in. His easy half smile, almost a look of innocent curiosity, assured me that, at least for now, the beating would wait.

"Hey, Main Man, do you mind if I come in?" I'm told that he had many terms of endearment for me, but Main Man is the one I remember. I didn't even look up but nodded slowly. He had to duck to clear the low doorway. He picked me up and, as he sat on the bed, placed me on his lap. As I sat there, all of my anxiety released. I could not have felt safer, more secure. He began to explain what I did wrong and why my mother was so angry. "Main Man, you just can't hit people, and particularly women. You must defend them, not fight them. Do you understand?"

I nodded, then asked, "Is Mommy mad at me?"

"No, Mommy loves you, like I love you, she just wants you to do the right thing."

My father and I sat talking for another five minutes before he led me downstairs to apologize to my sister, and my mother. With each tiny step I took with him, my whole hand wrapped tighter around his middle finger. I tried to copy his walk, his expressions. I was his main man. He was my protector.

That is one of only two memories I have of my father.

The other was when I watched him die.

My dad was his parents' only son. Tall but not physically imposing, he dreamed of being on television—having a voice that made an impact. Armed with an insatiable desire to succeed—and aided by his natural gifts, which included a deeply resonant voice—he made his dream come true soon after finishing up at Bard College in 1971.

As a young reporter, he went to many corners of the country, following a story or, in many cases, following a job. After stints in North Carolina, New York, Florida, Virginia, California, and a handful of other states, he returned home to southern Maryland and started work at a job that would change his life. He finally had the chance to host his own public affairs show. And he'd hired a new writing assistant. Her name was Joy.

Their working relationship evolved quickly into courtship, then love. She appreciated this up-and-coming reporter and the professional partnership they shared. Wes was calm, reassuring, hardworking, and sober. In other words, the antithesis of Bill. Wes was intensely attracted to this short woman with a broad smile who mixed a steel backbone with Caribbean charm. And he loved Nikki. Despite her not being his own child, he forged a sincere friendship and, eventually, an unbreakable bond with Nikki. It all became official when my mother and father married in a small ceremony in Washington, D.C. I entered the world two years later.

On April 15, 1982, my father ended his radio news broadcast on WMAL, a stalwart in the Washington, D.C., market, with his traditional sign-off—"This is Wes Moore, thanks again, and we'll talk next time"—as the on-air light faded to black. His smile was hiding the fact that for the past twelve hours he'd been feeling ill. His every breath was a struggle.

He came home to the smell of his favorite meal, smothered lamb chops. It was almost midnight and we kids were already in bed, but my parents stayed up, sat together, and ate. That night he couldn't get to sleep. He tried taking Tylenol, hoping it would help his severe sore throat and fever, but the pill lodged in his throat, refusing to dissolve. At 7:00 A.M., he woke my mother to tell her he thought he should go to the hospital. He threw on a tattered blue flannel shirt and a pair of worn blue jeans. He got in his red Volkswagen Rabbit and drove himself to the hospital. After my mother took Nikki to school and dropped Shani and me off with the babysitter, she rushed to meet my father. In the emergency room, she was shocked by the disoriented man before her. My father could not keep his eyes open. His head flopped from side to side. The doctors thought the cause of his discomfort was a sore throat and blamed his lack of neck control on a lack of sleep. To reduce the pain, they anesthetized his throat. In retrospect, that was the worst thing they could have done. He could no longer feel it closing.

The doctors didn't know what to make of his symptoms. They questioned my mother about my father's medical history, then shifted to questions about his mental state. "Does he have a habit of exaggerating?" "Is there anything going on in his life that would force him to make up symptoms?"

At 4:40 P.M., my father was released from the hospital and told to get some rest at home.

By six that evening, my mother was in the kitchen with Nikki, holding Shani as she cooked potato pancakes for our dinner. I sat at the dining room table adding colors to the black-and-white clown in my coloring book. I was months away from my fourth birthday. I heard my father coming down the stairs. His steps were slower than usual. I got up from the chair so I could be picked up as soon as he reached the first floor. Then I heard a crash.

His body was sprawled and writhing at the foot of the stairs. Hardly any sounds came from his mouth. I heard another crash, this one from the kitchen. The clatter momentarily stole my attention from my father. My mother heard his collapse and, in her rush to see what had happened, dropped the sizzling cast-iron skillet and potato pancakes on the floor. I looked back up to my father and saw him gasping for air, holding his throat. His normally strong features sagged in exhaustion, as if he were in the final hours of a battle he had been fighting for years. I stared at him, looking but doing nothing.

Mommy pushed past me and told Nikki to call 911. Nikki rushed to the phone and began speaking with the emergency personnel on the other end. I could hear her repeating again and again: "I don't know what county we're in." Minutes passed. Shani was crying hysterically. My mother attended to my father, improvising her own version of CPR while also minding Shani. My baby sister's screams only seemed to get louder. And I just stood there, staring.

Finally my mother told me to go outside with Nikki and guide the ambulance crew in. My older sister took my hand and led me out to wait. Minutes later, police and ambulance crews arrived. Nikki ordered me to stay outside while she led them into our home.

At this point my memories get less distinct. It was like standing in a field when a powerful gust of wind suddenly blows: everything around you vanishes, all you hear is the wind filling your ears, all you feel is the wind on your skin. Your eyes tear, and sight blurs. Your mind all but empties.

I stayed outside with the collection of neighbors who had come to see what was going on. Through my uncertain eyes I saw my friend Ayana holding her mother's hand. When Ayana caught my eye, I could see she was trying to force a smile, but all she got out was a look of uneasy confusion, which I mirrored back to her.

The ambulance crew loaded my father onto the gurney and raced back out. By this point dozens of people lined the street. They watched as he was placed in the back of the ambulance. The doors slammed shut behind him. The loud sirens and flashing lights broke the silence of the neighborhood. Mommy quickly loaded us into the car and followed the ambulance to the hospital. The car was full of sound—Shani crying and Nikki making goo-goo noises to try to calm her down, and the roar of the ambulance in front of us—but it felt as silent as a tomb. No talking. No questions. Just the white noise of the ambulance, one sister crying, and the other struggling to comfort her without words.

The hospital was only five minutes from where we lived, but it seemed like a long ride. We rushed out of the car and ran inside. They were already working on my father, so we were sent to the waiting area. Shani had quieted down and was playing with her shoestrings, while Nikki put me on her lap. My paternal grandfather and my aunts Dawn, Tawana, and Evelyn had all arrived to join our vigil.

Eventually an ER doctor walked into the waiting room. He asked to see my mother alone. "He's dead, isn't he?" my mother said before he could begin speaking. "I am sorry. By the time he got here, he was gone," the doctor said. "We tried, we tried hard. I am so sorry."

Then my mother passed out.

My father was dead five hours after having been released from the hospital with the simple instruction to "get some sleep." The same hospital was now preparing to send his body to the morgue. My father had entered the hospital seeking help. But his face was unshaven, his clothes disheveled, his name unfamiliar, his address not in an affluent area. The hospital looked at him askance, insulted him with ridiculous questions, and basically told him to fend for himself. Now, my mother had to plan his funeral.

He died on a Friday night. We were told at first that the hospital wouldn't be able to determine the cause of death until Monday, when they would perform the autopsy. But my father's radio station wanted to issue a news release about his death, so it leaned on the morgue to perform the autopsy sooner. The morgue acquiesced, and by Saturday afternoon we found out that he had died from acute epiglottitis, a rare but treatable virus that causes the epiglottis to swell and cover the air passages to the lungs. Untreated because of the earlier misdiagnosis, my father's body suffocated itself.

Nikki took his death worse than the rest of us. Not just because she was the only one old enough to really understand what was going on but because her biological father, Bill, changed abruptly after my father died. While my dad was alive, Bill supported Nikki financially and took the time to see her. After my father died, Bill no longer called, wrote, or bothered to check up on her. My father's love of Nikki had forced Bill to step up to his parenting responsibilities—it was almost as if Bill cared more because another man did. With my father no longer in the picture, the pressure was off. It was as if my sister lost two fathers that day.

While I knew something bad had happened, I still wasn't sure what it meant. All weekend, people came in waves to our home. The phone rang nonstop. I saw the hurt on people's faces but didn't fully understand it. I was still in the wind tunnel. I heard that my father had "passed on" but had no idea where he'd gone. At the funeral, my uncle Vin escorted us to the mahogany casket in the front of the church to have our final viewing of the body. The celebration of my father's life took place at the Fourteenth Street Baptist Church, the same church my parents had been married in six years earlier. We stood in front of my father's body for the final time. He lay in the casket with his eyes closed. It was the first time I had seen him in days. He looked more serene than he appeared at the bottom of the stairs. He looked at peace. I was holding my uncle Vin's hand when I looked into the casket and asked my father, "Daddy, are you going to come with us?"

"Wes, get up here and get your backpack together. You're going over to your grandmother's house." Mary Moore's raspy voice echoed through the house. Wes was in the living room watching television with the volume turned almost all the way up. *Speed Racer* was almost over. Packing his backpack could wait.

"You hear me talking to you?"

Wes reluctantly got up from the red plaid couch and turned off the television, but the truth was that he liked going over to his grandmother's house. He had never met his father, at least not that he remembered. But his father's mother spoiled him. She also had a rabbit living under the kitchen sink that he always played with when he visited.

He climbed the stairs and caught the scent of his mother's perfume before he even hit her doorway. He saw her sitting on the bed with her back to him. She was wearing the white dress he liked. Clearly, she was going out tonight.

Wes asked her what he should bring to his grandmother's house, but he was losing the battle with the radio, which was blasting George Benson's "Turn Your Love Around." He reached over and turned the volume down.

"Ma, what do I need to bring?"

When she saw Wes standing there, one hand flew to her face to wipe her eyes. The other slid a sheet of paper under her leg. Something was wrong.

"Ma, you all right?"

"Yes, Wes," Mary automatically responded. "Just bring some stuff to play with for tonight. Hurry up, go pack your stuff."

He wanted to ask what was wrong but decided against pressing his mother. He slowly turned around and headed toward his bedroom to pack.

The letter Mary was hiding explained that the federal budget for Basic Educational Opportunity Grants—or Pell Grants—was being slashed, and her grant was being terminated. Pells—need-based financial awards for college—were part of a larger federal budget cutback in 1982 (during his eight years in office, Ronald Reagan reduced the education budget by half). Mary realized the letter effectively closed the door on her college aspirations. She had already completed sixteen hours of college credits and would get no closer toward graduation.

Mary was the first in her family to even begin college. After graduating from high school, she enrolled in the Community College of Baltimore. When she completed her associate's degree, she decided to pursue her and her parents' longtime dream of completing her bachelor's.

Johns Hopkins University was only five miles from where Mary grew up, but it might as well have been a world away. To many in Baltimore, Johns Hopkins was the beautiful campus you could walk past but not through. It played the same role that Columbia University did for the Harlem residents who surrounded it, or the University of Chicago did for the Southside. It was a school largely for people from out of town, preppies who observed the surrounding neighborhood with a voyeuristic curiosity when they weren't hatching myths about it to scare freshmen. This city wasn't their home. But after completing her community college requirements, Mary attempted the short but improbable journey from the neighborhood to the campus. Her heart jumped when she received her acceptance letter. It was a golden ticket to another world—but also to the dizzying idea that the life she wanted, that she dreamed about, might actually happen for her.

She worked at Bayview Medical Center as a unit secretary in order to supplement the grant that was helping her pay for school. The $6.50 an hour she was making at Bayview was enough to keep the balance of her tuition paid, the lights on, and the kids fed, as long as her Pell Grant was in place. But with that grant now eliminated, it wouldn't be enough. The next day she called Johns Hopkins and let them know she was dropping out. That part-time job at Bayview would become permanent.

Wes got himself ready and went to check on his mother again. He felt he had to take care of her: his father had been a ghost since his birth. His older half brother, Tony, spent most of his time with his maternal grandparents or with his father in the Murphy Homes Projects in West Baltimore. Wes was the man of the house.

As Mary wiped her still-damp face, she told herself she was down but not out. She just had to quickly recalibrate her ambitions. She still had big dreams—maybe she could become an entrepreneur, open a beauty salon or her own fashion company. Growing up, she'd worked at a grocery store in West Baltimore owned by an older black couple, Herb and Puddin Johnson. She remembered looking up to them and wanting to own something the way they did. The Johnsons had achieved a level of independence that others in the neighborhood didn't know existed, let alone understood how to obtain. And their example had long driven her. But she couldn't deny it: without schooling she was worried.

She gazed out the window, down the same streets she'd been staring out at her whole life. The same streets she'd walked down when she began her first days at Carver High School. The same streets that had cared for her family, taught her family, looked out for her family for so many years. She wondered how long she would have to call these streets home.

This section of Baltimore had never fully recovered from the riots of the 1960s. After the death of Dr. Martin Luther King, Jr., Baltimore burned. No street saw more destruction than Pennsylvania Avenue. Mary could remember the days after the assassination when her parents forbade her and her seven siblings from leaving the house because just outside their windows a war was unfolding. The bitter riots were sparked by King's assassination, but the fuels that kept them burning were the preexisting conditions: illegal but strictly enforced racial segregation, economic contraction, and an unresponsive political system. Looters ran free as the city exploded with anger. White neighborhoods in Baltimore blockaded their streets, attempting to confine the damage of the Riots to its poorer, darker jurisdictions. National Guard troops patrolled the communities, but their presence created more resentment, not to mention fresh targets for rock-toting kids. Soon it became clear that the Riots were about more than the tragic death of Dr. King. They were about anger and hurt so extreme that rational thought was thrown out the window—these were people so deranged by frustration that they were burning down their own neighborhood. The Riots in Baltimore, particularly West Baltimore, got so bad that "Little" Melvin Williams, a legendary drug dealer and one of the most powerful men in the city at the time, was recruited by the mayor to help quell the violence. Tellingly, his influence had considerably more effect than the efforts of any politician or soldier.

By the end of the Riots, Baltimore stood eerily quiet. Almost $14 million in damage was recorded, and nearly five thousand men, women, and children were arrested, injured, or dead.

Mary was only a kid, but she made a pact with herself at that moment: she would get her education and leave the neighborhood no matter what it took.

Wes watched his mother as she moved from the window to her closet to look for a pair of shoes to wear with her white dress. She yanked the already stretched telephone cord a few feet farther so she could keep talking while digging through her closet. Mary was planning on doing what she always did to celebrate, commiserate, blow off steam, or just kill boredom. She and a couple of her friends would head out to Thirty-second Street Plaza, a popular nightclub where Mary knew the owner. She was only twenty-seven years old, and despite having two sons, Tony, who was eleven, and Wes, she was still young enough to enjoy partying, dancing, and being noticed by men—and noticing them back—much to the chagrin of her family and friends who ended up watching the boys so many nights. She noticed Wes walk back in her room. She sighed and told her sister she would call her back.

"Wes, didn't I tell you to go get ready?"

Wes stood undeterred and again asked her what was wrong. Being the man of the house, he wanted answers, and he wasn't leaving until he got them.

"Mommy got some bad news about school, and I want to go see some friends and talk about it."

Wes gave her an unsatisfied look, as if he knew that the story didn't end there. Finally, she sat him down at the edge of the bed and shared with him, in language he could understand, why school was so important. He listened intently as she explained to him the significance of being the first one in the family to go to college. She told him how much it meant to her parents that she finish. Then she explained why she had to quit.

Mary and her family had spent the years after the Riots in a house on McCulloh Street, one of the central arteries in West Baltimore. The home was a large, three-story, five-bedroom row house with a jagged gray brick façade. It sat on a relatively quiet block lined with similarly well-appointed houses, each by trees and grass. But, like so much in Baltimore, even this beautiful house was bloodstained.

After the Riots, Kenneth and Alma, Mary's parents, decided they wanted to move to a larger home with their ever-expanding family—they'd had eight children in eleven years. One night Alma said to Kenneth, "Did you hear about what happened on McCulloh Street?" He asked her to explain.

"A man killed his wife in their home. Chopped her up. She was there for a few days, and when the cops came looking for him, he decided to try to hide in the chimney. That's where they found him." Kenneth got the point. "I wonder if they are renting it out now." After a bit of inquiry, the landlord placed the home on the rental market with a severe discount to account for the sensational circumstances of the prior tenant's eviction. Kenneth and Alma proudly moved their family into their new home.

After their move, Alma's kidneys failed, and she began dialysis treatments three days a week. The painful and tiring treatments took their toll on her physically and emotionally. She maintained a cheery outlook, her hair pulled back into a bun that revealed her smooth, dark skin and bright smile. She was always a small woman, but her dialysis was forcing her to lose weight fast, and soon her short, gaunt frame was an almost comical mismatch with her husband's bulk.

When Mary told her mother that she was pregnant, at age sixteen, Alma said, "I don't care! You are going to finish school and go to college." Alma had never been to college, the great regret of her life, and like Mary, she became a mother well before she entered her twenties. As tears rolled down Mary's face, her mother told her she would be there to support her no matter what happened. Always the optimist, Alma kissed her daughter's forehead and gave her a reassuring smile.

One morning soon after, Alma got news: it looked like they had found the matching kidney she had been waiting for, praying for. Kenneth was elated. Alma was his heart. He needed her. But Alma seemed disturbed.

Alma called her mother before she went to the hospital and for the first time opened up: "I don't trust them, Mommy. They have never really given very good treatment, so I just don't feel like I will get it now." Her mother told her not to worry and launched into a diatribe about the medical technologies of the seventies until Alma interrupted her. "Mommy, I need to know that if something happens to me you will take care of my babies. I really need to know that." Without hesitation, her mother replied, "You know I will, baby."

Alma went to the hospital for the transplant, and the family did its best to maintain their routines. Mary longed for her mom's return. Learning the basics of child rearing is difficult at any time. When you are only three years past the start of puberty, the challenge is exceptionally daunting. Tony cried too much. He required so much attention. He was awake when she was trying to sleep, and he slept when she was awake. She could no longer see her friends, and her father wasn't much help. The baby's father was a neighborhood boy who had no interest in helping out with his son. Mary needed her mom back.

Three days later, Kenneth received the news that Alma's body had rejected the new kidney and she had died earlier that morning. Kenneth had to tell his children what had happened. But how do you share something with kids that you have not fully absorbed yourself yet? Kenneth, usually a gregarious and fun-loving person, also fought the demons of alcoholism. He would spend Thursday through Sunday getting drunk. Then he would spend the rest of the week recovering from a monster hangover, waiting for Thursday to arrive again. He was a "weekend alcoholic"—in his case, a long-weekend alcoholic—who battled over which version of himself he preferred, the drunk one or the sober one. He drank especially heavily when he needed drunk Kenneth to engage in conversations that sober Kenneth wouldn't dare.

He took one final swig of rum before calling the kids together.

"Sorry, guys, Mom's dead," he finally blurted out, blunt to the point of absurdity.

The silence that sat over the room wasn't broken until Mary ran out with Tony, tears streaming down her face. Weezy went over to hug their father, and the rest of the children simply sat in their places, still not sure if they fully understood what they had just heard, and not knowing how to react.

The morning of the funeral, Kenneth did an admirable job of trying to comb the girls' hair. He made sure all of the kids were dressed and ready to go on time, and he cooked breakfast, all jobs normally reserved for Alma. A few pieces of burnt toast later, the family was ready to pay their final respects.

Kenneth held everything together until he saw the casket at the altar. It was the first time he had seen his wife's body since he viewed her at the morgue. Something had changed, but not what he had expected. Now she looked more like his Alma. The makeup made her cheeks rosier, her skin more even, more alive. It looked almost as if she was flashing her trademark smile as she lay in the brilliantly polished wooden casket.

When he saw his partner of sixteen years stretched out in the coffin, Kenneth's eyes welled up. All of his strength evaporated. The weight that sat on his shoulders—the burden of losing his partner and raising this family without her—became unbearable. He wept, choking for air. He reached into the casket and grabbed her shoulders. He yanked Alma up and, supporting her head with one arm, tried to pull her body out of the casket. Some of the other mourners ran over to him, trying to loosen his grip from his wife's lifeless body. After a struggle, Kenneth was pulled from his wife's small frame and she was laid back down in her casket. He screamed as he was escorted out of the church. The congregation began to sing "Blessed Assurance."

Alma's parents soon moved into the home Alma and Kenneth shared, and they didn't leave until the last child was out of the house.

Mary was the first of the kids to leave home. Education was her escape in more ways than one.

After listening to his mother describe her letter, Wes quickly volunteered to get a job and help out. Mary laughed. "You can work later and make money. Right now I just need you to go get your bag so I can drop you off." Wes, finally satisfied, moved from his mother's bed so he could put the last of his toys in his backpack. Mary watched as he walked out of her room. Tall for his age—he was over four feet tall at six years old—and muscularly defined, he looked amazingly like his father. They were the same shade of dark brown and even wore the same short, even haircut. Like his father's, Wes's grin stretched across his entire face and had a way of putting everyone at ease. Where they differed was in personality. Wes carried himself with a reserved, quiet dignity, while his father was always loud and rude. At least he was like that when he was drinking, which seemed to be all the time.

Mary met Bernard, Wes's father, at her job after he showed up to visit one of her co-workers at Bayview. Bernard was struck by Mary's figure. She had that new-mother thickness and still-young-enough-to-flaunt-it confidence. Her smoky voice and welcoming smile all enticed Bernard. Within minutes of meeting her, he asked if she would see him again. She agreed.

It turned out that for most of their lives they'd lived only a few blocks apart. Bernard's parents lived on McMechen Street, which ran adjacent to McCulloh. A few months later Mary was pregnant with her second child. In 1975, Wes came into the world.

But the relationship between Mary and Bernard didn't even make it to their child's birth. Since leaving high school years prior, Bernard hadn't found a steady job. He spent most of his time searching for himself at the bottoms of liquor bottles. Mary was left with two alcoholic, abusive men who shared the DNA of her two children but no husband or dad for her boys.

Once, Bernard tried to be involved in his child's life. About eight months after Wes's birth, Mary was awakened by a loud banging on the front door of the home she shared with her sister on Pennsylvania Avenue.

"Mary, what the hell is going on?" her sister asked.

"It's Bernard's crazy ass out there. I ain't going out to talk to him. He's drunk and crazy."

Bernard continued to bang and scream. He stood on the other side of the door in faded jeans and a plain white T-shirt, his beard scruffy and his eyes bloodshot. He was slurring out demands to see his son. Mary simply sat on her bed, peeking through the blinds at the father of her younger child. All the noise woke Tony up, but when he arrived at Mary's bedroom door asking what was going on, she snapped her fingers and hushed him, telling him to go back to bed. Wes, not even a year old yet, slept on peacefully. Bernard kept up his racket for another twenty minutes, while Mary just peered out at him, disgusted. Finally, admitting defeat, he stumbled back home. That was the last time he tried to see his son.

Wes waited downstairs for his mother to take him to his grandmother's house. It was already late, almost six in the evening, so he wondered how long he would have to stay there. Mamie, Wes's grandmother, liked Mary, but she loved her grandson. Wes always felt true love when he went to her house. Despite the fact that her son had nothing to do with Wes, Mamie didn't want Wes punished for the circumstances through which he was brought into the world.

Wes sat in the front seat of the car for the short drive to Mamie's. Mary ran down the rules of the house, as she did every time Wes visited. No running indoors, no talking back, don't eat too much. Wes nodded at each commandment.

Minutes later, they arrived at McMechen Street. Wes ran up the three white marble stairs that led to the front door. He got on his toes and reached up to push the doorbell. Mamie's scintillating eyes met Wes's as she opened the door and her arms for a big hug. Wes loved the house. It was large, three stories, which gave him plenty of things to get into and out of. He sprinted inside the house and made a beeline for the kitchen. The smell of fried chicken cooking and the excitement of playing with the pet rabbit under the sink increased his pace.

He was running through the living room when he saw someone he had never seen before. A man sat on the couch leaning precariously to the side, his right elbow supporting his body and his head nearly flat against his shoulder. The strong smell of whiskey wafted from his clothes and his pores. Wes and the man returned each other's quizzical looks.

Mary entered the room and stopped in her tracks. She would have recognized that "hangover lean" anywhere. The man looked through his partially opened eyes and saw Mary.

A wide smile appeared on his face. "Hey, Mary. Damn, you look good," he loudly announced.

"Hey," she responded, her voice as emotionless as she could make it.

Wes looked at his mother, hoping she would explain who this man was. He moved closer to his mother's hip. Not only did he feel safer there than in the middle of the room but also because the smell coming off the man was beginning to bother him. The man on the couch looked up at Mary and asked, "Who's this?" Mary smirked and rolled her eyes. She could not believe his audacity.

Wes didn't understand why, but he felt a tension in the room. Mary looked down at her son and uttered the words she had never said before and never thought she would have to say.

"Wes, meet your father."

TWO

In Search of Home

The phone was up to its eighth ring. It was nine in the morning, and Wes hadn't seen nine in the morning since his summer break started. He climbed out of bed slowly, irritable, his eyes still half-masted when he picked up the phone in his family's narrow hallway.

"Hello?"

"Where's Mom at?" Tony asked.

"Probably at work already. Try her there." Their mom was usually out of the house by 8:30 and didn't come back until well into the evening. Wes, now eight years old, was free from any adult supervision till then. His brother, six years older, was the closest thing Wes had to a caretaker during the daylight hours and was fiercely protective of the little brother who idolized him. But lately even Tony hadn't been around much. Tony was spending most of his time in the Murphy Homes Projects, where his father lived.

The Murphy Homes were built in 1962 and named after George Murphy, a legend in Baltimore for his work as a groundbreaking educator, but just as often they went by a self-explanatory nickname, Murder Homes. The seventeen-story monoliths were among the most dangerous projects in all of Baltimore. The walls and floors were coated with filth and graffiti. Flickering fluorescent tubes (the ones that weren't completely broken) dimly lit the cinder-block hallways. The constantly broken-down elevators forced residents to climb claustrophobic, urine-scented stairways. And the drug game was everywhere, with a gun handle protruding from the top of every tenth teenager's waistline. People who lived in Murphy Homes felt like prisoners, kept in check by roving bands of gun-strapped kids and a nightmare army of drug fiends. This was where Tony chose to spend his days.

The conversation between brothers quickly turned to school. Tony knew Wes had just finished elementary school and asked him what he was doing to get ready for the start of middle school at Chinquapin, pronounced "Chicken Pen" by all of its students. Chinquapin Middle was 99 percent black. Close to 70 percent of the kids were on the school lunch program.

Wes mumbled the verbal equivalent of a shrug. Tony was enraged. "Yo, you need to take this shit seriously, man. Acting stupid ain't cool!"

Wes sighed into the phone. He had heard it before. He loved his brother but had learned to ignore his occasional "do as I say, not as I do" tirades. Tony, by contrast, was desperately trying to give his little brother information he thought he needed, the kind of information that Tony never got. Tony felt his brother's life could be saved, even if he felt his own had already, at age fourteen, passed the point of no return.

To Wes, Tony was a "certified gangsta." Tony had started dealing drugs in those shadowy hallways of Murphy Homes before he was ten. By the time he was fourteen, Tony had built a fierce reputation in the neighborhood. Despite his skinny frame and baby face, his eyes were lifeless and hooded, without a hint of spark or optimism.

Tony's dead-eyed ruthlessness inspired fear. He spent much of his time in West Baltimore but had decided to try to open up a drug sales operation in East Baltimore as well. Baltimore is a territorial and tribal city. Once the boys in East Baltimore heard that a West Baltimore guy was attempting to take over their corners, tempers flared.

Tony ended up in a shoot-out with a few of the corner boys. Ten minutes later, it was Tony's corner. But no matter how tough he was, or how many corners he controlled, what Tony really wanted was to go back in time, to before he'd gotten himself so deep in the game, and do it all over. He wanted to be like Wes.

There's a term in the hood for a face like Tony's, that cold, frozen stare. The *ice grille*. It's a great phrase. A look of blank hostility that masks two intense feelings—the fire evoked by *grille* (which is also slang for *face*), and the cold of the ice. But the tough façade is just a way to hide a deeper pain or depression that kids don't know how to deal with. A bottomless chasm of insecurity and self-doubt that gnaws at them. Young boys are more likely to believe in themselves if they know that there's someone, somewhere, who shares that belief. To carry the burden of belief alone is too much for most young shoulders. Tony had been overwhelmed by that load years ago. Now he wanted to help Wes manage his. Like a soldier after years of combat, Tony hated the war and wanted Wes to do whatever he could to avoid it. He was willing to risk seeming like a hypocrite.

When Tony finished his rant, Wes hung up the phone and went back to bed. As soon as he was comfortably under the covers, the phone rang again.

"Yo, you coming out today?" a gruff voice barked out.

"It's too early, man!" Wes replied. "Wait, okay, okay, give me ten minutes."

Wes was talking to his new friend, Woody, one of the first people he'd met when Mary moved the family to this neighborhood a year earlier. It was their third move since Tony was born. The first was from Pennsylvania Avenue to Cherry Hill to get away from Wes's father. The move from Cherry Hill to Northwood was to get away from Cherry Hill.

Wes spent his earliest years in the Cherry Hill Apartments, a planned construction built after World War II to provide housing to returning black veterans. A neighboring development, the Uplands Apartments, was the white counterpart, built at the same time under the city's "separate but equal" policies. The Uplands became home to a thriving middle class, while the over 1,700 units in Cherry Hill became a breeding ground for poverty, drugs, and despair. There was never a question that Cherry Hill wasn't built as a sustainable community for its families. Isolated and desolate, it had no main streets. Small, poorly constructed, faux-brick homes lined the streets like dormitories. There were three swing sets in the middle of the complex that sat vacant at all times because all of the children had been taught to stay clear of them. The rest of the courtyard remained busy with drug activity. If you're not from Cherry Hill, you don't go to Cherry Hill. Over half of the eight thousand residents lived below the poverty line.

Mary shuddered every time she left the house and was plotting her escape from Cherry Hill almost as soon as she got there. When she moved from public housing to a three-bedroom home in a suburban area in the Northwood section of town, she was trying to create more distance between her and the city's imploding center. Compared with the chaos of Cherry Hill, Northwood was a paradise of neat houses with fastidiously maintained lawns. Black professionals constituted the bulk of the residents, many of them graduates of the universities that sat on its borders, Loyola College and Morgan State University. Mary felt safe and hopeful here.

Wes searched around his room for his football jersey. He played defensive end for the Northwood Rams, one of the best rec football teams in the nation. Wes loved football, and his athletic frame made him a natural. Even if he was just going out to play in the streets with Woody and some other friends, he wore that jersey like a badge of honor. The crimson "Northwood" that blazed across his white jersey gave him a sense of pride, a sense of belonging. He found the jersey in the corner of his room. Grass still stained the white mesh from his last game.

As football became more important in Wes's life, his performance in school declined. His test scores were high enough to make it to the next grade, but not high enough to make a legitimate argument that he'd learned anything. He was skating by, and since this was his third elementary school, he was able to do so with fairly little notice. Wes didn't act up in class, which kept him under the radar; his teachers spent 90 percent of their time dealing with the 5 percent of kids who did. Wes's teachers gave his mother reports that said he was unmotivated, but Wes just claimed boredom. He always felt he was smarter than the other kids in class and that the work just didn't hold his interest.

Wes laced up his white Nikes, beelined to his mother's room, and started to look through her drawers and closets for change, his daily ritual after she left for work. His mother would notice missing bills, but he could steal coins with no worries. In the corner of her closet, there was a large green-tinted glass jar of loose change shaped like a teakettle. He permanently borrowed about a dollar, enough to grab a few quarter waters—the colored sugar water sold in small plastic bottles at the corner store.

He ran out the front door to meet Woody, who was sitting on the curb lightly tossing a football in the air.

"It's about time, man!" Woody yelled. Woody lived one street over, on Cold Spring Lane. When Wes moved to Northwood, Woody immediately noticed his size and speed and tried to recruit him for the Rams. They'd since become friends.

Woody came from a working-class, two-parent household. Woody's father was a former sergeant in the Army. During the peak of the Vietnam War, he volunteered for the Army in logistics as an alternative to being drafted and sent to the front lines like many of his friends. Wes loved his war stories, savoring every detail. But most of all Wes enjoyed the simple fact that Woody's father was there.

Before he met Woody, Wes had never really seen a father around. Single-parent households were the norm in his world. At best, kids would have a setup like his brother Tony's, whereby they would get to see their fathers regularly and even stay with them a lot. But a family where the father lived with the mother, happily? This was new to Wes, and he liked it. Sometimes he'd ask Woody to hang out, and Woody would reply, "Can't, I'm with Pops today," and Wes would feel a surge of conflicting feelings. He was genuinely happy for Woody, but he was also deeply envious.

Wes and Woody tossed the football back and forth, waiting for other kids to show up to play. The houses on the street were large by

Baltimore standards, two stories with small front yards. Wes's home was among the few on the block without flowers or colorful decoration in the front. It was also one of the few rentals on a block full of homeowners.

Wes and Woody were soon joined by their friend White Boy. White Boy's real name was Paul, but everyone called him White Boy because his father was Lebanese-American and his mother was white. In West Baltimore, white people were a rare sight, so White Boy took the brunt of constant teasing. Despite clowning him about it, they loved him. Wes would always say, "The only thing white about him is his skin. Everything else is black. He's a real black dude." White Boy would just shrug and say, "It's not my fault. I was born this way."

These had been Wes's boys since he'd moved out to Northwood, and they would remain his boys for life. The boys approached another group of kids toward the dead end on Wes's block and asked them if they wanted to play. Particularly during the summertime, the streets were full of kids, and this group looked like a good match for a game of street football. Wes, always up for a challenge, relished the opportunity to beat up on a new group of neighborhood kids.

Wes was playing defense, guarding one of the kids from the neighborhood who was playing wide receiver. The boy ran his pattern with Wes closely guarding him, pushing him slightly to throw him off-balance. Wes didn't believe in taking it easy. If he was going to play, he was going to play to win. That was his style. The boy told Wes to stop pushing him. Wes pushed the boy harder.

Wes was bigger and stronger than the other boy, a fact pointedly reinforced every time their bodies collided. The boy finally had enough and, after the final play of a drive, stood toe-to-toe with Wes, bumping his chest against the bigger boy. His nose brushed up against Wes's chin.

"Didn't I tell you stop touching me?" the boy yelled in Wes's face.

"Make me, bitch!"

The boy pushed Wes in the chest, creating a short distance between the two, then cocked his right arm and punched Wes square in his face. Wes stepped back and threw his hands up, not just to protect himself from another blow but to make sure his face wasn't damaged.

Wes had never been punched before, not like that. And he never expected this little dude to swing on him. The boy stared at Wes, seemingly as shocked as he was.

Woody stepped in front of Wes and urged him not to retaliate. The boy who punched Wes was still trying to maintain his strut but seemed to realize that he might have made a mistake by punching the bigger guy. Wes was stunned. Then he tasted the unmistakable bitterness of blood on his tongue. He stuck his lip out slightly and felt the skin splitting open. Blood flowed, staining his white Northwood jersey.

The sight and taste of his own blood set Wes off. He clenched his fists and forced his way past Woody. Everyone waited for the next punch to be thrown. Instead, Wes broke into a sprint, running right past the kid. His focus was elsewhere. He left the kid standing there confused, hands still up, preparing for a fight. Wes was running home.

The commotion caused a stir, and neighbors began to look out their windows to see what was going on. Many of them were already frustrated with the boys playing football in the street—lost in their game, the players would curse, run through flower gardens, and scatter their quarter-water bottles across the sidewalks. It was not unusual for the owner of a beautifully decorated and well-kept yard to wake up in the morning and see an empty bag of Lay's potato chips or Cheez Doodles drifting through. Woody and White Boy looked up at the neighbors' windows and saw unhappy eyes staring back at them.

Woody ran after Wes to see what was going on, while White Boy ran back to his house to avoid getting in trouble. Woody cut through the back door of Wes's house. As he entered, he looked into the kitchen to see Wes slamming a drawer closed. With his left hand, Wes held a wet paper towel to his lip, trying to stop the steady flow of blood. The lip had begun to swell, and his anger grew along with it. This was a pride issue for Wes. He had just allowed himself to be punched dead in the face, in front of his friends, by a smaller guy. He could have walked away. He could have fought back on the spot and settled it. But when Wes had looked into the other boy's eyes, he knew that he had to send a message.

Tony flashed through Wes's mind. Tony wanted the best for Wes, but he still felt that part of his mission as a big brother was to toughen him up for the battles Tony knew Wes would have to fight as he got older. Some days, Tony would have Wes and Woody meet him at the Murphy Homes, where he would assemble a group of Murphy Homes boys. The boys would circle up like they were getting ready to watch a gladiator fight. Tony would order Wes and Woody into the center of the ring. Then he would call out the names of a few of the Murphy Homes boys. At Tony's command, Wes, Woody, and the boys from the projects would start wrestling and punching one another, first tentatively but then with increasing viciousness until Tony jumped into the circle and grabbed the backs of their collars, separating them like pit bulls in a dogfight. If he ever slackened, Tony would pull an exhausted Wes to the side, get within inches of his face, and say, "Rule number one: If someone disrespects you, you send a message so fierce that they won't have the chance to do it again." It was Murphy Homes law and Wes took it to heart.

As Woody got closer, his attention was diverted from Wes's left hand to his right, where he held a long-bladed knife. Woody carefully approached Wes and said, "Don't do it, man. Dude is not worth this," but Wes moved toward the back door, which led to the alley that connected the homes on each block. The alleys were narrow, barely wide enough for a car to pass through.

Woody sensed where Wes was headed and ran to block the back door. Woody held on to Wes's arms and tried to talk sense to him, but Wes's rage blocked out every word his friend said. Wes tried to wriggle free, to no avail. He knew he couldn't overpower Woody, so he told him that he needed to change the paper towel stanching his wound. The moist towel that Wes held to his lip was almost solid red and beginning to drip blood on the living room carpet. As he walked back to the kitchen, Wes kept an eye on Woody.

Woody turned his head away to see if the boys outside had moved from the front yard to the back alley. To no surprise, they had. What did surprise Woody was that they weren't alone.

One of the neighbors must have called the police, because two cruisers had pulled up, flashing their red and blue lights. They blocked off the alley. The boys who were running from the front of the house to the back alley stopped, following orders from the police car that pulled up behind them. Woody began to think it was a good thing that he and Wes had come inside.

The slamming front door brought Woody's attention back to the kitchen. Wes was gone. Before Woody could tell Wes that the police were out back, Wes was on the other side of the front door, knife in hand, hurrying to settle the score with the boy who had busted his lip.

Wes was now in a full sprint, clearing the five steps of his front porch in one leap and then running around to the alley, figuring that's where the boys were. His pace slowed as he turned the corner. Right in front of him was the boy who'd split his lip. The anger he'd felt minutes before rushed back. He gritted his teeth and clenched his fists. His eyes started to stream with tears of anger, confusion, and fear. He began to scream. His vision tunneled till the only thing he saw was the boy who'd punched him. Nothing else was on Wes's mind or in his sights, not even the policeman who had just stepped out of his cruiser.

The policeman left his car just in time to see the other kids clearing out of the alley and sprinting away. Wes was still preparing to take this fight to the next level. He took a few quick steps toward the boy who'd punched him, holding the knife to his side. The police officer yelled at Wes: "Put down the knife." Wes didn't hear him. Wes continued to move toward the boy. His grip on the knife handle tightened. His forearms flexed.

Send a message.

After repeating the order one more time, and watching Wes ignore him again, one of the officers stepped forward. He lifted all eighty pounds of Wes off the ground, slamming him facefirst on the trunk of the police cruiser. Wes's chest collapsed against the trunk of the car, sending pain throughout his entire body. His hand loosened. The knife fell to the asphalt. The officer pinned Wes's body to the car with a forearm hard against the back of Wes's neck while he used his other hand to pull the handcuffs from the right side of his belt holster. Wes was incapacitated, the side of his head pressed against the cruiser, but he still had the boy who'd punched him in his sights. Wes wondered how it was that he was the one being arrested. He tried to plead his case to the police officer as he closed the second cuff on Wes's eight-year-old wrists.

Woody went through the back door. He saw Wes lying on the back of the police car in handcuffs. "Why y'all got my man in handcuffs? What did he do?"

Woody's screams were largely ignored by the two police officers. They were busy placing Wes in the back of one of the cruisers and told the other boys to go home. They ignored Woody until he shouted out, "If y'all don't let him go, I'm gonna have to kill somebody!"

Moments later, Woody was in handcuffs too.

Woody was taken to his house in one of the police cars while Wes was brought down to district booking. Wes sat there, pondering his next step. He didn't want his mother to know he'd been arrested. She would probably ground him at least. It was summer, and that was the last thing he wanted. He used his one phone call to call his brother in Murphy Homes. Tony agreed to ask his father to pick Wes up. Three hours later, Wes was released under the care of Tony's father, and he was back at his house before his mother got home from her job.

It was years before Wes's mom found out her son had been arrested that day. By the time she did, she had bigger things to worry about.

The extreme heat in my poorly ventilated room woke me in the middle of the night. I was dying of thirst. I crept slowly out of my room, careful not to wake Shani. Each stair let off an irritating squeak. As I reached the bottom of the alcove, I saw my mother half lying down, half sitting up on the couch, staring at me with wide eyes. It was obvious she had been sleeping just a few moments prior, but the sound of the stairs woke her. She asked what I needed, and after I explained that I just wanted some water, she insisted on getting it for me. I didn't need her help, but I didn't say anything as she rose from the couch to get a glass from the kitchen.

Since my father's death, my mother had made the tattered brown leather couch in the living room her bed. Our neighborhood was getting more and more dangerous; there had been a rash of break-ins in the houses around us. My mother slept in the living room to stand guard, she said. She didn't want me and my sisters to be the first people a trespasser ran into if they entered the house. She was determined to protect us. The fact that sleeping in the living room also allowed her to avoid the haunted bedroom she'd once shared with my father was never mentioned.

My mother still tortured herself with what-ifs concerning my father's death. Did she ask all the right questions? Should she have pushed the doctors harder for a clearer diagnosis? Could her CPR have worked better had she learned how to do it properly when she had the chance? Her protective vigilance for her surviving family had overtaken rationality. For the past two years, she'd slept on the couch listening, waiting, protecting.

The death of my father had created a major stir in the journalistic community. He was young, talented, and admired. My mother, concerned about the effects on her children of a drawn-out legal affair, opted to settle out of court, despite believing she had a larger wrongful death case. Intent to make some sense of the tragedy, she used the money to create a fund that would provide equipment and training to paramedics on a new procedure for dealing with respiratory or cardiac arrest, a technique that could have saved my father's life. At the time of my father's death, none of the first responders were trained in the technique. My mother hoped her gift would prevent other families from having to go through what we'd suffered. But her act of kindness could do nothing to ease our feelings of loss.

She rubbed her knees and grimaced as they straightened out. She had started to gain weight, and what had once been a sprightly step had begun to slow. Perpetual bags hung under her eyes. I watched her as she walked by me, looking worn, almost defeated.

After kissing me good night for the second time, she sent me up to my room and sat on the couch. With a glance back, I saw her rub her eyes again and rest her head in her hands. People around us didn't think she was coping well with her husband's death. They thought she needed help, not just in raising the kids but in raising her spirits. Although we were surrounded by her longtime friends from college and my uncles and aunts from both sides of the family, it wasn't enough. She was losing her grip. She needed help only her parents could provide.

A few mornings later, Mom woke up, made breakfast for us, and got Nikki and me off to school. Then she called her mother up in New York. Her mother had let her know that there would always be an open door for her in the Bronx if she needed it. But my mother had been determined to stick it out in the home she'd bought with her husband. Until now.

"Mom, if it's still all right, I think we need to move up there. I can't do this alone anymore."

My grandmother was thrilled. Before she even answered my mother, she called out to my grandfather, "Joy and the kids are moving up to New York!"

Three weeks later, Nikki, Shani, and I all stood outside our car, staring with something like disbelief at our now empty home. This was it. We were actually leaving Maryland.

"All right, guys, load up," my mother cheerily yelled as she threw in one final bag and slammed shut the trunk of our lime green Ford Maverick. Nikki helped me get my seat belt done while my mother secured Shani in the car seat. Even as a kid, I could tell my mother's aggressive good cheer was for our benefit. Before we took off, she paused to take one final look at our house, the house she'd lived in for six years. It already felt like a past life.

My grandparents weren't strangers to me; they'd spent quite a bit of time with us in Maryland. They were both recently retired—my grandfather from the ministry and my grandmother from twenty-six years as an elementary school teacher in the Bronx. I was excited by the idea of living with them; they spoiled us like crazy. But I was apprehensive about moving away from my friends, from the only world I'd known.

My mother prepared us for the move by telling us about her wonderful childhood and the glories of the Bronx. She told us about the neighbors who always had a hot meal for you and looked out for you if your parents weren't around. She told us about the amazements to be found at the Bronx Zoo, which was only ten minutes away from our new home. She told us it was safe, that in all the time she'd lived there as a kid, she had not once experienced crime or violence. But when we broke off the interstate and started navigating the burned-out landscape of the Bronx, we could feel her energy shifting. Things had clearly changed.

The Bronx is an amazing place, home to over a million people. The diversity of the borough is extraordinary: areas like the Italian-immigrant-settled Country Club neighborhood were among the most affluent of the city but were only minutes away from the poorest congressional district in the nation. When my grandparents moved to the United States, in the 1950s, the South Bronx had already begun its transformation from a majority Jewish borough to one dominated by blacks and Latinos. When my mother grew up in the Bronx, despite rising poverty levels, the sense of family and community were strong. With every decade that had passed since she left the area, things had gotten worse. In 1977, when President Jimmy Carter visited the Bronx, he said it looked like "a war zone." Seven years later, we were moving back.

We'd stopped at a red light at the corner of Paulding and Allerton avenues when we saw a woman walk up to a young boy standing on the corner. The woman was dressed in a blue shirt and faded blue shorts that showed off her scaly, ashy legs. She stumbled to the boy, with her right hand tightly gripping a wad of money. The boy, no older than sixteen, darted his head back and forth, apparently looking for cops, customers, or both. As she approached him and they started talking, the light turned green and my mother quickly hit the gas. Even craning my neck backward, I didn't see how that scene ended. We were now only two blocks away from our new home. When I turned back around, I could see the nervousness on my mother's face reflected in the rearview mirror. Moments later we arrived.

When my grandparents moved to the United States, their first priority was to save enough money to buy this house on Paulding Avenue. To them a house meant much more than shelter; it was a stake in their new country. America allowed them to create a life they couldn't have dreamed of in their home countries of Jamaica and Cuba. Their plan had been to return overseas once they retired, but they couldn't bring themselves to leave. They sensed that they were needed here. Today was exactly the kind of day they'd been anticipating.

The three-bedroom home always managed to somehow stretch itself when people were in need of a place to stay. The number of people who lived in the home at any given time fluctuated between five and nine, which made for tight living conditions. When we showed up that late summer day in 1984, we brought the number to seven.

I walked up the stone stairs to see the front door open and my grandparents waiting there. My invitingly plump grandmother stood in the doorway, her hair in a light Jheri curl and a smile settled so firmly across her face it seemed permanently engraved. "Welcome home!" she bellowed out to us in her Jamaican accent. She engulfed my entire body in her hug, folding me into her chest in a tight embrace. My grandfather stood directly behind her, waiting his turn to get at the grandchildren. My grandfather was a short man, no more than five foot six, but his presence dominated every room he entered. He was dark-skinned with a muscular frame that made him seem much younger than he was. People often compared him with his fellow man of the cloth Archbishop Desmond Tutu, but of course that didn't mean anything to me. His mustache tickled as he hugged me and kissed me on the cheek.

After unloading the car, my mother began to tell my grandparents about what she had seen earlier, the woman buying the drugs from the young boy. She also told them about a telephone pole she'd noticed outside their house that had been converted into a makeshift memorial. There was a picture of a young girl taped to the pole, and sympathy cards and tiny stuffed animals were scattered around it. Signs saying WE LOVE YOU and SEE YOU IN HEAVEN were taped around the little girl's picture. Her name was April. The shrine had unsettled my mother.

My grandparents told my mother about the changes that had been taking place in the neighborhood. As I sat next to her, trying to spin a basketball on my index finger, I heard my grandparents talk about how drugs and violence had slowly crept in. Fear and apathy had become the new norm in what had once been a close-knit community. They also talked about something I'd never heard of before. Crack.

My grandmother left the table and went into the kitchen. She returned a few minutes later with a large pot of codfish and ackee, the official dish of Jamaica, and a large helping of grits. They had spent days preparing the dish in anticipation of our arrival, my grandfather serving as sous-chef, deboning the light, salty fish and chopping up the onions and peppers while my grandmother seasoned and cooked it to perfection. Retirement had been wonderfully relaxing for them. That was all over now.

My grandparents, Rev. Dr. James Thomas and Winell Thomas, met when he was an eighteen-year-old ministerial student in a small Jamaican parish and she and her parents were newly arrived parishioners from Cuba. My grandmother's parents left Havana in the 1930s in search of work; at the time Jamaica was an island of relative prosperity amid the worldwide Great Depression. My great-grandparents loaded up on a boat in Havana Harbor with six-year-old Winell and prepared to create a new life in Jamaica.

The two largest islands in the Caribbean were only ninety miles apart, and my great-grandparents planned to return quickly after a temporary stay in Jamaica to make some money. In fact, my grandmother's older sister, Lurlene, was left behind. But the family never went back to Cuba, and my grandmother never saw her sister again.

When my maternal great-grandparents arrived in Jamaica, they searched for a church home. One Sunday, they entered Mount Horeb Church in St. James Parish and were immediately impressed by the young, dynamic pastor, Josiah Thomas. My grandmother, however, was even more struck by the pastor's son. Their friendship was quick and easy. As they got older, their love for each other developed; they were married in 1948.

My grandfather had a dream to follow his father's footsteps and join the ministry. Since he could remember, he'd wanted to lead his own congregation. But to do it, he needed to complete school. His father used to tell him, "Being a leader in the faith is about more than simply proclaiming the Word, you must be a student of the Word." The first step along that road was to leave his new bride and his homeland to attend Lincoln University, a historically black college in Pennsylvania.

When he arrived in the middle of November, he had his Jamaican wardrobe: shorts, short-sleeve shirts, and a few pairs of slacks for fancy occasions. On his first day on the picturesque campus, he walked briskly through the bracing Pennsylvania wind and fallen autumn leaves in open-toed sandals and shorts.

"Hey, you, come here quickly!"

The voice came from a man standing about thirty feet away. My grandfather hesitated—not only did he not know the man but also because it was too cold for small talk. The man jogged over to my grandfather, who speed-walked to meet him halfway.

"Where are you from?" the man asked. He wore an elegant black suit and black tie, and his demeanor was irresistibly cheerful, which put my grandfather at ease. His accent wasn't American, but my grandfather couldn't quite place it.

"Jamaica," my grandfather proudly responded.

"I knew you were not from here. We need to get you some appropriate clothes. Don't worry. When I first came here, I did the same thing."

The man took my grandfather to the store to buy him some warm clothes to wear until he could properly equip himself for the winter. The shopping excursion was the first of many encounters between my grandfather and this man, who would become a mentor, teacher, and friend to him. They spent many hours talking together about the changing world and the dawning of independence and liberation movements across the African Diaspora. He tried to convince my grandfather to go into politics, as he hoped to, and change the world through that means. But my grandfather insisted that God was calling him to serve through the ministry.

The two men's paths diverged over time. The man who mentored—and clothed—my grandfather followed his dreams and made history. That man, Kwame Nkrumah, became the president of Ghana, the first black African president of an independent African nation.

After completing his education, my grandfather moved to the South Bronx and brought his wife and kids with him. In 1952, my grandfather, son of a Presbyterian minister and now a Presbyterian minister himself, became the first black minister in the history of the Dutch Reformed Church. The Dutch Reformed Church, born in the Netherlands during the Reformation, had spread throughout Europe and around the world, and even eventually became the official religion of apartheid South Africa. My grandfather's pioneering ascent to the ministry was met with many cheers but some threats as well. He battled through them and made history.

Thirty-two years later, he hadn't changed. He sat across from my mother and told her that the changes in the neighborhood had not diminished his belief in the community. He was determined to stick it out and do his part to heal what was broken in the Bronx.

I continued to spin the ball on my finger.

The first few days after the move, I became antsy. I missed my old friends and my old neighborhood. I had thought my mother's rules were strict but soon realized that my grandparents' were many times worse. They made it very clear that Paulding Avenue was their home and their rules would apply. When the streetlights went on, we had to be back home. All chores had to be done before we even thought about going outside to play. If we heard any gunfire or, as my grandmother called it, "foolishness," outside, we were to immediately return home, no matter when it was. These were not Bronx rules, these were West Indian rules. And my grandparents figured if these rules had helped their children successfully navigate the world, they would work on their grandkids too.

My restlessness was cured only by heading out into these new streets. After completing my chores one day, I got permission to play basketball at a park five blocks from our house.

"Go, play, and come right back!" were the orders I heard as I began to dribble my basketball up the concrete sidewalks toward the courts. I took my time getting to the courts, practicing dribbling the ball between my legs, but I also tried my best to absorb the new neighborhood. There were many more people on the streets, sitting on the stoops, hanging out, than I was used to. The *boom-bap* of early hip-hop, still young and close to its Bronx roots, tumbled out of the apartment buildings, mixed with Spanish music blaring from boom boxes. The Bronx was in its postapocalyptic phase. Whole blocks were abandoned, buildings blackened and hollowed out by fires set by arsonists—many of whom were in the employ of landlords looking to cash out of the deteriorating ghetto. I didn't have much of a frame of reference back then, though. I didn't know that drug fiends were still making use of those abandoned buildings for activities that would've blown my mind, or that the swollen hands on the man leaning against a telephone pole by himself—eyes flickering, head nodding—were telltale signs of needle injections. I walked past neighbors whose eyes overflowed with desperation and depression, people who had watched their once-proud neighborhood become synonymous with the collapse of the American inner city.

With every step on those cracked sidewalks, I passed a new signifier of urban decay. But I didn't even realize it. I was a kid, and just happy to get out of the house. The people I passed would look me up and down, and I would look back, give the traditional head nod, and then go back to practicing my crossover dribble.

I finally arrived at the courts and saw a handful of guys playing three on three. They all looked a little older than me, or at least bigger than me. I quickly realized they were all better than me, too. The red iron rims had no nets, and since there was no real give on the rims, every shot ended as either a silent swish or a high-bouncing brick. Although I was intimidated, I called "next" because I knew my deadline for going back to the house was quickly approaching.

I was practicing my lefty dribble next to the iron gate that surrounded the courts when one of the guys fell hard to the ground. He had been accidentally hit in the face while driving to the basket. Blood trickled from his mouth. He quickly walked off to get some water and clean his face. No foul was called. I would soon learn that calling fouls just wasn't done.

The players realized they were short one man. The group looked at me, seemingly all at once, since I was now the only person on the sidelines.

"You good to run?" one of the boys asked me.

I dug up all the confidence I had, placed my basketball on the ground, and began to walk toward them. My oversize sneakers clopped on the court like a pair of Clydesdale hooves. My new teammates called out their names as I gave each of them a quick dap, an informal greeting of clasped hands and bumped chests.

"What's up. I'm Oz."

"What's going on. Deshawn."

I played hard, lost pretty bad, but enjoyed every minute of it. These kids were different from my friends back in Maryland. I quickly started to pick up on their lingo and style, the swagger of my new teammates and neighborhood friends.

From this first moment on a Bronx court, I could tell there was something special about it. The basketball court is a strange patch of neutral ground, a meeting place for every element of a neighborhood's cohort of young men. You'd find the high school phenoms running circles around the overweight has-beens, guys who'd effortlessly played above-the-rim years ago now trying to catch their breath and salvage what was left of their once-stylish games. You'd find the drug dealers there, mostly playing the sidelines, betting major money on pickup games and amateur tournaments but occasionally stepping onto the court, smelling like a fresh haircut and with gear on that was too fine for sweating in. But even they couldn't resist getting a little run in—and God help you if you played them too hard, or stepped on their brand-new Nike Air Force Ones.

You'd find the scrubs talking smack a mile a minute and the church boys who didn't even bother changing out of their pointy shoes and button-up shirts. You'd find the freelance thugs pushing off for rebounds, and the A students, quietly showing off silky jump shots and then running back downcourt eyes down, trying not to look too pleased with themselves. There would be the dude sweating through his post office uniform when he should've been delivering mail, and the brother who'd just come back from doing a bid in jail—you could tell by his chiseled arms and intense stare, and the cautious smile he offered every time a passing car would honk and the driver yell out his name, welcoming him home.

We were all enclosed by the same fence, bumping into one another, fighting, celebrating. Showing one another our best and worst, revealing ourselves—even our cruelty and crimes—as if that fence had created a circle of trust. A brotherhood.

We played that first night until I saw the streetlights come on, my cue to head to the house. I asked them when they would be back out playing, and they said tomorrow, same time, same place. So would I.

THREE

Foreign Ground

1987

"Just stand next to the white people. They'll get off by a Hundred and Tenth Street."

Justin broke down his strategy for securing a seat as we shoved ourselves onto the crowded Number 2 train heading uptown. We had spent the day in Manhattan, taking a break from the Bronx, prowling the city's sneaker stores, checking for the new Nikes we couldn't afford. Now on the subway back home, we stood in a crush of executives, construction workers, accountants, and maids—a multicolored totem of hands clinging to the metal pole in the middle of the car for dear life.

Six stops later, Justin's prediction proved out. A business-suited exodus emptied the train when we hit 110th Street, the last outpost of affluent Manhattan, and we were finally able to sit down. A subway car full of blacks and Latinos would continue the bumpy ride back up to Harlem and the Bronx. Justin smiled at me just as the train's last yuppie scurried out ahead of the closing doors.

Justin and I bonded from the first time I met him. We wore the same haircut, a towering box cut made popular by rappers like Big Daddy Kane, whose elegantly chiseled high-top was the gold standard. Justin loomed over me, standing at almost five foot six in fifth grade, and his skinny frame made him appear even taller. His voice was deep, an excursion into puberty that had left the rest of us behind. He lived in the Soundview Projects, just minutes away from our house in the Bronx. We knew each other's neighborhoods, each other's friends, and each other's families. There was one other thing that helped us bond quickly: he was one of the few other black kids at my new school.

My mother decided soon after our move to the Bronx that I was not going to public school. She wasn't a snob, she was scared. My mother was a graduate of the public school system in New York herself, and the daughter of a public school teacher in the same system. She knew the public schools in the area. The schools she'd gone to were still there—same names, same buildings—but they were not the same institutions. The buildings themselves were dilapidated—crumbling walls and faded paint—and even if you were one of the lucky 50 percent who made it out in four years, it was not at all clear that you'd be prepared for college or a job. Just as the street corners of the Bronx had changed, so had the public schools. Things were falling apart, and the halls of school were no exception or refuge from the chaos outside.

But no matter how much the world around us seemed ready to crumble, my mother was determined to see us through it. When we moved to New York, she worked multiple jobs, from a freelance writer for magazines and television to a furrier's assistant—whatever she could do to help cover her growing expenses. She had to provide for us, and she was helping out her parents, who were living off two small pensions and their small monthly Social Security check. My mother would wake us up in the morning for school, and before we had even finished getting dressed, she was off to work, leaving my grandparents to get us there. My grandparents would pick us up after school, prepare dinner for the family, and get us to bed. Late into the night, my mother would come in from her last job and walk straight to our bedroom, pull the covers tight around us, and give my sister and me our kiss good night. The smell of her perfume would wake me as soon as she walked in, and then comfort me back to sleep.

My mother first heard about Riverdale Country School when she was a girl growing up in the Bronx. It was the sort of school you might find in a storybook, a fantasy for a public school kid. It sat along the banks of the Hudson River, and the rolling hills and lush quadrangles of its campus gave it the grand appearance of a university. The ivy-covered buildings were like a promise to its students of what awaited them. It was the school John F. Kennedy attended as a child.

When my mom visited the school again as an adult, she was immediately convinced that this was where she wanted my sister and me to go. Riverdale was in the Bronx but was its own little island of affluence, a fact local residents were quick to remind you of in hopes of keeping their property values from collapsing to the level of the rest of the borough. My mother saw Riverdale as a haven, a place where I could escape my neighborhood and open my horizons. But for me, it was where I got lost.

Justin and I got off the subway—covered with graffiti tags and all-city murals—at Gun Hill Road and began the ten-minute walk home. Everything about the Bronx was different from downtown Manhattan, more intense and potent; even the name of the street we walked down—Gun Hill Road—suggested blood sport. As soon as we hit the Bronx bricks, our senses were assaulted. We walked through a fog of food smells blowing in from around the world—beef patties and curry goat from the Jamaican spot, deep-fried dumplings and chicken wings from the Chinese take-out joint, cuchifritos from the Puerto Rican lunch counter. Up and down the street were entrepreneurial immigrants in colorful clothes—embroidered guayaberas and flowing kente and spray-painted T-shirts—hustling everything from mix tapes to T-shirts to incense from crowded sidewalk tables. The air rang with English and Spanish in every imaginable accent, spoken by parents barking orders to their children or young lovers playfully flirting with each other. By now, all of this felt like home.

On the way to my house, we decided to stop by Ozzie's to see if our crew was around. Ozzie was our boy, tall and dark-skinned, with a close-cropped Caesar and a soft Caribbean accent like his father's. His basketball skills transcended his years; he was only in fifth grade when high schools started to recruit him.

As expected, there they were—our little crew, sprawled along the white stone steps of Ozzie's house. Before I could properly get into the flow of conversation, Paris turned to me.

"How y'all like it up there at that white school?"

Paris was a good-looking guy with a brilliant smile that he rarely cared to share. He leaned back as he spoke—his question was a challenge.

"It's cool, it's whatever," I quietly replied, looking down at the ground. It was a sore spot. In the hood, your school affiliation was essential. Even if you weren't running with the coolest clique, you still got some percentage of your rep from your school, and the name Riverdale wasn't going to impress anyone. If anything, it made my crew kind of suspicious of me. So I quickly changed the subject.

"What's up with the Knicks this year?"

Lame, I know, but I was desperate. Most of my neighborhood friends were attending public schools in the area; a few were attending Catholic school. But Justin and I were the only two who actually went all the way across town to attend a predominantly white private school. It would take as long as an hour and a half some days, depending on traffic, stalled trains, weather, and other factors, but we would make it there. And on time. At least initially.

"Nah, for real, what's up with *Riverdale*?" Paris asked, bringing the topic back. His voice rose on the last word, as he made his best attempt at a proper British accent. I had to admit that Riverdale sounded a little like something out of Archie Comics. It was embarrassing. I decided to try a different tack. "Yeah, it's cool, man, nobody messes with me over there. I have the place on lock," I started, unconvincingly. My feet shuffled and my voice lowered a few octaves. I caught Justin out of the side of my eye, shaking his head with amazement at the nonsense that was coming out of my mouth. I could feel the burn of his skeptical stare on the side of my face, but I pressed on.

"Let me tell you how I run things up there," I said and launched into the story of my recent suspension from school.

A few weeks earlier I had been suspended for fighting. I was play-fully wrestling with a kid from my grade when I decided to go for a killer move: I grabbed his right arm with mine and hoisted him over my shoulder, then dropped him hard on the ground. The fall was awkward, and he landed on his head, opening a small but surprisingly bloody cut. After the boy was rushed to the school nurse and eventu-ally to the hospital to get a few stitches, I was suspended for fighting.

That was the truth.

For my friends, I decided to juice the story up a little. Or a lot. The story I told had the boy disrespecting me and me getting in his face to respond. When he kept jawing, I picked him up over my head and slammed him to the ground. Then I stood over his bleeding body, taunting him like Muhammad Ali over Sonny Liston, daring him to get back up.

My friends looked over at Justin, who had a pained expression on his face. He knew the truth, and soon the rest of my friends did too. I became the butt of pretty unrelenting taunting. My attempt at creat-ing a Wes Moore legend had backfired.

I was saved after about twenty minutes when a man stumbled toward us. His hair looked like it hadn't seen a comb in weeks. There were laces in only one of his filthy sneakers.

"Can you young brothers spare some change? I need to make a phone call," he stuttered. An old and unpleasant odor preceded him.

Ozzie responded first, his Jamaican accent a little thicker than usual. "Get the hell out of here, man. Nobody has any change for you."

The man slowly moved away, peeking backward a couple times, hoping one of us would overrule Ozzie's rejection.

Ozzie shook his head in disbelief. "If dude wanted to buy some rock, he should have just said it. Who the hell was he gonna call if we gave him some change?" We all laughed as the panhandler staggered back up the block to look for sympathy elsewhere.

Drugs were not new to the Bronx. Marijuana, cocaine, and heroin all took their turns as the drug of choice. But crack was different. After it officially introduced itself in the early 1980s, it didn't take long for crack to place a stranglehold on many communities. The Bronx was one of them. I was an eyewitness.

Crack was different from the drugs that preceded it. It was crazily accessible and insanely potent—and addictive. My friends and I would regularly trade the most remarkable stories we'd overheard or witnessed: A father who left his family and robbed his parents for money to buy rock. A pregnant mother who sold her body to get another hit. Someone's grandmother who blew her monthly Social Security check on crack.

The other difference between crack and other drugs was its method of distribution. There was so much money to be made that drug gangs rapidly expanded their ranks, sucking in some of our best friends, and turf wars became deadly, aided by the influx of sophisticated firearms. The mayhem spread from the gangs to the rest of the neighborhood. Everyone felt threatened. Everyone was defensive. From the early 1980s to the end of the decade, there was an almost 61 percent jump in the murder rate. When I look back now, it's almost surreal. In 2008, there were 417 homicides in New York City. In 1990, there were 2,605. Those murders were concentrated in a handful of neighborhoods, and the victims were concentrated in a single demographic: young black men. In some neighborhoods, the young men would've been safer living in war zones. We laughed at the panhandler on the block, but he wasn't just an object of ridicule, he was an unsettling omen.

After sitting with the crew for a few hours, Justin and I decided to get back to the subway station so he could head home. The sun was beginning to set, so we knew we didn't have much time. We didn't need to check our watches—we were starting to feel the fear that crept around the edges of our consciousness at dusk. Justin lived a few train stops away from me, and taking the train home after dark was a different journey than the one we'd made earlier in the day. Justin knew the rules: Never look people in the eye. Don't smile, it makes you look weak. If someone yells for you, particularly after dark, just keep walking. Always keep your money in your front pocket, never in your back pocket. Know where the drug dealers and smokers are at all times. Know where the cops are at all times. And if night fell too soon and Justin was forced to go home by foot over the Bruckner Expressway overpass in the dark, he knew to run all the way.

We increased our pace; neither of our mothers would condone us coming home late. His mother and mine were kindred spirits. Both were born in 1950, both nicknamed their oldest children Nikki after Nikki Giovanni, both knew all about the public schools in the Bronx (my mother went to school in them and Justin's mother taught in them), and both were single mothers working multiple jobs to send their kids to a school outside their neighborhoods. Justin's mother looked after me like I was one of her own. The same way my mother did for Justin.

The sun continued its rapid descent. We tried to keep a bop in our step, tried to keep it cool, but by now we were pretty explicitly speed-walking. Breathing a little heavily, we did our best to keep up appearances. We laughed about our day, talked about school.

Riverdale. The pristine campus and well-dressed kids had stunned me on my first visit—the Bronx was not the homogenous ghetto I thought it was. I felt a crazy-making crosscurrent of emotions whenever I stepped onto campus. Every time I looked around at the buildings and the trees and the view of the river, I was reminded of the sacrifices my mother was making to keep me there. And every time I looked at my fellow students, I was reminded of how little I fit in.

I tried to hide the fact that my family was so much poorer than everyone else's at school. Every week I sat down to create a schedule for my clothes. I had three "good" shirts and three "good" pairs of pants. I would rotate their order, mixing and matching so that each day I had on a fresh combination. Later I even borrowed Nikki's clothes to show some further variation, thinking that nobody would notice the zippers at the bottoms of the jeans or the way the hips hugged a little tight. I would just nonchalantly say that I was trying to "bring the seventies back." This claim was usually met with polite smiles when I was in the room, but I can only imagine the hysterical laughter and conversations about my cross-dressing when I wasn't around.

When the kids would talk about the new videogame system that was out or how their family was going to Greece or Spain or France during summer vacation, I would sit silent, hoping they wouldn't ask me where my family planned on "summering." At times I would try to join in, chiming in about the "vacation home" my family had in Brooklyn, not realizing how ridiculous I sounded. The "vacation home" I was speaking about was the parsonage my grandparents had moved into when my grandfather came out of retirement to lead a congregation. Not until I got older did I learn that Flatbush Avenue inspired a lower level of awe than the French Riviera. Whenever I hung out with Riverdale kids, I made sure we went to their homes, not mine. I didn't want to have to explain. But, in the sixth grade, I broke my own rule.

My uncle Howard was my mother's younger brother. He had recently made a decision with his medical school that becoming a doctor was not in the cards for him, and he moved to the Bronx, where he worked as a pharmaceutical salesman. He came up with the idea to invite some kids from the neighborhood to play a game of baseball with the kids from my school in a park near our house. I think he sensed my frustration at living in mutually exclusive worlds and thought a game of baseball would bring together my neighborhood friends and my wealthier Riverdale classmates and broaden the horizons of both. His intentions were good. I jumped at the idea. I invited ten friends from school to come and play against my friends from the neighborhood.

In the first inning, my neighborhood friend Deshawn, who was playing first base, started trash-talking Randy, a lanky Riverdale kid with a mop haircut, after Randy hit a single. Innocent stuff—until Deshawn finally said one thing too many and Randy, the pride of super-affluent Scarsdale, playfully tipped the front bill of Deshawn's hat, knocking it off his head. It was as if he were a king and someone had knocked his crown into the dirt. Before we were even fifteen minutes into the game, a brawl had broken out. Three fights and four innings later, I conceded that the experiment wasn't working out. The game was called. Everyone retreated to their separate corners, to their separate worlds. Everyone except me, still caught in the middle.

I was becoming too "rich" for the kids from the neighborhood and too "poor" for the kids at school. I had forgotten how to act naturally, thinking way too much in each situation and getting tangled in the contradictions between my two worlds. My confidence took a hit. Unlike Justin, whose maturity helped him handle this transition much better than I did, I began to let my grades slip. Disappointed with Ds, pleasantly satisfied with Cs, and celebratory about a B, I allowed my standards at school to become pathetic. In third grade I was reading at a second-grade reading level. Later in life I learned that the way many governors projected the numbers of beds they'd need for prison facilities was by examining the reading scores of third graders. Elected officials deduced that a strong percentage of kids reading below their grade level by third grade would be needing a secure place to stay when they got older. Considering my performance in the classroom thus far, I was well on my way to needing state-sponsored accommodations.

When we finally got to the train station, Justin asked me a question.

"Did you study yet for the English test for Wednesday?"

"Nope," I replied.

"You know they are going to put you on probation if you don't start doing better, man."

I knew, but I broke it down for Justin: the problem wasn't what I knew or didn't know, the problem was that they didn't understand my situation. My long trip to and from school every day, my missing father, my overworked mother, the changing routes I took every day from the train just so no one with bad intentions could case my routine. I continued throwing excuses at Justin but started to wither under the heat of his glare. Justin had it worse than I did but was still one of the best-performing kids in the class. My litany of excuses trailed off.

After a moment I broke the awkward silence by telling him my mother had begun to threaten me with military school if I didn't get my grades and discipline together.

"For real?" he asked and laughed.

My mother had even gotten her hands on a brochure that she'd haul out as a visual aid to her threats. But I knew there was no way my mother would allow her only son to be shipped off to military school. Regardless of the grades. Regardless of the suspensions. It was too remote, too permanent. Maybe she'd shift me to a school closer to home, maybe a public or Catholic school, but not a military school.

My mother couldn't send me away. She needed a man in the house to look after Shani and Nikki, not to mention her, right? She had to be bluffing. Plus, in Caribbean households, boys were often indulged like little princes. Minor infractions were tolerated and "he's just being a boy" was an all-purpose excuse for anything short of a felony. And what was military school anyway? A bunch of countrified folks yelling and screaming, waving flags and chewing tobacco, forcing confused kids to crawl through mud, preparing them to get killed in a war? My mother wouldn't even let me have toy guns in the house. It was absurd.

"We'll see what happens," Justin said with a smirk.

"Yeah, we'll see," I replied.

The cloudless evening sky had gone dark. Justin ran up the metal staircase to the train entrance. The streetlights blinking on were a silent siren. Time was up. Justin laced up his sneakers and boarded the train, preparing for his run home.

Wes walked through his new neighborhood, the fourth he could remember living in so far in his short life. He'd called this place home for only the last four months. Despite its being only ten miles from his old home, the thick old-growth trees that lined streets with names like Biscayne Bay, March Point Park, and Whispering Woods were evidence of how far removed he was from the Baltimore City row houses he'd been accustomed to. They now lived in Baltimore County, which sits on the northern, eastern, and western borders of Baltimore City, a horseshoe that fits around its more well-known neighbor. Baltimore City residents increasingly bled into it, exchanging the city for the county's spacious neighborhoods, quality schools, and higher per capita income. Mary Moore was part of that flight.

Dundee Village, where Wes's new home was located, was a collection of connected, whitewashed homes. The houses were modest but well cared for—flowerpots were filled with geraniums or black-eyed Susans, and floral wreaths hung from each wooden door.

He hadn't lived there long, but the closeness of the homes allowed Wes to get to know the neighbors and their idiosyncrasies well. He stared thirty yards across the road and saw Mrs. Evers, a middle-aged black woman, standing in front of her house talking with Joyce, an older white woman from Brooklyn, Maryland, who worked at the Royal Farms up the street. Aside from the carbon-copy houses, there was nothing uniform about this working-class neighborhood; it was filled with people of all shapes, colors, and backgrounds. The only thing most of them had in common was that they came from somewhere else, and for most of them, Dundee was a better place to be.

Back in Baltimore, a new young mayor had just taken over. He ran on a platform of improving the school system, fighting illiteracy, and trying to find innovative solutions to the metastasizing drug trade that was poisoning life in major areas of the city. Mayor Kurt Schmoke was himself a proud product of Baltimore City who went from the city's public schools to Yale University, Oxford, Harvard Law School, and then, improbably, back to his beloved and deeply troubled city. He served as Baltimore's state's attorney for four years and at age thirty-eight was elected the first African-American mayor of Baltimore City, which at the time was over 60 percent black.

A few months into his administration, Mayor Schmoke was lambasted for saying, "I started to think, maybe we ought to consider this drug problem a public health problem rather than a criminal justice problem." Most people heard this as a cry for drug legalization in Baltimore. But Schmoke was desperate. He knew that unless someone figured out some way of controlling it, the drug trade—and the epidemics of violent crime and untreated addiction it left in its wake—would stifle any hope for progress in the city.

Change couldn't come fast enough for Mary. Tony was now full-time in the streets, splitting his time between his father's and girlfriend's apartments in the Murphy Homes Projects. He was a veteran of the drug game at eighteen. He'd graduated from foot soldier and now had other people working for him. School was a distant memory; Tony hadn't seen the inside of a classroom on a regular basis since eighth grade.

Two incidents were decisive in Mary's decision to move. First, Tony got shot in the chest during a botched drug deal. It was the first of three times that he would feel the searing heat of a bullet enter his body. Second, Wes failed the sixth grade at "Chicken Pen" and had to repeat it. Baltimore City had a 70 percent dropout rate at the time. Tony had already joined that statistic; Mary wanted to keep Wes away from the same fate. And now here Wes was, walking around Dundee Village, hoping these bucolically named "avenues" and "circles" would lead him to a better place than the city streets had.

Wes finally turned from his neighbors. He was wearing his unlaced, beat-up Adidas, a T-shirt, and an orange Orioles hat with the bill facing the back. He'd pleaded with his mom earlier in the week for an upgrade to his wardrobe. Tony, he complained, was wearing all the newest clothes and was now sporting a thick gold rope chain on top of it. His mother came back at him hard. "And you see Tony just ended up in the hospital, right? Be thankful for what you got!"

It meant nothing to Wes. All he knew was that, when he got back to the city and walked its streets, breathing in the noise and bustle and craziness he was used to, he did it in secondhand gear.

Back in the county, he walked away from Dundee Village, trying to kill time on a lazy Saturday afternoon. A few blocks from his house he noticed something he had never seen before: a kid, maybe a couple years older than Wes, standing on a street corner. The boy was wearing a headset right out of the Janet Jackson "Control" video. A gold ring with a small diamond cut into the middle of its crown caught the light every time the boy moved his hand. The ring was not exactly flashy, but the shine coming off it told a short story: the kid had some money. The whole tableau—the ring, the headset—was the coolest thing Wes had ever seen. The boy's tall and muscularly broad frame made him look older than he probably was and he had a few people around him, all of them laughing and joking. But it was obvious, both by the size difference and by his cool gadgetry, that this kid was the leader of the pack. Wes wanted to know more and, never shy, he approached the boys.

"Hey, where can I get one of those headsets—"

"Who are you?" one of the boys snapped back, cocking his head and narrowing his eyes.

Wes knew to choose his next words carefully. "I just moved here. From the City. I live over on Bledsoe." He kept his tone level, non-confrontational, but not scared. Never scared.

The tall kid looked him over carefully before he responded. "You want one of these, it's pretty easy. All you have to do is wear one, and every time you see jakes roll by, you just push this button and say something. When your shift is over, you come by, and I'll give you your money," he said.

Money? Wes just wanted to get his hands on one of the headsets. There was money involved too?

After hearing more details, Wes was sold. It seemed like a sweet setup. Simply wear a headset, hang out with new friends, notify people when you see police coming, and get paid at the end of the day. He knew what game this was, the same game that had consumed Tony and put a bullet or two in him. The same game Tony continually urged Wes to stay out of.

But Wes rationalized. *I am not actually selling drugs. All I'm doing is talking into a headset.* He wasn't exactly excelling in the classroom, and his disenchantment with school was beginning to wear on him. All he really wanted to do was either play football professionally or become a rapper. If he could earn some cash in the meantime—just a little pocket money to hold him over till he was running in the end zone of RFK Stadium or rocking a sold-out crowd in Madison Square Garden—why not? This game didn't require studying or exams. It didn't require a degree or vocational skills. All he needed was ambition. And guts. And, as Wes was soon to understand, an ability to live with constant fear. But Wes wasn't focused on that yet. He didn't bother thinking about Tony's warnings, that no matter what job or position you took within it, this was a game for keeps—you could be in jail or dead in a matter of months.

Besides watching Tony, Wes's first real interaction with drugs had taken place a few months earlier, just before the move out to Baltimore County. It was late November, early in the morning. Wes was already up and showered, finishing some cold breakfast cereal with his book bag next to his leg, when Mary left to go to work. The moment he heard the door slam, Wes rushed to the window and watched as his mother slowly pulled out of her parking spot and joined the flow of city-bound traffic.

Wes had no intention of going to school. He was supposed to meet Woody later—they were going to skip school with some friends, stay at Wes's house, and have a cookout. Woody was bringing the hot dogs and burgers, Wes would be responsible for firing up the grill. Just the thought of hanging out with his boys and imagining the smell of barbecued hot dogs made Wes happy. He moved toward his mother's bedroom. Wes began his ritual search for change in her closet, but the jar was not in its usual place. Wes paused. Had she caught on?

As Wes rummaged through the closet, moving clothes and boxes from one side to the other, he came across a small see-through bag packed with a green substance. It looked like a collection of moss held together by some small sticks. But Wes knew exactly what he had stumbled on. He had just found his mother's weed stash. After a moment to think about whether he should take it, he came to the obvious conclusion: he was going to turn this barbecue into a real party.

Wes put the bag in his pocket and went outside to wait for Woody. As soon as he saw his friend turn the corner, he yelled in excitement, "Wait till you see what I've got!" Woody hustled over, and after they exchanged dap, Wes pulled out the bag. Woody instantly knew what they were working with. His eyes lit up, and he snatched the bag from Wes, opened the top a crack, and took a deep whiff like an old pro. Then he smiled. "Where did you get this, man?" Woody asked.

Wes told the story, and they exchanged a conspiratorial look. Their plans for the day had changed.

Within minutes, Wes and Woody had hooked up with some older

kids who were also skipping class that day. The boys all hopped on their bikes and rode to the corner store, where they picked up some Mad Dog 20/20 and rolling papers and, within a half hour, the party was getting started.

The boys found a spot under a bridge near the Morgan State University campus. Since Wes had been the one to discover the smoke, he was granted the privilege of the first hit. Wes knew all about weed but had never actually tried it. He cautiously put the rolled-up joint to his mouth and inhaled. He broke out into a spastic fit of coughing almost as soon as the joint passed his lips. The older boys laughed. But Wes kept at it. With each inhalation, the smoke passed more easily, and by the third toke, he was taking deep puffs and holding them in his lungs for several seconds before blowing a white cloud back out through his nose and mouth.

But after a few hits, Wes was disappointed. "I don't see what the big deal is, man."

"Just wait a little while. You'll feel it," Woody said.

The boys sat under the bridge drinking malt liquor and smoking as the morning quickly turned to afternoon. After a while they got hungry and decided to head to ABC, the fast-food Chinese food restaurant up the hill from their neighborhood. As soon as Wes stood up, he stumbled back to the ground.

"Told you he would feel it soon," Woody said, laughing. Wes slowly rose again, this time making it to his feet, and shuffled along, trying to get his bearings.

The bike ride to ABC usually took around five minutes, but this time it took the boys almost twenty because of Wes's slow pace. Wes joked about it, putting on a charade around his friends, but it was the most uncomfortable and vulnerable he had ever felt. Once they entered the restaurant, Wes quickly sat down to avoid collapsing. The rest of his boys got in line to order their food.

"You see that girl over there!" Wes shouted to Woody, as Woody stood in line to order a carton of fried rice.

"What girl?" Woody responded, looking puzzled.

"The one right there, with the red dress." Wes pointed to the other side of the restaurant. "Honey is thick!"

Woody looked at Wes and then turned to look at the other guys. Once they caught one another's eyes, they started cracking up.

"Dude is tripping! No more bud for you, yo!" one of the boys said. It didn't hit Wes until a few seconds later as he cleared his eyes. The "girl" he was admiring on the other side of the room was actually a trash can. Wes was a lot higher than he thought.

After the Chinese food stop, Wes decided it was time to head home. He began the slow, painful journey back down the hill, his stomach still empty after he'd tried unsuccessfully to eat at the restaurant, his head aching from the THC now swimming through his body. Each revolution of the bike pedals was more painful than the last, and all Wes wanted to do was lie down and forget the morning. The barbecue was canceled. Lying in bed was the only thing on the agenda.

When Wes got to the house, his mother's boyfriend, who was living with them when he wasn't back home with his wife, was sitting in the living room, directly next to the front door.

"What's up, Wes, you're home early," Wes heard as he stumbled through the door. The television blasting in the background made Wes's head throb even more. He closed his arms around his head and rushed past his mother's boyfriend with a quick "hey," beelining it to his room. He was in bed with all of his clothes on and his pillow over his head when he heard a knock at the door. It was his mother's boyfriend checking on him.

"Please leave me alone. I'm fine, just a little sick," Wes yelled out, but his voice was barely audible through the pillow pressed tightly against his face.

The boyfriend knew exactly what was bothering Wes. He'd smelled the liquor as soon as Wes staggered through the door.

Hours later, when Mary walked into Wes's room, the high had begun to wear off, but Wes was still in bed, thinking about the day's events.

"How do you feel?" Mary asked, intentionally speaking loudly. She gave her son a sarcastic yet toothy smile.

"Please hold it down, Ma! I hear you just fine," Wes pleaded, feeling his head begin to pound again.

Mary laughed, watching him squirm. "Well, at least now you

know how bad it feels and you will stay away from drinking," she said.

Wes now knew for sure how powerful drugs could be. He felt a strange sense of having passed a test, graduated to a new level of maturity. It was exhilarating. As he lay in bed, he realized how time seemed to stop when he was high, how the drug—smoking it, feeling its effects, recovering from it—made him forget everything else. And he understood, faintly, how addictive that feeling could be, and how easy it would be to make some money off selling that feeling to people who needed it.

As Wes placed the headset over his freshly cut fade and adjusted it, he remembered this story. The headset now fit perfectly. There was definitely money to be made.

Part II

Choices and Second Chances

"Happy birthday!"

Wes gave me a half smile. "Thanks, man, I almost totally forgot."

As the rest of the country celebrated independence, Wes spent his thirty-second birthday in prison. He's allowed to have visitors only on odd days of the year, so he was prohibited from seeing people on the Fourth of July. I visited a couple of days after his actual birthday.

When I arrived at Jessup that morning, my eyes flickered up to the sign mounted above the institution's steel front doors, the name of the prison—Jessup Correctional Institution—inked in bloody crimson. I stopped walking for a moment and stood in silence. It was midday. Over the towers of the prison the summer sun was high in the center of a cloudless sky. I looked up at the vast canopy of blue above, then took a deep breath, feeling the fresh air race through me. For the first time in a long time I was reminded of the daily miracle of my freedom, the ability to move, explore, meet new people, or simply enjoy the sun beating down on my face.

After going through the requisite security checks, I waited for Wes to walk into the waiting area. I studied the reunions taking place around me. One inmate, a young man seemingly in his early twenties, sat across from a woman with a baby squirming in her arms—he was apparently meeting his own child for the first time.

His girlfriend complained that since the kid hadn't slept through the whole night since he was born, neither had she. Another inmate listened wide-eyed as his grandmother ran down a list of his friends from the neighborhood, updating him on what they'd been up to since he'd gone away. He hung on her every word.

When my conversations with Wes had begun years earlier, we'd said only what we thought the other wanted to hear. What the other needed to hear. But over time it was hard to keep up the act, and our conversations drifted toward an almost therapeutic honesty.

"When did you feel like you'd become a man?" Wes asked me, a troubled look on his face.

"I think it was when I first felt accountable to people other than myself. When I first cared that my actions mattered to people other than just me." I answered quickly and confidently, but I wasn't too sure of what I was talking about. When did I actually become a man? There was no official ceremony that brought my childhood to an end. Instead, crises or other circumstances presented me with adult-sized responsibilities and obligations that I had to meet one way or another. For some boys, this happens later—in their late teens or even twenties—allowing them to grow organically into adulthood. But for some of us, the promotion to adulthood, or at least its challenges, is so jarring, so sudden, that we enter into it unprepared and might be undone by it.

Wes, feeding off my answer, attempted to finish my thought. "Providing for others isn't easy. And the mistakes you make trying are pretty unforgiving." He paused. I waited. He rubbed his chin, softly pulling at the long strands of his goatee with his fingers. "And second chances are pretty fleeting."

"What do you mean?"

"From everything you told me, both of us did some pretty wrong stuff when we were younger. And both of us had second chances. But if the situation or the context where you make the decisions don't change, then second chances don't mean too much, huh?"

Wes and I stared at each other for a moment, surrounded by the evidence that some kids were forced to become adults prematurely. These incarcerated men, before they'd even reached a point of basic maturity, had flagrantly—and tragically—squandered the few opportunities they'd had to contribute productively to something greater than themselves.

I sat back, allowing Wes's words to sink in. Then I responded, "I guess it's hard sometimes to distinguish between second chances and last chances."

FOUR

Marking Territory

"Dude, I am going to ask you one more time. Where did you get the money from?"

Tony's fists were clenched and his jaw tense as he eyed his little brother up and down. His stare was serious, and his stance like that of a trained boxer preparing to pounce. Wes's body language was evasive. He refused to look his brother in the eye.

Tony had come by the house that morning to see Wes and his mother. When he strolled past Wes's room, he noticed it had changed significantly since the last time he saw it. One wall was covered with a tower of sneaker boxes—inside the boxes were a rainbow assortment of Nikes, each pair fresher than the last. The smell of barely touched leather seemed to fill the room. It was like walking into Foot Locker.

Tony found his younger brother and asked for an explanation for the leaning tower of Nikes. Wes stuttered out a story: he'd become a popular DJ in the neighborhood and was making incredible loot DJing parties. It was the story he'd used with Mary, and she'd bought it whole. Maybe because she really believed him. Maybe because she really wanted to believe him. She'd asked Wes about the shoes when they started to multiply, but after her first inquisition, she'd left the subject alone.

Tony knew better.

Tony had now spent over a decade dealing drugs and knew how much money could be made in the game. He also knew there was no way for someone as young as Wes to make that kind of money DJing. There were not enough records to spin, enough beats to play, to buy that many sneakers.

Tony grabbed Wes's shirt collar and pulled him in close. "How many times do I have to tell you to leave this stuff alone, man?" His tone was low and serious, but he barked his words out like a challenge as the two boys squared off on their front lawn, out of sight of Mary, who was inside the house.

Wes's eyebrows arched up and his voice rose, his best play at sincerity. "I told you, man, I made this money DJing!" he repeated, almost convincing himself that it was the truth.

Tony closed his eyes and asked again, pounding out every word. "Wes. Where. Did. You. Get. The. Money?"

"I made the money D——"

Before Wes could even finish his sentence, Tony cocked back his arm and punched him dead in the face. Wes tumbled backward onto the grass. His left eye immediately began to swell. Tony jumped on top of him, pinning Wes's arms to the ground with his knees. Once he'd locked Wes's arms down, Tony unloaded blows, striking his younger brother's chest, ribs, and face with wild abandon. Wes was trying hard to wriggle free, but his stronger and tougher older brother was getting the best of him.

Mary heard the commotion and ran outside. She rushed over to the boys and tried to pull Tony off Wes, screaming for an explanation. After a brief struggle, Wes wrestled free and jumped back from his incensed brother.

"What the hell is going on here!" Mary screamed.

"Wes is out here hustling! I told him to leave this alone, but he won't listen!" Tony yelled back.

"No he isn't, he is making the money DJing," Mary said.

Hearing this, Tony pulled back his anger at Wes and turned it on his mother. "Are you serious? You really believe that? Are you blind?"

Mary hesitated. Her voice was less assured when she responded. "Well, that's what he told me, and I believe him," she said. Her eyes turned to Wes. He stood about ten feet away from them, head tilted back, trying to stop the bleeding from his nose. He suddenly jerked his head down to spit out the blood pooling in his mouth. Mary knew her younger son was no innocent. In addition to the knife fight when he was younger, Wes had been arrested a few years back after being caught stealing a car. But the sight of Tony punching Wes in the face infuriated her. Maybe it was because Wes was younger than Tony and Mary knew well how violent Tony could be. Or maybe it was because she wanted so much for Tony to be wrong. She knew what her older son was into but didn't think there was anything she could do for him now. She hoped that Wes would be different.

Wes was completely taken aback by his brother's anger. Tony had tried to keep Wes in school and away from drugs for as long as Wes could remember. But Tony was still deep in the game himself. Wes didn't think Tony was a hypocrite exactly—he knew why his brother felt obliged to warn him off. But it was clear that Tony himself didn't have any better ideas or he would've made those moves himself. And the truth was, Wes now had more money in his pocket than he'd ever had before, which kept him outfitted in new clothes—including the two-hundred-dollar Cross Colours set now covered with grass stains and dirt.

Tony looked over at Wes, his clothes, his crisp green footwear, the laces gleaming white even after their tumble through the grass. They were a long way from their days of youthful innocence: catching lightning bugs in jars, playing freeze tag on the Cherry Hill streets, and going to the Ocean City beach on summer days with their mother. The days of using a shopping cart as a go-cart, pushing it to the top of a hill, and letting gravity pull them down to the bottom were over. He realized he was staring at a mirror image of himself.

"You know what, dude," he said, "I'm good." Tony was exhausted. Tired from the beating he just gave Wes. Tired from repeating himself. "If you won't listen, that's on you. You have potential to do so much more, go so much further. You can lead a horse to water, but you can't make him drink, right?"

Tony leaned over to pick up his hat—it had fallen to the ground during their fight. He spun it around and placed it backward on his head. He walked off the lawn and into the street. Mary called out to him, asked where he was going. Tony yelled back over his shoulder, "Home," and kept walking down the block. He didn't look back again.

That was the last time Tony ever tried to talk to Wes about the drug game.

Mary raced over to Wes and examined his nose. The bleeding had slowed. "I am so sorry, Wes. That's just how Tony gets sometimes," she said.

Wes looked back at her but said nothing. They walked together into the house, where Mary wet a rag and started to clean up the scrapes and bruises Tony had left on his brother's face and body. The wet rag felt good over the open cuts on Wes's face. The deeper bruise, however, Mary could do nothing about. Wes knew he was disappointing his brother, which hurt much more than the beating he'd just taken. Wes was so confused. He loved and respected his brother. Tony was the closest thing Wes had to a role model. But the more he tried to be like his brother, the more his brother rejected him. The more he copied him, the more Tony pushed back. Wes wanted to be just like Tony. Tony wanted Wes to be nothing like him.

Tony's outburst did accomplish one thing, though. It motivated Mary to dig a little deeper into Wes's new income flow. The next day, after Wes went off to school, Mary began searching through his drawers. She hoped that he was not involved in drugs. "Please let it be DJing money. Please let it be DJing money," she prayed.

She lifted his mattress and found a few extra shoe boxes under his bed. She placed them on the mattress. They were light, so she knew they didn't hold sneakers, but something was rattling around in them. As she reached for the top of one of the boxes, she pulled her hand back. She whispered to herself, "Don't ask a question unless you are ready to hear the answer."

She reached again for the first Nike box and opened it. Inside were pills, marijuana, half an ounce of powdered cocaine, and half a dozen vials of "ready rock," or crack cocaine. She felt like she'd been punched in the stomach. She sat down on the bed, unsure of what to think. She wasn't only upset about the drugs, she was upset about the lying. She didn't even bother looking in the second box; she already knew all she needed to know. Both of her sons were drug dealers.

She sat paralyzed on the bed for fifteen minutes before springing up, suddenly decisive. She took the boxes into the bathroom, lifted their tops, and emptied the contents into the toilet. She watched every ounce, every rock, every leaf, every crystal float to the bottom of the toilet bowl, until the water was cloudy and white. She flushed it away once, and then again and again until the water in the bowl returned to its normal clarity. She put the tops back on the boxes and placed the boxes on Wes's bed.

A few hours later, Wes walked into his room and saw the two shoe boxes. His heart plummeted. These were his work boxes. He knew he was busted.

He started to think about what he would say to his mother as he slowly walked toward his bed. Maybe he would blame it on someone else. Maybe he could say he was holding them for a friend and never knew what was in them. Maybe he could say they were planted, that this was part of a larger conspiracy against him. But who would bother conspiring against him? When he reached the boxes and picked them up, he was struck by how light they were. He opened one of them and saw that it was empty. Had she thrown his drugs out? His anxiety about getting caught flipped to anger. He threw the boxes across the room. He tried to calculate how much weight he had lost, and how much money he now owed the connects who supplied him with the drugs.

"Damn!" he shouted. "Ma! Where are you? Do you know what you just did!"

"I'm in my room," Mary responded.

Wes stepped quickly to his mother's room, gaining anger with every creaky floorboard. When he walked into the room, Mary was calmly folding laundry on her bed. She didn't stop when he busted in.

Wes was senseless with anger, but Mary just coolly looked at him, eyes opened in an expression of exaggerated innocence.

"Ma, do you have any idea about what you just did? Where are the drugs?"

"I flushed them down the toilet."

"That was over four thousand dollars in drugs! I have to pay someone back for that!" Wes had completely forgotten about his conspiracy argument. The only thing on his mind was trying to figure out how on earth he was going to come up with four thousand dollars—and fast.

Mary was not the least bit concerned about her son's new dilemma. "Not only did you lie to me but you were selling drugs and keeping them in my house! Putting all of us in danger because of your stupidity. I don't want to hear your sob story about how much money you owe. You will stop selling that stuff. I will be checking your room, and I don't want to ever see it in here again. Now get out of my room."

Wes was stunned. He went back to his room and desperately tried to devise a plan. He owed money but had no drugs to sell—he had to figure out how to make that money back quickly. The only way to do that was to go see his connects and hit the street again. He'd realized very early in the game that the drug market was a simple supply-and-demand equation. The demand was bottomless. Your money was determined by how hard you worked, and how feared you were. He focused. He knew the streets would get him that money back, and more. But next time, he'd be smarter about where he kept the stash and how often he moved it around.

Wes left the house and began to walk toward his girlfriend's place a few blocks over. She was older, about seventeen. Wes complained to her about his mother's abuse of his privacy. His girlfriend sympathized. Before she realized what she was doing, she'd agreed to make her home his new headquarters.

As Mary heard the door slam behind Wes, she sat back down on her bed. She pressed her fingers against her temples and began to massage them. She closed her eyes; her mind raced: Who is to blame for this? Tony, the neighborhood, the school system, Wes's friends? She put them all on trial in her mind. She was furious at Wes for what he'd done and knew that this probably would not be the end of it. Tony, who was about to become a father—making Mary a thirty-six-year-old grandmother—had been right.

Leave the smack and the crack for the wack
Or the vial and the nine; keep a smile like that

My eyes were closed, and my hands moved along with the beat, as if I were onstage laying down the tracks on a DJ set. I was in a zone, concert mode, even if I was only in the front seat of my mother's blue Honda Civic. I recited a verse from the Chubb Rock song as it blared out of the car's speakers.

The road lost my mother's full attention momentarily as she stared down at me. She looked incredulous.

After a series of unsatisfactory report cards, my mother had begun to think that what many of my teachers were telling her was correct: I might have a learning disability. My teachers broke it down for her more than once: "Wes is a nice boy, but he has real problems retaining information." She remembered this as she listened to me reciting lyrics like I'd written them myself.

Anyway the shunless one brings forth the fun
No hatred; the summer's almost done

"How long have you known that song?"

"I don't know, not long," I mumbled out, lazily opening my eyes but never picking my head up to look at my mother. I'd first heard the song two days earlier.

"Well, your grades obviously aren't bad because you can't pick this stuff up or because you are stupid, you are just not working hard enough," my mother said, her voice rising into the epiphany. My academic failures had forced her to go through the stages of grief: denial, anger, bargaining, depression, and acceptance. She'd been stuck in depression for a long time and hadn't quite made it to acceptance, no matter how much I'd hoped she'd get there. It seemed like there was faulty wiring in the system, because now she was reverting to anger.

"You think I'm playing. Just try me," she said, the last note in a short conversation she seemed to be having with herself, and then returned her full attention to the road. As she did so, the new EPMD song came on. She must have noticed my slight head nod to the beat, because she quickly killed the radio.

Hip-hop had begun to play a special role in my life. It wasn't just music and lyrics. It was a validator. In my struggle to reconcile my two worlds, it was an essential asset. By the late 1980s, hip-hop had graduated from being the underground art of the Bronx to a rising global culture. My obsession with hip-hop kept me credible with the kids in my neighborhood. It let them know that, regardless of my school affiliation, I still understood. Hip-hop also gave the kids in my school a point of entry into my life: Public Enemy's black nationalist anthems or KRS-One's pulpy fantasies about gunning down crack dealers offered a window into a world that before hip-hop had seemed foreign to those who even dared to look through. But even more than that, I found in hip-hop the sound of my generation talking to itself, working through the fears and anxieties and inchoate dreams—of wealth or power or revolution or success—we all shared. It broadcast an exaggerated version of our complicated interior lives to the world, made us feel less alone in the madness of the era, less marginal. Of course, all that didn't matter to my mother. All she knew was that I could effortlessly recite hip-hop lyrics while struggling with my English class.

What she didn't know was that my problem in school was much more basic than a learning disability. The problem was that I wasn't even showing up half the time. It's tough to do well in school as an eleven-year-old when you're picking and choosing which days to go.

It was weeks before I had my schedule down pat. I realized the only time anyone really cared about my attendance was during homeroom, the first class of the day. Two days of the week, I had homeroom with my English teacher, Mrs. Downs, a young blonde who had taught only one other class in her life. I sensed her weakness and spent most of class coming up with creative ways to burnish my status as class clown. One day, she flatly told me that it didn't matter to her if I showed up because the class ran smoother when I wasn't there. From that moment, I understood Mrs. Downs and I had an unspoken agreement, a "don't ask, don't tell" pact that worked like a charm for both of us. Here's how a typical day would go: My grandmother would drop Shani and me off at school or at the train stop and we would wave goodbye, book bags in hands and smiles on faces. We would turn around and begin marching toward the school building or train stop until my grandmother's car pulled away. At that point, I'd have to decide how I would play it. Some days I would check into homeroom; other days I'd head directly back to the train and return to the neighborhood, where I'd meet up with one of the guys who had a similar arrangement. My sister, always the loyal accomplice, never snitched.

With our mother working so much, and our grandparents obviously slowing in energy, my sisters and I were supposed to look after one another. Nikki was older, so she was always the one looking after me, and it was my responsibility to look after Shani. But Nikki's hands were full with her own turbulent high school experience, which was about to come to a close. The move to the Bronx had been hard on her. Nikki never fully adjusted to the new social and academic environment; she attended three different high schools in four years. Shani, by contrast, was a prodigy. She did not go outside much, except to play basketball with me and my friends, and she seemed to have a book with her wherever she went. In fact, by the time I hit fifth grade and she was in third grade, she had overtaken me in reading scores, a distinction she carried through our entire academic lives and probably holds to this day. As much of a screwup as I was becoming, I still tried hard to look after her.

A few months earlier, Shani went out to play with one of the neighborhood girls, Lateshia, and came back home with her face covered in blood. When I returned home later that day, she was sitting on the couch in the living room, a red-stained napkin stuck in one of her nostrils and my grandmother's arms wrapped around her shoulders. They told me what had happened: Shani, Lateshia, and a Puerto Rican girl named Ingrid were jumping rope outside the house. A dispute broke out, words were exchanged, and Shani found herself on the receiving end of a punch to the nose. Shani was much bigger than the other girl and was used to wrestling with me, but she didn't fight back. She just started crying and headed into the house, pinching her nose to stop the bleeding.

By the end of the story, I was furious. First, at Shani for not punching Lateshia back, but then at Lateshia, who had the audacity to go after my sister. Just recently off my first encounter with the movie *The Godfather*, I pulled a Sonny Corleone and flew out the door to find Lateshia. My actual godmother, who was standing by the door, also wanted in on the action. Aunt BB, a tall, light-skinned Alabamian who had known my grandparents since she moved up to New York thirty years ago, was one of our family's fiercest defenders, and she was not going to let me go out there to avenge my sister without her being there. She had also just moved into the house with us, making it eight of us in our small row home. Just as fired up as I was, Aunt BB followed me up the street. In retrospect, we made a comical pair of enforcers, a forty-something-year-old woman trailing an eleven-year-old boy. But we were deadly serious.

When we rolled up to her house, Lateshia was sitting on the front steps with her older brother. She straightened up with a surprised look. Aunt BB demanded to know why she'd hit Shani. Lateshia stumbled through an answer, claiming that she was defending herself. Aunt BB cut her off.

"Little girl, don't you ever touch her again. I don't know who you think you are, but you are really messing with the wrong one."

Lateshia stared back. She was too cool to show submission and too scared to show defiance. As we started to walk away, I decided I could not let my aunt handle the fight solo, so I turned around to face Lateshia while keeping an eye on her older brother. "And let me tell you," I said, "if I ever hear about you touching her again, the last thing you will have to worry about is a bloody nose."

Not only was her brother older and bigger but he had a rep as one not to be played with. But I just stood there in my B-boy stance, empowered by strains of "The Bridge Is Over" running through my head, until I felt like the message had gotten across. Satisfied, Aunt BB and I took off for our house. I was a little shaken as we walked back home in the twilight. Little things like this had a way of escalating into blood feuds. Big brothers called bigger brothers, who called crews. But Shani never played with Lateshia again and, fortunately, I never saw her brother again.

The Bronx streets had become a fixture in my life. Whether it was playing ball at Gun Hill Projects basketball court, heading over to Three Boys on Burke Avenue to get a slice of pizza, running to Saul's to get an edge-up on Bronxwood, or just sprawling out on stoops with my crew, some of the most important lessons I learned, I learned from these streets. I learned about girls getting periods not from biology class but from my friend Paris. I learned the realities of gang violence not from after-school specials but when my boy Mark got jumped and beaten down for wearing the wrong color jacket. And I learned that cops were smarter than I thought on the corner of Laconia Avenue.

I was rocking my Olaf's basketball shorts and Syracuse T-shirt on an unseasonably warm Saturday in October. I'd always wanted to go to Syracuse like my uncle Howard and play basketball for the Orangemen. I was to find out later that I wanted them a whole lot more than they wanted me. We'd just finished playing a game of basketball and were leaving the courts when out of the corner of my eye I saw Shea, one of my friends from the neighborhood. Shea was my age but shorter, with reddish hair and light skin, light enough for a spray of freckles to shine through. I broke off from my friends and walked over to him—we met halfway and greeted each other. I asked him what he was up to, and he said confidently, "Nothing, just finished working." I checked out his gear: black jeans, a white tank top, and a black backpack. Work. I knew exactly what that meant.

Shea was a "runner," an entry-level position in any drug enterprise. A runner was the one who moved packages for local suppliers who needed to make drop-offs for the street-level dealers but didn't want to carry the weight themselves. Kids like Shea were used because they were less conspicuous, and less likely to be stopped by police officers. Shea was making decent money, but ever since he'd started "working," we'd seen less of him.

Shea and I sat in front of the Cue Lounge, a bar and billiards club whose façade was painted black. The Cue Lounge sat next to a Kentucky Fried Chicken and an hourly-rate motel. Cars whizzed by as we spoke. We were checking out the black wall of the lounge, which was plastered with spray-painted tags. Some we recognized as friends we knew, and others from other walls around the neighborhood. It seemed as if everybody in the hood had their own nickname and tag, some more elaborate than others. Even me. Mine was simple: a "KK" with a circle around it, standing for Kid Kupid, an alter ego I assumed to advertise my largely imaginary prowess with the young ladies. I had redecorated a few corners of the Bronx with it.

As we stared at the markups on the wall, admiring the work of some of our contemporaries, Shea reached over his shoulder, pulled the backpack in front of him, and slowly unzipped it. I quickly looked inside. Beside a small bottle of water and a white headband were two spray-paint bottles, one with a white top and one with a blue. He looked at me with a sly smirk.

"You wanna tag?"

I couldn't say no. First off, Shea was one of the most respected young hustlers in the neighborhood. He was a worker, we all knew that—and while some of the kids were smart enough to be disgusted by what he did, other kids, even the ones who weren't in the game, respected his position. Plus, I loved throwing my name up on a wall; it felt like splashing in the shallow end of the criminal pool.

I scanned the streets for cops and nosy neighbors as I reached into his bag and pulled out the can with the white top. My eyes continued to scan as I shook the can, making sure the contents were mixed so that the paint would come out even and clean, creating a crisper result. Once I felt the coast was clear, I began, first drawing the connected Ks and finishing with a wide circle around them, my custom style. I placed the can back in Shea's bag, satisfied with my work—and our speed. Seven seconds and done. I had added my indelible

My grandparents right after they moved to the United States. They were married for fifty-seven years.

Mom and Dad at their wedding. My grandmother made my mom's dress.

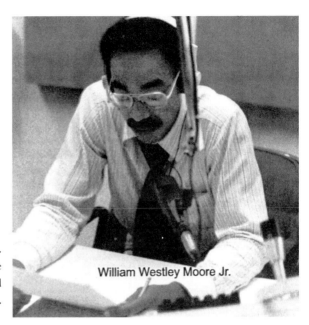

My father at work. His passions in life were his family and good journalism.

William Westley Moore Jr.

Me posing with my sister Nikki. I was two years old in this picture.

With my grandfather at SeaWorld.

Leaning on Uncle Howard's shoulder. I was eleven in this picture and having difficulty in and out of the classroom.

Admiral Thunman and I during my first year at Valley Forge.

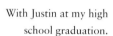

With Justin at my high school graduation.

More than a dozen members of my family came to Pennsylvania for my high school graduation. I felt honored to have so much support.

Wes being held by his older brother, Tony. Even at that young age, Tony was Wes's protector.

Nine-year-old Wes on vacation with his mother.

Wes on Christmas Day
in Dundee Village.

Woody (number 55) playing for
the Northwood Rams.

Tony at fourteen years old.

Wes at home in Cherry Hill.

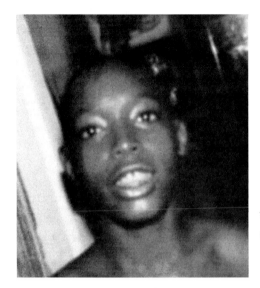

Wes's smile always put people at ease.

Aunt Nicey was a second mother to Wes when he was growing up.

mark to Laconia Avenue, a testament to the world that Wes Moore lived—or at least Kid Kupid did. Nobody could ever deny I was there. Not even me as a police cruiser rolled up around the corner.

Wuap, wuap! The distinctive sound of the police siren rang out. Shea and I looked at each other and then sprinted off in different directions. Foolishly, I headed right past the police car; it took one of the officers seconds to wrap me up and throw me against his vehicle. Shea at least had a shot. I saw him sprinting off in the opposite direction. He turned around, saw me being patted down, and realized my escape had lasted a mere four steps. He tried to speed up, but seconds later, he too was wrapped up by a policeman. As I lay on the hood of the car, with the officer's hands pressing against every part of me, searching me, I watched Shea twenty feet away on the ground getting the same treatment.

My uncertainty about what to expect ended when the officer reached above my head and began to pull my left arm behind my back. Now I understood where this was going. I was being arrested.

"Chill, man, I didn't do anything!" I began screaming as I tried to wrangle my hands free.

"Stop resisting," the officer warned as he cuffed my left wrist and roughly pinned down my flailing right arm.

The relationship between the police and the people they served and protected changed significantly during the 1980s. For almost as long as black folks have been in this country, they've had a complicated relationship with law enforcement—and vice versa. But the situation in the eighties felt like a new low. Drugs had brought fear to both sides of the equation. You could see it in the people in the neighborhood, intimidated by the drug dealers and gangs, harassed by the petty crime of the crackheads, and frightened by the sometimes arbitrary and aggressive behavior of the cops themselves. On the other end of the relationship, the job of policemen, almost overnight, had gotten significantly tougher. The tide of drugs was matched by a tide of guns. The high-stakes crack trade brought a new level of competition and organization to the streets. From my supine perch on the back of the police car, I noticed an older woman staring at me, shaking her head.

After he finished cuffing me, the cop opened the rear door of his cruiser and pushed my head down while shoving me into the back-seat. I was terrified. I had no idea what was next. A thought raced around my head—my mother was going to have to pick me up from jail. She had just finished talking to me about my grades, and now this. My relationship with my mother was in a strange place. My desperation for her support was in constant tension with my desperation for independence and freedom. I projected apathy about her feelings, but I wanted nothing more than to make her proud. In other words, I was a teenager, deathly fearful of disappointing her but too prideful to act like it mattered. Now I was afraid this incident might turn my only stalwart supporter against me.

Loneliness enveloped me. I felt my fate suddenly twinned with that of Shea, an aspiring drug dealer who I knew didn't really give a damn about me. My friends seemed far away, and in that distance I became aware of the contingent nature of my relationship with my crew. We loved one another, but how long would we mourn the absence of any one of us? I'd seen it happen a million times already, kids caught out there in one way or another—killed, imprisoned, shipped off to distant relatives. The older kids would pour out a little liquor or leave a shrine on a corner under a graffiti mural, or they'd reminisce about the ones who were locked down, but then life went on, the struggle went on. Who really cared? Besides my mother, who would even miss me?

My eyes watered as I sat in the backseat of the cruiser, watching out the window as the two cops picked Shea up off the ground and led him toward the backseat with me. Shea winked at me as he walked up to the car with his hands behind his back. *Is this dude serious?* I thought.

The car door opened, and Shea was thrown into my lap. "Fuckin jakes, man," he coolly stated as he straightened himself up.

"Yo, shut up, man! We are in serious trouble! I can't go to jail, man." I was almost hyperventilating.

"Just say you didn't do anything. Just say you don't know what they are talking about," Shea said.

I looked out the window, saw the two cops searching Shea's bag with the spray-paint cans, and realized that Shea's strategy was one of the dumbest ideas I had heard in a long time. Even I, who could come up with an excuse for everything, was at a loss for a good one in this situation.

The cops stood outside for what seemed like forever, discussing our fate. I wanted to ask Shea if he had any of his "work" inside the bag too but decided against it, feeling it was better for me not to know. In fact, I didn't even want to talk to him. I wanted to wait in silence.

One of the officers, a stocky Italian with jet-black hair, moved toward the passenger side of the car and opened the front door. He folded himself in and looked back at us over his left shoulder. Shea and I sat silently, me with wet eyes and a look of uncertainty, Shea staring back with cocky, smug indifference. The cop turned back around and began to write something on a clipboard. Finally he looked back at us and said, "What the hell are you thinking?"

Almost simultaneously, Shea launched into his brilliant "It wasn't us" story while I loudly attempted to overrule him by apologizing profusely. When we were done with our overlapping monologues, we glared at each other.

The cop shook his head and pointed his right index finger in our direction. "You kids are way too young to be in this situation. But you know what, I see kids like you here every day. If you don't get smart, I am certain I will see you again. That's the sad part."

He paused and looked into our eyes, searching for a reaction. Mine were probably filled with tears. I was wincing because the handcuffs were beginning to hurt my wrists, but I was also sincerely fearful about what was going to happen next. And the self-righteous look on Shea's face was starting to piss me off. I'm sure in my outlaw fantasies I would've been as defiant as Shea, but something about this situation had soured me on romantic rebellion. It may have been the moment when the officer finally pulled my second arm behind my back and tightened the handcuffs. In that moment, I became aware of how I had put myself in this unimaginably dire situation—this man now had control of my body; even my own hands had become useless to me. More than that, he had control of my destiny—or at least my immediate fate. And I couldn't deny that it was my own stupid fault. I didn't have the energy for romantic rebellion—the possibility of losing all control of my life was like a depthless black chasm that had suddenly opened up in front of me. All I wanted to do was turn around, go home, and never find myself at this precipice again for such a stupid reason. Kid Kupid! What was I thinking?

The cop opened his car door, allowing himself out. The other officer began to move toward his side of the vehicle. Within moments they'd opened the back doors. The officer who'd been lecturing us reached in and grabbed me by the shirt until he could get a good grip on my shoulder and pull me out of the vehicle. As I cleared the door, he stood me up straight, and I noticed the same happening with Shea on the other side of the car. The officer reached down and, with a quick turn of his wrist, the cuff on my left wrist opened up.

"I hope you really listened to what I told you," he whispered in my ear, opening up the other cuff to let both of my hands free.

"Yeah, thank you," I replied as I rubbed each wrist with the opposite hand, trying to ease some of the pain of the metal handcuffs pressing against my skin.

"All right, guys, the bag is ours. Now get moving."

Shea looked as though he was about to start protesting to them about keeping the bag until I grabbed him by the left arm, telling him it was time to get moving. We began to walk back down Allerton Avenue, turning around every few seconds to see the cops, who were still staring at us. The cops gave us a gift that day, and I swore I would never get caught in a situation like that again.

A week later, Kid Kupid was on the loose again, adding my tag to another graffiti-filled Bronx wall.

FIVE

Lost

"Get up, get up, get out of your racks, plebes!"

It was 5:30 in the morning, my room was pitch-dark, and the sound of half a dozen teenagers screaming at the top of their lungs startled me out of the light sleep I'd just drifted into. I was on the top bunk of a metal bed that was more sturdy than comfortable—and probably built during the Second World War. My roommate was awake too—I could tell because he jumped out of the bottom bunk and stared up at me; even in the dark I could see that his face was masked with panic. He was wearing an oversize white T-shirt that draped over his bony shoulders and gray thermal underwear that covered his legs, which were now trembling in fear.

"Moore, we have to get up and go in the hallway!" he said. His pubescent voice was cracking from the stress.

He stood there for a moment, waiting for me to respond, shuffling his feet as if he had to go to the bathroom. His face was aimed at me, but his glasses sat on the wooden desk next to the bunk bed. The lenses were as thick as Coke-bottle bottoms, so I doubt he saw much.

I watched him do his pee-pee dance for a moment, then peeked over at our clock, which sat across the room. I couldn't believe it.

"Bro, it is five-thirty in the morning! You tell them to come get me around eight," I said and yanked my covers tighter around me. "I should be ready to go then."

My roommate somehow managed to look even more dumb-founded. Just as he was opening his mouth to say something, another yell came from the corridor, a single voice now, ordering us into the hallway. My roommate's attention shifted; he wasn't going to waste his time trying to convince me to get up. I was either really brave or really stupid, and he was not going to wait around to see which. Within moments, I was left alone in the room.

Once I had the room to myself again, I rolled over, turning my back to the door, and pulled the covers over my head to avoid the commotion coming from the hallway. Seconds after getting comfortable, I heard the yelling voice with a new clarity. It was right on the other side of my door.

"Why is there only one person outside this room?"

My door slammed open, and in walked First Sergeant Anderson, a high school senior with an impressively premature five-o'clock shadow, a scruffy voice, and the posture and mannerisms of a bulldog. Still half-asleep and turned away from the door—I refused to believe this was happening—I heard the sound of boots approaching my bunk and then stop. And that's when the screaming started. Anderson's anger, efficiently transmitted through his sonorous, full-toned voice, had shifted from general displeasure with all of us to a focused rage pointed in my direction.

"Get your goat-smelling ass out of the rack!

"I am going to smoke you so bad, they will need dental records to identify your body!

"You better get that z monster off your back, turdbird!"

Some of the curses he used I hadn't heard before. But I could figure out they weren't compliments or normal pleasantries.

I turned around so I could face him and was met with a fusillade of saliva as he continued his tirade. Why in the world was he yelling so early in the morning? And who did he think he was, screaming at me like that?

I slowly sat up and wiped the cold out of my eyes. The first sergeant paused for a moment—he saw me moving and must've figured his tantrum had done the trick. As silence finally returned to my room, I moved my hand from my eyes and calmly spoke: "Man, if you don't get out of my room . . ."

His eyes widened, then slitted. His angry face broke into a devilish smile. Just as quickly as he'd come into the room, he walked out.

This was my first morning at the military school.

I knew my mother was considering sending me away, but I never thought she'd actually do it. The final straw came one evening while she sat downstairs on the phone listening to my dean from Riverdale explain why they were placing me on academic and disciplinary probation. It wasn't pretty. Bad grades, absence from classes, and an incident with a smoke bomb were just some of the reasons he rattled off as my mother sat silently on the couch with the phone to her ear. Her conviction was increasing with every bad report. Meanwhile, upstairs, Shani and I sat in my room watching television—or trying to. Our eighteen-inch color television, topped with a wire hanger where the antenna should have been, was a blizzard of snow. I got bored and looked around for alternative entertainment. The only thing available was my sister. I began to lightly punch her in the arm, first with my right fist, then with my left, trying to get her to pay attention to me. She stubbornly kept staring at the ghostly images of Pat Sajak and Vanna White flickering through breaks in the snow. Eventually she told me to stop, never taking her eyes off the screen, but I kept on aiming blows at her shoulder. Boredom in teenage boys is a powerful motivation to create chaos. At that moment, Shani's arm was my time filler.

Finally fed up, Shani turned to tell me to stop and, as she did, my right knuckles skipped off her shoulder and into her bottom lip, which immediately stained red.

In more shock than pain, Shani saw this as an opportunity.

"Oooooh, Ima get you now," she said. She smiled slyly as the blood covered her bottom row of teeth.

The smile faded, and her bottom lip began to tremble. Her eyes filled with tears. And then came the scream. . .

"Mommy! Westley hit me in the face, and I'm bleeding really bad!"

Damn.

I tried to stop her from running to my mother, but she beat me to the door and began a full sprint down the hallway. Her screaming continued as she disappeared down the stairs. Her acting was stellar, and since she still had the blood on her rapidly swelling lip and the crocodile tears streaming down her face, I knew the evidence was against me. There was nothing left to do but wait. I sat back in front of the television and watched as Vanna came briefly into view, strutting across stage to turn a blank tile into the letter *R*.

When I heard my mother coming up the stairs, I braced myself. She walked into my room, tired from her long day at work, disappointed by the conversation she'd just had with my dean, and furious after seeing her youngest with a split lip that her only son had given her. As soon as she came close enough, I tried to plead my case, but as it turned out, she had nothing to say. She simply pulled her right hand back and slapped me.

The burn consumed the entire left side of my face. Not willing to show fear or weakness, I stood there looking back at her. I guess she was expecting tears or apologies. When neither came, she reached back and unloaded another slap to my face. She looked at me again, waiting for a reaction. My jaws clenched, and my hands balled into fists. By this time, I was five inches taller than she was, and my recently defined shoulders, biceps, and triceps made me look older than my age. Every reflex inside said to strike back, but I didn't. How could I? She was my everything, the person I loved and respected most in my world. I had no idea what to do.

Neither did my mother, it seemed. Her almond-shaped eyes were overflowing with anger, disappointment, and confusion, and maybe even a little fear. I would never have hit my mother. But in my room, at that moment, she was not so sure. She looked at me as if for the first time. The days when she could physically intimidate me were clearly over.

She turned around and walked out of the room. She was devastated. She was losing her son, and she was not sure how to turn the tide. We didn't know it at the time, but once alone, we both started to cry.

After my first sergeant left the room, I lay back down and pulled the covers back over myself. As my head hit the pillow, I smirked to think that I could make them leave my room so easily. I was from the Bronx, after all, maybe these country jokers were intimidated. Maybe I could manage this military school thing.

Moments later the door slammed opened again, hitting the wall so hard flakes of the crusty blue paint chipped off. My entire chain of command, eight large and angry teenagers, entered the room and, without saying a word, picked my mattress up off the top bunk and turned it over, dropping me five feet to the cold, hard, green-tiled floor.

Welcome to military school.

Valley Forge Military Academy is in Wayne, Pennsylvania. It's on the prestigious Main Line, just twenty-five minutes outside Philadelphia, on a rolling campus surrounded by overgrown foliage. It was a more austere version of Riverdale, a far cry from my Bronx neighborhood. Our days began before the sun came up and ended well after it retired. Over our first few days we would learn how to shine our shoes using Kiwi black shoe polish, a cotton rag, and a pretty disgusting amount of saliva. We would learn how to execute military commands and repeat our drill and ceremony so many times that "right face," "left face," and "parade rest" became as familiar as our own names. We would learn how to "square our meals," a way of eating that forced us to slow down and savor the sometimes unidentifiable cuisine we were forced to eat, and "square the corridors," which required marching around the entire hallway to leave the building, even if the exit was only a few steps away from your room. Our birth names were irrelevant, as were our past acquaintances and past accomplishments and past failures. We were the same now. We were nothing. In fact, we were less than nothing. We were plebes.

My squad leader, Sergeant Austin, a blond sophomore from Connecticut with green eyes and a sneaky smile, would go off on one of us and then announce, "Don't take this personally, I hate you all just the same." I was given this dubious reassurance more than others.

For those first few days, I woke up furious and went to bed even more livid. The target of my rage was my mother. How could she send me away? How could she force me into a military school before I was even a teenager? When she dropped me off the first day, I was in full ice grille mode, lip curled, eyes squinting, with my "screw the world" face on, ready for battle—but inside I was bewildered. I felt betrayed. I felt more alone than ever.

By the end of the fourth day at military school, I had run away four times. I had heard that there was a station somewhere in Wayne where I could catch a train that would take me to Thirtieth Street Station in Philadelphia. From there I could transfer to a train that would take me to Penn Station in New York, which would take me to the Number 2 subway train, which would drop me off on the grimy streets that would take me home. I had the entire plan set. The only thing I couldn't figure out was how to get to this train station in Wayne.

One morning, my roommate and I were in our tight five-by-eight room, sitting on our respective wooden chairs, shining our shoes. My roommate was from Brooklyn, and we were the only two New Yorkers in the entire unit. I partially blamed him for my being in military school, because it was his grandmother who'd first told my mother about Valley Forge. My roommate's uncle had graduated from the school years earlier and was now a successful business executive. So when my mom, who was friendly with their family, was looking for a new environment for me, they enthusiastically recommended this school. Paralleling my mom's insistence that I attend Riverdale because John F. Kennedy had once gone to school there, she was won over to Valley Forge when she heard that General Norman Schwarzkopf was a graduate. This was right after the first Gulf War, and General Schwarzkopf was seen as the second coming of General

MacArthur. There was no military history in my family, but for them, as for many immigrant families, American heroes—and the schools they attended—carried a certain cachet. I glanced at my roommate, burning with resentment.

I had just finished shining the tip of my left shoe and was scooping out a helping of polish for the right shoe when our door opened.

"Ten-hut!" my roommate yelled, jumping to his feet upon seeing our squad leader enter the room. I followed suit.

Sergeant Austin looked directly at my roommate and told him to leave the room. My roommate quickly dropped the rest of his shining kit and scurried out, shutting the door behind him. I had no idea what I'd done this time, but it couldn't be good. I was afraid that something serious was about to happen, and Austin had cleared the room because he wanted no witnesses. I stood at attention but braced myself for whatever was about to go down.

To my surprise, Austin told me to sit down. I dropped into my chair but stayed tense. Austin grabbed my roommate's chair, turning it around like we were old buddies about to have a heart-to-heart. He looked at me, almost with pity, and said, "Listen, Moore, you don't want to be here, and quite honestly, we don't want you here, so I have drawn you a map of how to get to the train station."

He handed me a guidon, a manila-colored book the size of a small spiral notebook that contained all of the "knowledge" we had to memorize in order to make the transition from plebe to new cadet. The book included items such as the mission statement of the school, the honor code, the cadet resolution, and all of the military and cadet ranks. More important to me at the time, the back of the book had an aerial map of the Wayne area and, on this particular copy, handwritten notes with clear directions to the train station.

I looked at the map and was momentarily struck dumb. There was nothing I wanted more than to join my friends, to see my family, to leave this place. To see my mother. Here was my squad leader, for whom I had no love, giving me what felt like one of the greatest gifts I had ever received. The burden of loneliness was suddenly lifted. Someone finally understood me. This map was my path to freedom. This map was my path home.

When I looked up from the map and into the eyes of Sergeant Austin, happiness overwhelmed me. I smiled uncontrollably and thanked him. "I will never forget you!" I proclaimed. He rolled his eyes and simply said, "Yeah, just get out of here." He stood up from the chair, and I got up and snapped to attention, showing the first real sign of respect I had given him since walking through the gates. As he exited the room, shutting the door behind him, my mind was spinning. I began to plan my great escape.

At 10:00 every night, "Taps" was played by a military bugler in the main parade area. "Taps" denoted the end of the day. The hauntingly slow anthem played loudly as the entire corps stopped and stood in the deferential parade rest position until the final note ended. "Taps" is also played at funerals, a way of paying homage to lost comrades. I bowed my head but couldn't suppress a smile. I knew this would be the last time I would have to endure this depressing song.

I set my alarm for midnight, thinking that would be late enough for everyone to be asleep but early enough to give me a significant head start before the predawn nightmare of wake-up call repeated itself. I could begin my journey back home undisturbed. My alarm clock, which was no larger than the palm of my hand, sat under my pillow so when the alarm went off, it would be loud enough for me, and only me, to hear. My night bag, which contained only a flashlight, a few changes of clothes, and a granola bar, sat under my bunk bed, packed and ready to go. It was *The Shawshank Redemption,* and I was about to become Andy Dufresne.

Two hours after "Taps," I was up and tiptoeing through the hallways until I hit the bloodred door that took me into the night. With nothing but a bag over my shoulder, a map and directions written on the back of the guidon in my left hand, and a tiny flashlight in my right hand, I was gone. I never looked back at Wheeler Hall, my residence building, as I quietly bolted through the door. Goodbye and good riddance, I thought.

I followed the map to a tee, pacing my steps, trying to identify the landmarks that my squad leader had highlighted. The quarter moon was not providing much light, so I trained my pen-size flashlight on the guidon. The map was leading me in directions I hadn't seen in my brief time at the school, through bushes and brush that quickly turned to trees and forests. But I stuck to the directions, and to hope, and imagined that, in a short time, the trees would open up and reveal the train station sitting there waiting for me. Minutes later, that hope was rapidly diminishing. In its place was a different feeling. Terror.

As I patrolled through the forest, my movie-saturated imagination began to run wild. I was having hallucinations. I started to hear snakes and bears and other wild animals. The affluent suburb of Wayne might as well have been the Serengeti the way I imagined animals surrounding me. I was against the ropes in my battle with fear, and I lost my bearing, my pace count, my control. Finally, I sat down on a rock that I could have sworn I had just tripped over ten paces back and began to cry. I was defeated. I had never wanted anything more in my life than to leave that school, and I was slowly coming to the realization that it was not going to happen.

As I sat on the rock weeping, I heard the rustling of leaves and brush behind me. I had been imagining wild animals for a while now, but these sounds were more intense. My ears perked up, and my head snapped to attention. I turned in the direction of the sounds and suddenly heard a chorus of laughter. Out of the darkness came the members of my chain of command, including my new "friend," Sergeant Austin.

Bastard, I thought.

The directions he had given me were fake. They'd led me nowhere but to the middle of the woods.

Without a fight, I got up from the rock and walked with them back to campus. With my head bowed, we entered the main building and went straight to my tactical officer's office.

Colonel Battaglioli, or Colonel Batt, as we called him, sat in his office as my chain of command led me in. I was broken, dead-eyed, with my night bag still on my shoulder and the utterly useless folded map in my pocket. Colonel Batt was a retired Army officer with twenty-six years in the service. He had served all over the world, including combat tours in Vietnam. He walked fast, his body at a forty-five-degree angle to the ground, as if he was leaning into every step. When he saluted, it seemed like the force of his entire body went into it. He spoke like an understudy for Al Pacino, all spit and curved vowels. He was new to the job at Valley Forge, we were his first plebe class, and I was his first major challenge.

Plebe system is a process all new arrivals must go through in order to earn the title of new cadet. As a plebe, you refer to yourself in the third person: "This plebe would like to go to the bathroom." "This plebe requests permission to eat." In plebe system, your plebe brothers are all you have to make it through. And to ensure that, there is no communication with the outside world. No phone calls, no televisions, no radios, no visits.

Colonel Batt looked at my eyes—which were downcast and barely open—and realized that if he didn't bend the rules just slightly, he would lose me for good.

"Look at me, Moore," he firmly commanded. I lifted my eyes.

Colonel Batt continued. "I am going to let you talk on the phone for five minutes, and that is it for the rest of plebe system. Call who you need to, but you had better be snapped out of this when that phone hangs up."

I looked around the room and saw four members of my chain of command looking down on me. I also noticed a man I had not seen before but whose presence dominated the room, demanding not only focus but respect. He was black, stood about five ten, and carried a muscular 210 pounds or so. He peered down on me through his glasses with a laserlike intensity. His uniform was pressed so sharp you could have cut paper with the cuffs on his khaki shorts. He appeared to be still a teenager but carried an old soul and a frighteningly serious demeanor. He didn't say a word, but he didn't have to. His look said it all.

Colonel Batt handed me the phone, and I dialed the only number I knew by heart. As the phone rang, I began to think about what I would say in five minutes to convince my mother to let me back home.

"Hello?" Her voice was groggy, reminding me that it was one o'clock in the morning.

"Hey, Ma, it's me!" I said a little too loud, excited to hear her voice after what had been the four longest days of my life.

She got nervous at the sound of my voice. She wasn't supposed to hear from me for at least another month. She asked if everything was all right, and I assured her I was fine. Then I started my five-minute campaign to come home.

"Ma, I know I haven't been perfect, but I promise to do better. I will pay attention in school and go more often. I will clean my room, I will clean your room, I will—"

She cut me off. "Wes, you are not going anywhere until you give this place a try. I am so proud of you, and your father is proud of you, and we just want you to give this a shot. Too many people have sacrificed in order for you to be there."

I had no idea then, but I later found out just what sacrifices she was talking about. When she first heard about Valley Forge, she told my grandparents about her plan. They were strongly in favor of the idea. The problem was that military school is not free. It's not even cheap. The price tag for Valley Forge was even steeper than that for Riverdale. My mother had written to family and friends, asking them to help her however they could. "I wouldn't ask if I didn't really need it," she wrote. Weeks later, she was still thousands of dollars short.

My grandparents knew that I was at a crucial juncture in my life. These forks in the road can happen so fast for young boys; within months or even weeks, their journeys can take a decisive and possibly irrevocable turn. With no intervention—or the wrong intervention—they can be lost forever. My mother made the decision to intervene—and decided that overdoing it was better than doing nothing at all. She felt my environment needed to change and my options needed to expand. Drastically. My grandparents agreed.

They put most of their money into the home, hoping to use their equity to support themselves in retirement, when they would return to Jamaica to be with family and friends. Now that my grandparents knew they were needed in the Bronx, their desire to move back to Jamaica had faded. Their children and grandchildren were here. Their friends and doctors were here. And more than that, they now considered themselves not Jamaicans who were living in America but Americans of Jamaican descent.

My grandparents took the money they had in the home in the

Bronx, decades of savings and mortgage payments, and gave it to my mother so that she could pay for my first year of military school.

As I sat on the other end of the line, listening to my mother talk about "sacrifice," I had no idea what my grandparents had given up. The five minutes went fast, and Colonel Batt signaled it was time for me to hang up and go to bed. "I love you, and I am proud of you. And, Wes, it's time to stop running," my mother said as I hung up.

I was sent back to my room to lie down for the three hours before I would be driven awake again by the same trash-can-drumming, light-flashing, music-blaring, insult-laden wake-up call as every other godforsaken morning in this hellhole.

The next day, as we prepared to head to second mess, which was what they tellingly called lunch, I noticed the black man from the night before standing next to Colonel Batt. They were talking and looking in my direction. Even when I was standing at attention with my eyes to the front, their piercing gazes felt like they were burning a hole through me. Finally the two men saluted, and the black man walked back toward F Company, the college freshmen and sophomores. It was known around the entire corps as the most squared away, the most impressive company. Its members were the best marchers, the most athletic, the most disciplined. Whoever was in charge of them was doing an amazing job. I wondered whether that man who was talking to Colonel Batt was going to fall into the ranks, but as my eyes followed him, I heard the thunderous sound of 120 men all snapping to attention. Nineteen-year-old Cadet Captain Ty Hill took his place at the front of F Company.

In spite of myself, I was impressed. I had never seen anything like that before. I had never seen a man, a peer, demand that much respect from his people. I had seen Shea demand respect in the neighborhood, but this was different. This was real respect, the kind you can't beat or scare out of people. That's when I started to understand that I was in a different environment. Not simply because I was in the middle of Pennsylvania instead of the Bronx or Baltimore. It was a different psychological environment, where my normal expectations were inverted, where leadership was honored and class clowns were ostracized. I was still watching Captain Hill out of the corner of my eye when Colonel Batt moved toward me.

After I'd left Colonel Batt's office the night before, my mother had called back and asked to speak to Captain Hill. She had met him once, through Colonel Bowe, the admissions officer who'd convinced her to send me to Valley Forge. I placed Bowe right up there with my roommate as a person to blame for my current existence. Colonel Bowe had told my mother—when she was still on the fence about military school—that he wanted to introduce her to a college sophomore from Texas who was about to become an officer in the Army and was one of the true stars of the school. When she saw Captain Hill on the day she went to the campus to drop me off, she asked him to keep an eye out for me. That night on the phone, she reminded him.

When Colonel Batt got to me, he came close to my face and whispered in my ear with his fast-talking, raspy voice: "Moore, after you are done with chow, go over to F Company and ask to see the company commander. He wants to talk to you."

Wes and his godbrother, Red, moved toward the cheese bus as it slowly rolled to a stop in Dundee Village. The cheese bus—yellow and boxy like a block of government-issue cheese—picked kids up from Dundee Village and delivered them, twenty-five minutes later, to Perry Hall High School in West Baltimore. It had taken a while, but Wes was finally getting accustomed to the long route, the new school, and the new environment. He missed the city life, its speed, its intensity, its hustle. But Wes also came to understand that the county life was not exceptionally different from what he had known before. Life in the county was deceptively green and quiet—but he soon discovered that the hood came in different shapes and sizes.

Wes and Red boarded the bus, giving the daily head nod to the driver and walking down the aisle looking for a seat. Simultaneously, they spotted two girls they had never seen before. They slowed to take a second look.

"You see them?" Wes whispered to Red, lifting his chin at the two teenagers.

"Yeah, man, I want to holler at the skinny one," Red said.

The line of students was beginning to pile up behind them, so they pushed ahead, finally throwing themselves into two open seats a few rows behind the girls they were admiring. Then they started strategizing.

Wes's athletic physique and laid-back style, combined with the obvious trappings of a kid with disposable income—a new pair of sneakers every day, brand-name clothes—made him very popular with the girls around town. He had a dozen girlfriends, but nothing serious. He was just enjoying his teenage years and, at the moment, he was enjoying the view in front of him.

Both girls lived inside Dundee Village with Wes, but this was the first time he had ever noticed them. They looked about the same age; one was a few inches taller than the other, and noticeably thinner, while the thick one had a frame that looked more mature. The weather was warm, so their clothes were short and tight, leaving little to the imagination. Wes and Red debated: Should they wait until they got to school or make a move during the ride? It was a short debate.

"You ready, man, I'm gonna go holler," Red said. "Remember, I got the thin one."

After seeing Red jump from his seat, Wes followed, his book bag lightly slung over one shoulder. He put on his shy grin as they wheeled around to face the girls.

"What's y'all names?" Red abruptly asked, interrupting the girls' conversation.

The two girls gave each other the "how rude" face. Finally they looked up at Wes and Red and answered. They were twins, as it turned out, even though they didn't look anything alike.

Wes was amazed. "I thought twins was supposed to be the same," he marveled.

Wes and his new friend continued to talk all the way to the school. She was a few years older than he was and found his shy half smile cute. He liked her sense of humor—and the way her shirt tugged against her teenage curves. Her dark eyes shone as she let her hand lightly brush against his forearms.

As the cheese bus entered the school grounds, Wes asked if he could get her phone number. She pulled a pen out of her book bag and began to write her number down. As she was writing, Wes spied Red standing alone, looking agitated. Obviously, "the thin one" wasn't working out.

As Wes's new friend left, he excitedly walked over to Red, unable to hide his grin. "What happened, man?" Wes asked.

"She has a boyfriend! I knew I should have tried to holler at that thick one!"

Wes and Alicia quickly became more than friends. After school they would head to each other's houses, since neither had parents at home during the day. Within two months of their meeting, Alicia told Wes that her period was late. Four tests and eight matching plus signs later, it was confirmed. They were going to be parents.

Wes was dazed. He kept the news to himself for an entire month. How could Alicia have let herself get pregnant? He thought maybe it was a mistake. Maybe the result would change. Maybe she was just reading the tests wrong. Time went on, and Alicia started having morning sickness, her period was still AWOL, and her belly began to rise. It was undeniable. Wes finally decided it was time to tell his people what was going on. The first person he thought to share the news with was Tony, who had just become a father himself. Wes caught up with Tony when he stopped by the house.

"Tony, I got to talk to you."

"What's up?" Tony replied.

"I am going to tell you something, but you need to promise you won't say anything to anybody, especially Mom."

Tony was smirking, but when he caught the weight of his brother's voice, his face became serious. "What's going on, man? You know I won't tell her."

"Alicia's pregnant. Like three months."

Tony stared at his brother, paused for about ten seconds, and then cracked up laughing. Their mother had had a baby a year ago, making it three boys in the Moore clan, and Tony thought that Wes having a brother and a son—and a nephew—all around the same age was hysterical.

"This is some sitcom shit, man!" Tony declared, laughing.

It *was* crazy. Wes smiled, but just a little. "Whatever, man, just don't tell Mom yet."

The idea of becoming a father depressed Wes, but he wasn't sure why. He didn't have to worry about feeling alone or like a pariah. Wes and Alicia's situation was anything but exceptional. In Baltimore in 1991, 11.7 percent of girls between the ages of fifteen and nineteen had given birth. More than one out of ten. He also didn't feel burdened by the thought that early parenthood would wreck his future plans—because he didn't really have any future plans. And he wasn't overly stressed about the responsibilities of fatherhood—he didn't even know what that meant. But in some unspoken way, he did sense that he was crossing a point of no return, that things were about to get complicated in a way he was unequipped to handle.

A week later, Wes and Tony took their girlfriends to their mother's house to celebrate the first birthday of their baby brother. An ice cream cake with HAPPY 1ST written in icing sat in the middle of the dining room table. Wes and Alicia sat on one side of the table, Tony and his girlfriend on the other. Mary, with her newest son on her lap, sat at the head of the table. When Mary stood to cut the cake, Tony was struck by the absurdity of the scene.

"Ma, isn't it crazy that you just had a baby, and we just had a baby, and there is someone else at the table pregnant—" Tony cut himself off and assumed a surprised expression, as if he couldn't believe he'd let the news slip out.

Wes's eyes shot over to Tony, Alicia's eyes shot over to Wes, Mary's eyes shot over to Alicia. Wes whined that Tony was ruining what was supposed to be a nice family gathering.

Mary didn't bother with their squabbling—her attention was on Alicia. "Alicia, are you pregnant?" she asked, still standing with a cake knife poised in the air.

Alicia's eyes did not leave Wes as she slowly nodded her head.

Mary closed her eyes and took a deep breath. She put down the cake knife and locked her fingers behind her head, then arched her back as if trying to work out some deep tension. After a moment, she brought her arms back to her sides, exhaled, and looked around the table.

"So who wants cake?"

The news of his imminent parenthood did not stop Wes from making time for other girls. Not surprisingly, this bothered Alicia, but she knew there wasn't much she could do about it. She hoped that she and Wes and the new baby would become a family. She hoped she could give her child the two-parent household that she'd never had. But before the baby even came into the world, she realized how unlikely that would be.

Wes's nonexistent relationship with his father probably contributed to his seeming indifference about becoming a father himself. All he knew was his mom. He had no idea what his role would be in this new situation—he wasn't even sure he had a role.

The third, and last, time Wes met his father had been just a few months back. Wes and Tony were heading over to Shake and Bake, a popular West Baltimore roller-skating rink. The rink was very close to the home of Wes's aunt, his father's sister, so they decided to stop by to say hello. Wes would often visit his paternal aunts, cousins, and grandparents when he went to Shake and Bake—they all lived in two houses on the same block.

But when Wes and Tony entered his aunt's house, Wes's father was the first person they saw. He slept alone on the couch in the living room, oblivious to the blaring basketball game on the television, or the fact that his son had just walked in the house. Tony looked at Wes and said, "You see your pops over there?" Wes nodded but then stood there silent, as if grasping for an emotion that was just out of reach. He had not seen his father in years and didn't know what he would say to him, or if he cared to say anything at all. At first Wes considered leaving the house, just heading to the roller-skating rink, but eventually he thought better of it. This was his father. He should at least say hello.

Wes slowly walked up to the couch. His father was motionless.

Wes put his hand under his father's nose, testing to see if he was even alive. After feeling the air coming in and out of his father's nostrils, Wes started poking his father in the side with his middle finger. The first few nudges didn't wake him, so finally he just pushed at his father's shoulder. He pushed so hard the man's entire body rolled a little, but he stayed asleep. Finally, after some more jostling, his father's eyes cracked open. He saw Wes standing over him. Still squinting, he looked his son in the eyes.

"Who are you?"

Tony began to laugh hysterically. "I would punch that dude right in the face if I was you," he said to his brother in between laughs.

Wes again found himself adrift emotionally, unsure where to anchor. Part of him was hurt, part ashamed, part relieved that the awkward conversation he had been dreading wouldn't be happening. Wes looked down at the man on the couch and clenched his fist, almost as if he was going to follow Tony's advice, but then his fingers eased, and he simply let off a smirk. Without knowing it, he was mirroring the smirk his mother had left his father with when she saw him on the couch years earlier.

Wes nodded at Tony, and they left the house without another word. He never answered his father's question.

Soon after hearing the news about Alicia's pregnancy, Wes met another girl. She told him that she didn't live in Dundee but her cousin did, on the other side of the complex. It wasn't long before Wes got a chance to see the inside of her cousin's house, and the water bed in her cousin's bedroom. Wes's visits became a regular thing. She returned the favor and visited Wes at his house.

During one of those visits, Wes's new girl woke up in a panic, realizing how late it was. "Wes, I have got to get home! It's one o'clock!"

She sprang from the bed and began to put her clothes back on while Wes slowly sat up and wiped his eyes. He stretched and grumbled out a groggy command: "Make sure you be quiet when you leave so you don't wake up my mother." Wes's mother slept in the room next to Wes's and was unaware that her son had company.

"Get up and walk me out! Be a gentleman," she replied. Wes was amused. This chick was a jump-off, a sexual time filler, and he felt she had forfeited her right to be treated like a lady a long time ago. He laughed to himself but got up and put on a pair of basketball shorts and a T-shirt so he could walk her to the door.

The two tiptoed down the stairs, careful not to make any noise. When they reached the bottom of the stairs, they hugged and Wes told the girl he would call her sometime soon. She stepped through the doorway, and before she could close it behind her, Wes heard another voice coming from outside.

"What're you doing coming out that nigga's house?"

A tall, muscular, older teenager had stood up from the curb when he saw Wes's door open. It was not clear how long he had been waiting there, but it was clear that he was not happy.

"Why the hell are you out here spying on me, Ray?" she yelled back, quickly regaining her composure as she walked down Wes's stairs. The man quickly moved toward her, and they started shouting louder and louder, even as the distance between them closed.

Wes stood at alert on his porch and watched for a few moments. Once he realized the man's anger was directed at the girl and not him, he decided to stay out of it. He wished they would quiet down, but other than that he figured it wasn't any of his business. He turned his back on the two and moved toward the door so he could get upstairs and resume his night's sleep. As Wes stepped into his doorway, the man finally noticed him. He stopped yelling at his girl and launched himself toward Wes. He reached him in an instant, grabbed the back of his shirt collar, lifted him off the porch floor, and slammed him onto his back. Wes found himself splayed on his stairs looking up at the night sky, the back of his head throbbing, unsure of what had just happened.

Ray wasn't done. He began to take unmerciful swings at Wes's face. His left and right fists took turns hitting their target while Wes tried to block the blows. The girl pulled at the man, trying to give Wes a little room to escape. Finally, Wes came to his feet and ran inside, but not before the man had significantly bloodied him up.

Wes went inside, but he had no intention of staying there. He ran to his room and straight to his closet. He reached up to the top shelf and pulled out the shoe box that held his 9mm Beretta and a few full clips. Wes opened the box, grabbed the gun and clips, and threw the empty box on the floor. As he left his room, he shoved a clip into the gun and cocked the slide hammer back, fully loading the weapon. He ran down the stairs and out the door, only to see the girl standing there by herself. Her eyes immediately trained themselves on the gun in Wes's hand.

Wes could only see red. He was blind with rage. Instincts kicked in. Tony's words rang through his mind. *Send a message.*

"What are you going to do with that?" the girl demanded and tried to block Wes's path.

"Shut up and get out of my way," Wes commanded. He pushed her to the side and started scanning the block for a sign of the dude who'd just worked out on his face.

Wes noticed one of his boys leaning out of a window along with dozens of other people, who were now curiously watching. The boy was one of Wes's partners in his drug operation, and when he saw Wes standing in the night air, face bloodied, with a gun in hand, he had his cue to join the fight. As Wes continued to scan the block for any clue of where Ray ran to, his friend joined him with his own trusty burner ready to blast.

The girl was still screaming at Wes, begging him to leave Ray alone, but for Wes her voice faded into the background noise of a now alert Dundee Village. After slowly pacing his street, looking for any movement, he finally saw what he was looking for. Ray leaped up from behind a car farther down the block and began sprinting, ducking behind cars as he moved around the enclosed complex. Wes chased after him. As they ran, he and his friend pointed their weapons in Ray's direction and began taking shots. Wes quickly figured out where Ray was heading and realized that this must be the "cousin" his jump-off was always visiting. Wes and his friend cut into an alley, trying to intercept Ray before he could get to his house.

Every time Ray rose from a hiding position, Wes and his friend would take turns firing shots at him, not only to try to hit him but to keep him from getting to his house. Shots rang through the development and car windows were shot out while the people staring out their windows backed away, trying to avoid stray gunfire. Wes and his friend ran through a dark alley, jumping over trash cans and fences, trying to get to the other side of the complex as fast as possible. Multiple shots had been fired, but the footrace to the house continued. All three of their hearts pounded—none of them would have imagined hours earlier what kind of night this would turn out to be.

As Ray's house came into view for all three young men, Ray decided to make a run for it, ducking behind a row of parked cars. Wes and his friend traded shots and finally heard Ray scream as he fell behind a black Toyota just fifty feet from his house. Wes and his friend stopped running. They saw no movement and figured the job was done. Not only that but the entire neighborhood seemed to be awake now, so they ran back to their homes, hoping to avoid identification. Adrenaline was rushing through Wes's body, followed quickly by fear, but no regret. Ray was a fool for stepping to him like that; he'd started something that Wes had no choice but to finish.

The girl Wes had been with was crying and screaming when he arrived back at his house. She was saying she was going to tell the police on him. Wes ran right by her, ignoring her threats as he slammed his front door behind him.

He was met by his mother, who was now awake and irate. "What is going on, Wes? What did you do?" she demanded.

Wes ran by her and, without even looking back, told her nothing was wrong and to go to bed. The blood on Wes's face and clothes, and the weapon in his hand, told a very different story.

Wes went straight to the bathroom. He shut and locked the door and began filling the sink with warm water. The pool of water quickly turned red as the blood fell from his face into the sink. He picked up his washcloth and a bar of soap and began to clean the blood coming from his nose and mouth. His mother was outside the door, knocking ferociously, demanding to know what had happened. Wes continued to clean his face, as if she weren't there.

Finally, vexed and frustrated, Mary called the only person she knew could find out what had happened. "Tony, Wes was involved in something out here, and I can't figure out what is going on. He's all bloody."

Tony jumped in his car and started driving toward Baltimore County.

Wes finished cleaning his face and removed his bloody shirt. After throwing his ruined clothes into the bathroom garbage can, he went to his bedroom and closed the door behind him.

He still had the gun in his hand and knew he wouldn't be alone for long. In the corner of the room was a large fish tank that was only a quarter full, but the bottom was covered with rocks and dark mud that clouded the water. Living in the tank were not fish but a large, green snapping turtle that took up almost half the sixty-five-gallon tank. The gun was still hot, so it created a small sizzle as it hit the cool water of the tank. Wes moved the sand around, clouding the already murky water even more, hoping it would hide the gun.

Wes heard commotion downstairs and knew his time was just about up. He reached into the wooden drawer next to his bed and got a clean blue shirt with white stripes on it. He pulled the shirt over his head and pushed his arms through the sleeves as he heard a parade of feet charging up the stairs. Wes hurriedly smoothed the shirt down and put his hands in the air, not wanting the cops to think he was armed. He knew how that scenario would end. Seconds later, Wes was being pushed facedown onto his own bed, his hands locked in cuffs behind his back.

He was escorted downstairs by three police officers, led to the back of their car, and shoved in. Wes could see police officers talking to witnesses about what they'd seen. He eyed the crowd; the jump-off he blamed for starting this mess was nowhere to be found. Wes's mother walked up to the backseat of the police car where her son sat and began to yell at him in between her tears. Through the car window and over the commotion in the streets, Wes tried to tell his mother to calm down. While the cops were still speaking to witnesses, he told her where the gun was. She asked him if he was the one who'd shot the boy, but Wes didn't answer. He simply stared at his mother with a blank expression, his head still spinning from the last hour's events. She asked him again, softly pleading with him to tell her something. Just then, the cops showed up and ordered her away from the car.

Two officers entered the cruiser and prepared to head back to the station. They had all the information they needed. They started the engine and the blue and red lights on top of their cars began to flash. As the cruiser began to pull off, Wes asked them to stop for a moment so he could say something to his mother. The driver slowed to a stop and rolled down the window next to Wes's head just a crack.

"Ma!" Wes yelled.

She was on her way into the house when she heard his voice. She ran to him. When she got closer, Wes craned his head to speak through the crack in the window.

"About your question. I don't know the answer."

The car pulled off. Wes closed his eyes and leaned his head against the black, plastic seat. The street began to clear, and after watching the car fade into the distance, Mary headed back inside her house.

Minutes later, Tony arrived. His mother stared at him, her face drained of emotion. "It's too late," she told him. "Wes is already gone."

SIX

Hunted

The steady flow of people entering the Northern High School gymnasium had slowed to a trickle as the three o'clock start time for graduation arrived. The wooden bleachers that circled the floor were full of family, friends, and supporters of the crop of graduates, who had yet to enter the room. Within an hour they would watch the high school experience of their children, grandchildren, siblings, nieces, and nephews come to an end. Many in the audience had thought the day would never come, but all were happy it did.

The state of Maryland had one of the highest graduation rates in the nation. Seventy-six percent of high school students who began high school in Maryland completed. In Baltimore County, the number was as high as 85 percent in some years. But in Baltimore City, where Northern High School was located, it was a dismal 38 percent. For many in the audience, this was the first high school graduation they had ever attended.

The procession of black robes entering the room was replaced by a wave of forest green robes—the students trailed shortly after the faculty. Smiles, waves, cheers, and whistles rang out. Camera flashes blinked over the parade, parents and friends shooting as wildly as paparazzi. Because his last name put him toward the front of the class, Woody was one of the first to enter the gym, walking with a confident strut. He saw his parents, sister, and grandmother, and smiled. He grabbed the edge of his green cap between his thumb and index finger and tipped it to them. A sign of respect, and gratitude.

Woody was one of the students who made it across the finish line kicking and screaming. He'd needed two points in the last few weeks to pass English. Gym was his favorite class. Every other class tied for last place. But as he entered the area where all the students were sitting to prepare for the ceremony, he knew none of that mattered. All that mattered was that he was here. He had accomplished his mission of completing high school.

The principal, valedictorian, guest speaker, and the rest of the graduation speakers gave their speeches as Woody fought to stay awake. Finally the moment he was waiting for arrived. The principal asked the class to rise, and one by one they walked across the stage to receive their diplomas. If the entire class that had started the ninth grade here had finished, it would have been a very long ceremony. But only eighty-seven seats were filled that spring morning. This wouldn't take nearly as long as it should have.

When it was Woody's turn, he practically danced up to the principal. The crowd laughed as Woody shook the principal's hand and looked up at his family, throwing his arms in the air in a triumphant stance. He carefully jogged down the steps at the end of the stage. As he turned the corner and looked at the dozens of folding chairs where the graduates were sitting, his mind wandered to the people who weren't there. He thought about Daemon, a ninth-grade classmate who didn't make it to the end of the year. Dae took a month off from school to care for his mother, who was sick with sickle cell. That month turned to two, and finally Dae stopped being a student. Woody thought about White Boy, his boy from the neighborhood, who picked up a job working at a restaurant called Poor Folks. He was tired of school and decided joining the workforce was a better option.

Most of all, Woody thought about Wes, who had stopped going to school two years earlier.

Wes returned to Dundee Village six months after being locked up for the incident in which he shot at Ray. Wes caught two breaks that night. The first was that the bullet entered Ray's shoulder and went straight through. No major organs were hit, and Ray left the hospital a day later, so Wes was charged with attempted murder rather than murder. The second break was that Wes's case was sent to juvenile court instead of adult court. His attorney argued he should be tried as a juvenile because "he would not be a potential threat to the community."

Wes went back to school immediately after leaving the juvenile detention facility, the Baltimore County Detention Center in Towson. He enrolled at Lake Clifton High School in East Baltimore but knew pretty quickly that he would not last long. He was two years older than the other kids in his grade from repeating a grade and losing time locked up. Teachers already dealing with overcrowded classrooms didn't have the time to teach Wes the basics he'd missed. Wes's attendance became sporadic, and once his first child was born, he just stopped going.

Not surprisingly, without a high school diploma or job training—and with a criminal record—Wes found it almost impossible to find a job to support his growing family. Alicia was living with the baby in her mother's house while Wes stayed with his aunt Nicey. Nicey was strict and made it clear from the day Wes moved in who was in charge: "You need to either get a job or go to school, one of the two, but neither is not an option."

Wes found another option: he decided to make himself scarce. In the mornings while Nicey was at work, Wes would play videogames in the house and then head out to check on his drug operation. When she was home in the evenings or the early morning, Wes would normally be out, "trying to find a job," as he would tell her. This charade went on for months. Wes didn't live there so much as he used Nicey's home as a place to rest and, increasingly, a place to hide his drugs.

Wes had his entire operation organized with the precision of a military unit or a division of a Fortune 500 company. The drug game had its own rules, its own structure. He was a lieutenant, the leader of his small crew. Everyone in the crew had a specific job with carefully delineated responsibilities. On the lowest rung of the ladder and in most cases the youngest kids on the team, were the corner boys. These were the kids, sometimes as young as seven but normally no older than eleven, who served as the lookouts for cops. They would huddle on the corners, and when they saw a cop—or anyone who looked like a cop—they would yell "Hey, Tina," or "Hey, Susan," or whatever name the crew had designated for the week. That way they could alert the crew that cops were creeping, but if the cops questioned them, they could simply say they were calling for a friend and walk away unscathed.

The hitters were the ones who dealt with the money. This job was very important, for obvious reasons, and you needed to trust your hitter. This was also one of the most dangerous jobs, because if the money ever came up short, the hitter was the one whose neck was on the line.

The housemen were in charge of distribution. The drugs were usually cooked and cut in a house, and the housemen would have to make sure the sellers had their supply for the day. The housemen also resupplied the ground soldiers if they sold their allocated amount.

Last, you had the muscle, who were there to protect the crew and the lieutenant. They were usually carrying weapons of various kinds and were not afraid to use them. A crew's relevancy—their ability to hold their own corner and expand the business—was dependent on the amount of muscle they controlled and the level of violence their muscle was ready to get into. Sometimes entire crews were muscle.

This was the crew. They would work together, fight together, stay together. An unbreakable bond united the crew—for many members, it was the only support system they had. It was family.

Wes managed his team extremely well. At their peak, his team brought in over four thousand dollars a day. He wasn't one of the main players by any stretch, but he was not doing badly in relation to others in the neighborhood. There were over 100,000 known addicts in Baltimore, and the real number was arguably higher. Given that the city had a population of just under 700,000, there was an obvious glut of addicts. With a demand like that, and an ample supply, it was hard not to make money. Still, Wes would find himself wondering about the percentage of that money that found its way into his pocket. He and his team were taking all the risks; they were the ones who faced the arrests and the danger. His bosses, the connects, and the ones bringing the drugs into Baltimore were making the real money. They never had to show their faces on the hard corners where the supply looked the demand in the eye. It started to become clear to Wes: the drug game was raw capitalism on overdrive with bullets, a pyramid scheme whose base was dead bodies and ruined lives.

Wes stood on the corner in Dundee Village. He no longer lived there, but he had a little operation there—he would bring drugs into the county because he could sell them for a higher premium than in the city. He was surrounded by some guys from his crew. His day was ending; it was 3:00 P.M., and he planned to pick up a girl from around the way to go to the movies. He had to get moving, but he lingered. He liked the feeling of holding down a corner with his boys. It was the one place he felt safe, or at least in his element. Wes's green jumpsuit hung over a glossy green T-shirt. His Gianni Brunelli shoes matched his outfit. Wes stayed fresh.

He was saying his final goodbyes when a man sidled up to him. He was clean-shaven, wearing jeans and an oversize T-shirt. Wes had never seen this cat before.

"Do you guys know where I can buy some rocks?" the man asked, his voice conspiratorially gruff.

There are a few major tip-offs that tell dealers something isn't right:

If a person looks unfamiliar or really out of place, it's probably a cop.

If a person you saw arrested a few minutes ago is suddenly back on the street and trying to buy from you, he's probably doing it for a cop.

If a person is usually a dime-bag customer and is now trying to buy a brick, he's probably working for the cops.

> If someone's lingo is wrong—if he comes up to you saying, "Do you
> guys know where I can buy some rocks?"—there's a good chance
> he's a cop.

"Nope," Wes replied, eyeing the man up and down.

The man began to walk away with his head swiveling, seemingly searching for someone else to get drugs from. Wes moved in the opposite direction, toward the girl's house. But for some reason, he couldn't let the sale go. He paused, taking a second look at the man. Wes thought about the small change he was turning down. The man threw up red flags, but Wes had dealt to people like that before and gotten away with it. He saw the man approach another corner boy and then walk away. Wes got antsy: the movie was starting soon, and if he was going to change his mind and make the sale, he'd better do it fast. He couldn't stop thinking about the money he could make off that sale—almost exactly enough to take care of this date. The logic felt right.

Wes looked to his right, saw a public phone booth, and began to move in that direction. As he approached the booth, he reached into his pocket and pulled out two dime bags of crack cocaine, twenty dollars' worth. He placed the small, clear, zipper-lock bags in the phone's metal-covered coin return bucket. He quickly scanned his surroundings, checking to see if anyone had seen his drop. When he felt sure that he'd been undetected, he moved toward the potential buyer.

It was a risk, and Wes knew it. But taking risks is at the heart of the drug enterprise, and scared money didn't make money.

"Hey, come here real quick," Wes yelled to the man, still wandering aimlessly around the block.

The man's head snapped up quickly. Wes looked him up and down again, desperate to recognize him and put his mind at ease. He couldn't. The man moved closer. Wes grabbed his right shoulder and pulled him in close. "I don't know who it was that told me, but if you give me twenty dollars, you can go over to that phone booth and they said you would be taken care of." The man nodded as his eyes met Wes's.

As Wes took the money, their hands touched briefly. The man's hands were smooth, and his nails were clean. *Damn.* It was time to get moving. Wes started walking, never looking back. He placed the twenty-dollar bill in his pants pocket and picked up the pace to the girl's house. He popped a breath mint in his mouth.

As he turned the corner, he heard a yell behind him. "Stop moving and get your hands up!" Wes kept walking. He looked forward, hoping they weren't speaking to him, hoping they'd just disappear. He maintained the same pace until he caught sight of two men running toward him.

Guns in hand and silver badges swinging from metal chains around their necks, the men pointed their weapons at Wes and ordered him to the ground. Wes saw another man, wearing a woodland camouflage shirt, crawling from beneath the bushes, reaching in his waist, and pulling out a weapon. In total, ten police officers moved toward Wes. He got down on his knees and laced his fingers behind his head.

"What did I do, man? I didn't do anything wrong," Wes pleaded with the cop who was reaching over to cuff him while the rest kept their weapons on him. Getting arrested was starting to feel routine. Wes wasn't shocked or afraid anymore, just annoyed. Why him? Why now? Why couldn't they just leave him alone? He had enough to worry about.

Wes continued to plead his case as the police read him his rights.

Ding, ding.

Two bells rang through the mess hall, signaling the corps of cadets to leave lunch and head back to barracks for their afternoon classes. At the sound of the bells, the corps moved en masse toward the cafeteria doors at the end of the building.

I stood up from my chair and ordered my platoon to "stand fast," or remain still, as I reminded them about the room inspection that was going to take place immediately after school. My platoon responded with a coordinated "Yes, Sergeant," and began to join the flood headed toward the door.

I was now a platoon sergeant, a cadet master sergeant, and the youngest senior noncommissioned officer in the entire corps. Three years ago I'd been one of the insubordinate kids first entering the gates of Valley Forge. In an ironic turn, I was now one of the ones in charge of them.

My mother had noticed the way I had changed since leaving for military school. My back stood straight, and my sentences now ended with "sir" or "ma'am." My military garrison cap was intentionally a size too big, forcing me to keep my head up, walking taller with every step. Our standard motto, "No excuses, no exceptions," and our honor code, "A cadet will not lie, cheat, or steal, nor tolerate those that do," were not simply words we had to memorize but words to live by. With the support of people like Cadet Captain Hill and the others in my chain of command and on the faculty, I'd actually started to enjoy military school. They made it clear that they cared if I succeeded, and eventually so did I. The financial strain Valley Forge brought on my mother was lessened significantly after the first year, when the school gave me academic, and later athletic, scholarships.

On my way back to the barracks, I met up with my friend and "plebe brother" Sean. Sean, from a single-parent household in central New Jersey, had lost his father when he was young as well. We'd started Valley Forge at the same time and lived down the hall from each other. We were among the few still at the school from our plebe class. We were the "survivors," the "old men" who were on pace to go the long haul.

We stopped in the mail room. In my box were three letters, two branded with the logos of colleges, and one from Justin, my best friend back in the Bronx.

I was a starter on the Valley Forge basketball team, the only sophomore on the starting squad that year and the first sophomore starter in over five years. I was making a name on the court, and colleges were taking notice, writing to me fairly frequently. These two letters, from Lafayette College and Georgetown, were just the most recent.

I spent my summers at prestigious basketball camps like 5-Star

Basketball and Eastern Invitational, camps where college coaches prowl, looking for fresh prospects. I was almost six feet tall at the time, with a quick first step, a passion for defense, and an okay jump shot. But I was cocky as hell. I would sit in my room and practice the "grip and grin" that would take place the day the NBA commissioner announced my name as the Knicks' first-round pick in the NBA draft. I would pantomime putting the hat on my head and work on just the right bland lines for the press: "Our team works hard in practice, and it pays off in the games." "When the game was on the line, my team put its confidence in me, and I am just thankful things worked out." "I believe we can beat any team on any given day, as long as we play our game."

One day a few months earlier, my uncle Howard took me out to shoot hoops at a park in the Bronx. I was telling him about receiving the recruiting letters from colleges, talking about how I knew I could make it to the pros. My uncle was still much stronger than I was and would use his size to post me up down low and then execute a quick turnaround hook shot or layup, reminding me that I wasn't quite in the NBA yet.

After he finished beating me, we sat next to each other on the side of the court and he started to spin the ball on his finger. "You know, your game is getting pretty good, and I hope you do make it to the league, then we would all be living nice," he said with a smile on his face. "But it is important that you understand that the chances are not in your favor, and you have to have some backup plans." I took the ball out of his hands, wanting to practice my midrange jump shot instead of listening to a lecture about my future prospects. I stood up, dribbled the ball from side to side, but never took my eyes off him, probably more to practice keeping my head up than for any other reason.

"Think about it, man. It's simple math. Only 60 players are chosen in the NBA draft every year. There are 341 Division One schools, each with 13 players on the roster. This makes 4,433 college players who could declare eligibility for the NBA draft. These numbers don't even include Division Two or Three players. Or international players, for that matter." My uncle had obviously been practicing this speech.

The dose of reality hidden in the impressive math exhibition was beginning to bother me, so I cut him off and asked him if he wanted to get another game going. A small smile appeared on his face again, and he pulled himself up using the metal fence that surrounded the court as support. I thought about him now, as I stared at the college seal on the top left corner of the envelope I held.

Next, I slipped my finger into the opening of the letter from Justin. Justin and I exchanged dozens of letters after I left the Bronx for Pennsylvania. I was one of the few outlets Justin had, and my leaving wasn't easy on either of us. We'd always been best friends, despite the urging of one of the deans at Riverdale, who'd once pulled Justin to the side and given him a stern warning: "Justin, you are a good kid, you need to stay away from Wes or you will end up going nowhere just like he will." Justin simply shook his head and ignored him. It amazed Justin how easily they would write off a twelve-year-old.

The letter opened with the normal trivial catching-up jokes, but it soon became more serious. Two pieces of news took the wind out of me.

First, Shea had been arrested on drug charges. These weren't simply running or possession charges either. Possession with the intent to distribute was a charge of a completely different magnitude—with serious mandatory sentences. Justin hadn't seen Shea around the neighborhood in a while and, from the sound of it, was not sure when he would again.

The even more devastating piece of news was that Justin's mother was dying. We had noticed changes in his mother for a few years. She moved more slowly than usual and seemed just a beat off. Justin's mother had Hodgkin's disease, a rare form of cancer. The survival rate is around 90 percent for those who discover it early. Unfortunately, his mother was in the other 10 percent. With Justin's older sister away in college, and his father living in Harlem, Justin's role in the family was changing.

Justin was now spending his mornings with her at the hospital, his afternoons at school, then running to basketball practice and back to the hospital. His grades fell dramatically as the burden began to wear him down.

I was halfway through reading the letter when Sean's voice broke my concentration. "You ready, man? I got nothing." I took one final glance at the letter, then carefully folded it back into its envelope and put it in the cargo pocket of my camouflage battle dress uniform. Sean noticed the look on my face and said, "You all right, man? Everything okay?" I told him everything was fine, but a few seconds later I spoke up again. "Hey, Sean, do you ever think about what life would be like if we never came here?"

He looked at me quizzically. "I don't know. About the same, I guess."

"Yeah, I guess."

Even though I'd grown to love military school, I still had mixed feelings about being there, and they were eating at me. I wanted to be home, to talk to Justin after he left the hospital. I didn't know what I'd say, but at least I'd be there. I wanted to be there as my mother and Shani moved back to Maryland and Shani began high school. I remembered what Baltimore could be like, and I wanted to be there to protect Shani and help my mother through the move. I felt like being at military school was keeping me in a bubble, ignorant of what was going on with my people on the outside. There was a comfortable distance between my life now and the levels of confusion that had engulfed me just a few years ago. This uniform had become a force field that kept the craziness of the world outside from getting too close to me, but I wondered if it was just an illusion.

H Company was broken up into two platoons. I was the platoon sergeant for one of them, and a cadet named Dalio was the platoon sergeant for the other. In the Army, there is an old expression that the officers make the orders and the sergeants do all the work; this year, as a cadet platoon sergeant, I was learning how true that was. From the moment I woke up to the moment I went to bed, my day was consumed with thinking about my platoon, taking care of them, making sure they were doing well in class, making sure things were fine at home, making sure the building was clean, and on and on, an exhausting litany. Saturday evening, after "Taps," Dalio and I put our guys down to sleep but still had a few hours of leave before we had to be back on campus.

"Want to go grab a stromboli?" Dalio asked. The stromboli is a staple in Pennsylvania cuisine, essentially consisting of a pizza folded on itself, a bread, dairy, and meat concoction held together with copious amounts of grease, classic adolescent comfort food. I was in.

We threw on our dress gray uniforms, including the gray wool pants that scraped every blade of hair off our legs and dark blue cotton shirts. I tightened the navy tie that accompanied the uniform—the tie was wrapped in the same knot I'd used as a freshman.

When you know how to get there, downtown Wayne is only fifteen minutes away from campus. We strolled down the barely lit street, gossiping about the antics of our platoons. About ten minutes into the walk, a red Toyota slowly drove up to us. Thinking the driver just needed directions or help navigating the dark, signless streets, we stopped and peered in. As the driver's window rolled halfway down, the sound of loud rock music and the smell of alcohol met us.

"What are you guys doing?" a slightly overweight teenager with unkempt black hair and a distinctive scar across the top of his forehead asked us.

"Nothing," I replied. Who is this guy? I wondered.

"Don't you mean 'Nothing, sir'?" A voice rang out from the backseat, but with the tinted windows, we couldn't see its source.

"Nothing, sir," I reflexively corrected myself, even without knowing who made the order. I was so accustomed to the rules and protocol on campus that it took me a second to realize I might be responding to the orders of some random drunk kids from town.

"I am Colonel Bose's son, and not only are you rude but your uniforms are in disarray. I am going to report you both." Dalio and I looked at each other, confused about whether this was a legitimate complaint or simply a prank.

Dalio realized the pizza shop would be closing soon, so he tried to end the conversation. "Well, you have our names, so do what you have to do," he said. The car sped away, leaving a trail of blaring music behind it. Dalio and I continued walking down the middle of the street, but our conversation now turned to the odd interaction we'd just had.

"What do you think?" Dalio asked me.

"Probably nothing. Just a bunch of idiots."

Suddenly a speeding car came roaring up behind us. We turned around with just enough time to jump out of the way as the red Toyota from before came within feet of running us both over. We lay there in complete bewilderment, unsure what to do next. The car slowed to a creep after missing us, like a confused predator who'd overrun his prey. Finally, the brake lights appeared. Dalio and I got off the ground, looked at each other, and broke into a sprint, running away from the car now sitting ominously a few yards from us. Just then, another car came down the street. Our drunk attackers were forced to keep moving.

Dalio looked at me and said, "What the hell are we supposed to do?"

That's when the kid from the Bronx started to elbow the cadet sergeant aside. "We keep going to get our pizza. They're done for the night, and if they aren't, we'll see them when they get out of the car," I told him. Dalio was not as convinced, but after kneeling behind a parked car for a few minutes and not hearing or seeing any sign of the red Toyota, he decided that I might be right. Besides, he was still hungry.

We picked up our pace as we walked in the shadows of the tree-lined sidewalks, now avoiding the center of the street. I felt like I was doing my speed-walk to the subway in the Bronx again. Every car that passed made our hearts stop. This was military school, I thought to myself. We were supposed to be protected from this kind of stuff.

We came to an intersection, one of the few lighted paths on our entire journey. Only two hundred yards away from our final destination. The quiet streets and passing minutes without incident had returned our focus to the oozing stromboli and not the Toyota. We were crossing the intersection when I heard a voice yelling.

"Go home, nigger!"

As I turned my head to see where the yell came from, a rock or bottle—something hard—slammed against my mouth.

"I just got hit," I yelled to Dalio, spitting out blood and pieces of tooth into my hand. My tongue searched my top row of teeth, scratching against my now sharp and jagged front tooth, while my mouth filled with blood. We realized the car had been sitting with its headlights off, waiting for us.

After their direct hit, they put on their lights and screeched off. Inside they were still screaming with laughter.

Going to the pizza shop was now off the table. We realized who the target was. I reached into my mouth and wiggled my loose tooth. We moved to a completely dark area behind a collection of bushes to regroup. Dalio, not panicking, said, "Bro, we have got to get back to campus, now."

My mouth was aching. I was beside myself with anger—and still confused. And embarrassed. Embarrassed to be called a nigger in front of my comrade. And embarrassed by my reaction. Because after being called a nigger and having my tooth broken, I'd decided to flee back to campus. Should I have stayed there in the middle of the street, waiting for the boys to come back, somehow gotten them out of their car, and tested them blow for blow? Part of me was aghast when I decided that the answer was no.

I'd only waded into street life in the Bronx; I never got into its deepest, darkest waters. But I'd been around enough street cats to know the code: they hit you with a knife, you find a gun. And I didn't have to be a Black Panther to know that *nigger* was the ultimate fighting word. This was the kind of knowledge we understood, the kind of code that was so deeply fundamental it never had to be fully articulated. But I had to let this one go. I had to look at the bigger picture. My assailant was unknown, unnamed, and in a car. This was not a fair fight, and the best-case scenario was nowhere near as probable as the worst-case scenario.

If I was successful, who knew how the fight would've ended? If I failed, who knew how the fight would've ended?

I thought about my mother and how she would feel if this escalated any further. I thought about my father and the name he chose for me.

We sat silent for a moment, waiting for any movement or lights, but as we'd just learned, darkness and silence did not translate to safety. I told Dalio we had to get back to campus by a different route, one where there were no lights and no streets. I told him to follow me and began to run through a series of front yards to a dark, empty field about a quarter mile from where we started. Dalio was trying to ask me where we were going, but I never slowed or turned around to explain. We did not have time. Hiding behind trees and cars along the way, we systematically moved closer to our goal. The veil of security I thought the uniform provided had been lifted, and now we hustled in our black dress shoes and stained wool pants through dirty fields and grassy yards. Our hearts pounded under our navy blue shirts.

"Where are we?" Dalio asked again when we stopped behind a large rock, staring at the wooded landscape in front of us.

"It's the field that leads us back to school," I replied. This was our chance to get on campus without having to meet up with our attackers again. Dalio had never been here, and most cadets never had a reason to. I had, however; it was one of the first memories I had of my school. This was the same area I'd run through trying to find the Wayne train station, trying to escape.

"Let's go," I whispered and we bolted into the woods. Scared, and angry, we navigated the darkness holding on to trees, using the moon as our guide. Minutes later, we saw the light from the cross perched on the chapel's roof, which was only fifty yards away from our barracks.

The irony of the situation forced me to smile, featuring my newly cracked tooth. Years earlier, I had run through these same woods with all of my might, looking for safety, trying to get away from campus. Tonight, I ran through the same woods looking for safety, but in the other direction.

Part III

Paths Taken and Expectations Fulfilled

*I sat again in that large, gray, windowless room with about thirty
other people waiting to see their fathers, husbands, sons, boyfriends,
and friends. The air in the room was heavy and cold, the chairs
hard. There was a vending machine with only a few sad items dan-
gling inside. Small lockers lined the gray walls. We were told to
place whatever we carried with us inside them. Nothing unac-
counted for could go in—or out of—the secured room that would be
our next stop. Out of the thirty people in the room, I was one of
only two men. The rest were women and children.*

*One by one, the guards called out numbers. After about an hour
of waiting, I finally heard mine. I quickly rose and walked over to a
desk where bulletproof glass separated me from a corrections officer.
The officer threw out the same barrage of questions they always ask.
"What is your relation to the inmate? Do you have any electronic
equipment or sharp items? Do you have any items you plan on passing on to the inmate?" Eventually they let me into the visitors'
room, where I waited for Wes to be escorted in.*

"I wasn't even there that day."

I looked at Wes, speechless. He still *didn't* admit to the armed
robbery that had led to his final imprisonment.

There were days when our unexpected relationship started to seem absurd. What was I doing here, anyway? More than three years earlier, I'd written a letter to a stranger whose story had sat with me for years. We shared a name, but the truth was that I didn't know this man. He was simply an address, a P.O. box, and a personal identification number. A man convicted of murder. And, inevitably, as in every convict cliché I'd ever heard, he claimed innocence.

But I started to think more about his repeated defense, offered again and again in earnest: "I wasn't even there that day." Did he think that through repetition it would become true? That if he just incanted the phrase enough the prison walls would collapse and he'd be able to walk back home? Did he think it could reverse time? How far back would he have to go to be innocent again?

Wes folded his hands together; his broad shoulders leaned in. We were nearing the end of our get-together. Silence now overrode the conversation. He smiled.

I decided not to respond directly to this latest protest of his innocence. Instead, I asked a question: "Do you think we're all just products of our environments?" His smile dissolved into a smirk, with the left side of his face resting at ease.

"I think so, or maybe products of our expectations."

"Others' expectations of us or our expectations for ourselves?"

"I mean others' expectations that you take on as your own."

I realized then how difficult it is to separate the two. The expectations that others place on us help us form our expectations of ourselves.

"We will do what others expect of us," Wes said. "If they expect us to graduate, we will graduate. If they expect us to get a job, we will get a job. If they expect us to go to jail, then that's where we will end up too. At some point you lose control."

I sympathized with him, but I recoiled from his ability to shed responsibility seamlessly and drape it at the feet of others.

"True, but it's easy to lose control when you were never looking for it in the first place."

An hour later, our time was up, and he was escorted out as quickly as he entered. I sat in the room alone, collecting my thoughts. I had more questions than I came in with.

SEVEN

The Land That God Forgot

1997

"Five minutes!" the jumpmaster yelled from the front of a C-130 military aircraft.

"Five minutes!" my entire chalk of Airborne candidates yelled back at him in the military's famous call-and-response cadence. We all knew what was next, and now we knew how long we had before it was time to face it. Five minutes.

I stood toward the middle of the C-130, staring at the back of another soldier's Kevlar helmet. The late-summer Georgia heat beat down on the metal shell of the airplane that we'd been packed into for over an hour. Sweat that had been beading all over my face was now streaming uncontrollably but, afraid to move, I simply let it fall. The only relief came from the open door at the front of the plane that our instructors—the Black Hats, we called them—occasionally looked out to inspect our drop zone. A Black Hat would brace his hands against each side of the door and stick his head into the open air, slowly turning from side to side to check for any potential obstacles. I had gotten used to the fifty pounds of gear cumbersomely strapped to my back, torso, and legs. My bladder verged on explosion because of the crazy amount of water we were forced to drink to stay hydrated. None of this now mattered. I was about to jump out of the plane. I was about to become a paratrooper.

An excited nervousness overwhelmed me. It had been a little more than a year since I decided to make the Army a fundamental part of my future. As my high school career was coming to an end, I was still being avidly recruited by college programs. *The New York Times* had even run a two-page article on my high school sports career and future prospects. I got a firsthand taste of the athletic campus visitation process, complete with young and attractive "tour guides" who showed me around and made me feel welcome—and wanted. It was a seductive ego stroke. Initially, it just reinforced my belief that I was special, that I was chosen. The young female admirers who seemed to come along with the package added to the allure. But eventually, all of these treats started to feel meaningless.

As I began to play against nationally ranked players at various tournaments and camps, I realized that the disparity between my potential and theirs was glaring. I played hard while they played easy, with a gracefulness and effortlessness that I lacked. When you step on the court with players like Kobe Bryant or six foot eight point guards who can dunk from the free throw line, your mind begins to concentrate on your other options.

I realized that I had to make sure these schools knew my name regardless of what I did on the ninety feet of hardwood that had brought me to their attention. Just as military school had slowly grown on me, so had academic life. I actually liked reading now. My mother, sensing my apathy toward reading, had bought me the Mitch Albom book *Fab Five*. The book is about the Michigan basketball team led by Chris Webber, Jalen Rose, and Juwan Howard, a team with five freshman starters who made it all the way to the national championship game. The Fab Five sported baggy shorts, bald heads, and a swagger I recognized from the streets of the Bronx, all reflective of the way the hip-hop generation was changing the face of sports, and college basketball in particular. I was riveted by that book. The characters jumped off the page, and I felt myself as engulfed in their destiny as I was in my own. I finished *Fab Five* in two days. The book itself wasn't what was important—in retrospect, I see that it was a great read but hardly a work of great literature—but my mother used it as a hook into a deeper lesson: that the written word isn't necessarily a chore but can be a window into new worlds.

From there, I leaped into every new book with fervor. My fresh love of reading brought me to the transformative writers who have worked their magic on generations of readers. I explored Spain with Paulo Coelho. I listened to jazz on the North Shore of Long Island with F. Scott Fitzgerald. I was reminded by Walt Whitman to think of the past, and I awaited "The Fire Next Time" with James Baldwin. But there was a more recent author and public figure whose work spoke to the core of a new set of issues I was struggling with: the Bronx's own Colin Powell. His book, *My American Journey,* helped me harmonize my understanding of America's history and my aspiration to serve her in uniform. In his autobiography he talked about going to the Woolworth's in Columbus, Georgia, and being able to shop but not eat there. He talked about how black GIs during World War II had more freedoms when stationed in Germany than back in the country they fought for. But he embraced the progress this nation made and the military's role in helping that change to come about. Colin Powell could have been justifiably angry, but he wasn't. He was thankful. I read and reread one section in particular:

The Army was living the democratic ideal ahead of the rest of America. Beginning in the fifties, less discrimination, a truer merit system, and leveler playing fields existed inside the gates of our military posts more than in any Southern city hall or Northern corporation. The Army, therefore, made it easier for me to love my country, with all its flaws, and to serve her with all of my heart.

The canon of black autobiography sensibly includes scores of books about resistance to the American system. For instance, reading *The Autobiography of Malcolm X*—a book that begins and ends in the madness and pathology of America's racial obsessions—is a rite of passage for young black men. Malcolm never stopped pursuing truth and the right course, based on the best information he had at any given moment. His response to the world he confronted in the middle of the twentieth century was profound and deeply felt, but he didn't speak to my experience as well as Colin Powell did. Powell, in his pragmatic way, wanted what I wanted: A fair shot. A place to develop himself. A code that would instill discipline, restrain passion, and order his steps. A way to change the world without first unleashing the whirlwind. In the chaos of the world I grew up in, those were as appealing to me as Malcolm's cry for revolution was to his generation. I don't claim that Powell had it all figured out: American history bedevils the most earnest attempts to make sense of it. And, of course, the problems of race that Malcolm confronted have not disappeared by any means. But Powell gave me another way to think about the American dilemma and, more than that, another way to think about my own life.

As I started to think seriously about how I could become the person I wanted to be, I looked around at some of the people who'd had the biggest impact on my life. Aside from family and friends, the men I most trusted all had something in common: they all wore the uniform of the United States of America.

I thought about Lieutenant Colonel Murnane, my tenth- and eleventh-grade history and social studies teacher, who lit a fire in me about the importance of public service. I sat in the front of his class entranced as he spoke about the Constitutional Congress and the Federalist Papers, and their relevance to our existence today. I thought about Rear Admiral Hill, the former superintendent of the Naval Academy, who served as the president of Valley Forge in my last three years of high school. Admiral Hill had thousands of cadets, faculty, staff, alumni, and trustees to deal with on a daily basis but always made it a point to know the names and stories of as many cadets as he could. He also taught me an important lesson about leadership: it always comes with having to make tough decisions.

I thought about Colonel Billy Murphy, the commandant of cadets. He was one of the most intimidating but fair men I have ever met. He and his command Sergeant Major Harry Harris demanded excellence from every unit, every platoon, and every cadet. They believed that excuses were tools of the incompetent and forced every cadet to believe the same. One of the last times I saw Colonel Murphy was in our chapel. I sat toward the front. The hard wooden pews forced us to sit up straight, and the message coming from the pulpit demanded everyone's attention. Colonel Murphy ascended to the podium, looking as strong as ever, his eyes still alit with a sense of purpose. Then he announced that he was leaving Valley Forge to undergo treatment for his advanced-stage cancer. He said something I will never forget. "When it is time for you to leave this school, leave your job, or even leave this earth, you make sure you have worked hard to make sure it mattered you were ever here." The notion that life is transient, that it can come and go quickly, unexpectedly, had been with me since I had seen my own father die. In the Bronx, the idea of life's impermanence underlined everything for kids my age—it drove some of us to a paralyzing apathy, stopped us from even thinking too far into the future. Others were driven to what, in retrospect, was a sort of permanent state of mourning: for our loved ones, who always seemed at risk, and for our own lives, which felt so fragile and vulnerable. But I started to see it a little differently that day. Life's impermanence, I realized, is what makes every single day so precious. It's what shapes our time here. It's what makes it so important that not a single moment be wasted.

My next decision was clear. I wanted to stay at Valley Forge and attend its junior college, which would allow me to go through the early commissioning process, receive my associate's degree, and become a second lieutenant in the Army. I wanted to lead soldiers.

"Three minutes!" the Black Hat yelled out.

"Three minutes," we replied with a good deal less gusto. I looked around the plane at the faces of my fellow prospective paratroopers. U.S. Army Airborne School is a collection of soldiers, sailors, airmen, Marines, Coast Guardsmen, cadets, and anyone else who has received the funding and possesses the will to become Airborne-qualified. Some of the attendees needed the qualification to advance in their careers. For example, those planning to join a Ranger battalion or one of the elite Army units like the 82nd Airborne Division needed to be qualified as paratroopers. For some attendees, whose career goals didn't involve combat, it was a way to get a taste of what the combat experience feels like. For all of us, however, it was, at this moment, terrifying. For some in my chalk, this was the first genuine military activity they would engage in. For a few, this was the first airplane ride they had ever taken. These few, even after today, still wouldn't have had the experience of landing in an airplane, just taking off and jumping out.

Broad smiles and hollow laughter were undermined by trembling legs and shaking hands. Our sweat-stained uniforms, still dusty from the endless push-ups and practice jump landings in man-made pits overflowing with sawdust from our first week, clung to our skin.

My left hand grasped the yellow ripcord for dear life as my right hand pressed against the side wall of the C-130 for balance. That bright yellow cord was my lifeline. If it failed, the reserve parachute that was strapped to my belly like a baby kangaroo would be my last hope.

A week before I boarded the most memorable plane ride of my life, Valley Forge had selected me to be the regimental commander for the 70th Corps of Cadets. This meant that I would be the highest-ranking cadet in the entire corps of over seven hundred people. I would be responsible for their training, health, welfare, morale, and success. I remembered watching the regimental commander my first year at Valley Forge with simultaneous fear and awe. On his command, the entire corps moved. Wherever he stepped on campus, cadets snapped to attention. Every cadet possessed a burning desire to be recognized, but never noticed, as his piercing blue eyes evaluated his corps. Now, days after I became a qualified paratrooper, I would take on that role.

The plane steadied as we neared our drop zone. At eighteen hundred feet in the air, the large aircraft began to cruise and prepare to off-load its twenty aspirants. I was only eighteen years old, the youngest in my chalk. When I was commissioned, less than a year from that moment, I was told I was one of the youngest officers in the entire United States military. My platoon sergeant would probably be older than my mother. My company commander would probably have over a decade of life on me. It was one thing leading cadets, but would I honestly be ready at such a young age to lead soldiers?

My mind began racing again when a command brought me back to reality.

"One minute!"

"One minute!"

My mind retraced my three weeks of training in fifteen seconds. I remembered the components of landing. When I landed, I needed to make sure that my feet and knees stayed together, that my eyes stayed focused on an object in the distance, not on the ground, and that my "five points of contact" hit the ground in order (balls of my feet, sides of my calves, hips, lats, and shoulders). It seems much easier than it actually is: jumping from a plane the wrong way or landing the wrong way could lead to serious injuries, even the kind after which you can't tell the war stories the next day.

Step out with one leg. Chin tight against my chest. Right hand on the handle of my reserve parachute.

Do I count to three or count to four before pulling my reserve?

Which way do I pull my parachute slips if the wind is blowing left to right?

Damn, I can't remember.

Is that minute up yet?

My mind and my nerves were on edge. The Black Hats yelling "Get ready, Airborne!" brought me back to task.

Our Black Hats always told us to remember three things as we were jumping: "Trust your equipment, trust your training, and trust your God." As we were seconds away from taking the leap, the multitude of prayers that left the plane were palpable.

I stared at the yellow light at the front of the plane, waiting for it to turn green; I spoke with God, asking Him to watch over me and the others in the plane. The excessively hot and cramped conditions, coupled with the fact that some of the toughest schools in the military take place at Fort Benning, have earned the base the nickname "the land that God forgot." I was hoping He'd remember us today. The formalities that usually accompanied my prayers—"dear most heavenly father" and "most gracious and everlasting God"—were replaced with very simple, blunt, and direct requests like "Help!" and "Please don't let me die like this."

Before I could even finish my prayer, the yellow light disappeared and a bright green one lit up right above it.

"Green light go!"

The soldiers, airmen, Marines, sailors, Coast Guardsmen, cadets, and everyone else in front of me began to shuffle their feet toward the door; it reminded me of commuters leaving a packed subway car, an odd resonance as I approached the open door two thousand feet in the air. We had heard stories during training about people who, after the Black Hat yelled "Green light go," had tried to stay in the plane. They were lifted off their feet by the jumpmasters and thrown out to keep the flow of bodies moving in rhythm and to make sure all of us landed in the drop zone and not in somebody's yard somewhere in Alabama. I shuffled my feet toward the door as the population of the aircraft methodically decreased; my colleagues, I realized, were all now flying through the air beneath me. Suddenly, the only person in front of me was the jumpmaster. He stared at me—we were so close that I could see my distorted reflection in his large Ray-Bans. His cheeks were flapping from the wind blowing against his face. I handed him my yellow rip cord, yelled "Airborne, Jumpmaster!" and turned my body to face the open door. I closed my eyes and felt the air just below me flying by. I assumed the proper position, and somehow my left leg stepped out over the edge of the doorway.

Instantly, my entire body was sucked out of the plane, and I heard—felt—the aircraft speed away. I thrashed around in the wind. It wasn't me who controlled my movements but the rushing air around me. I rotated in darkness because I refused to open my eyes. I was counting in my mind, as I was instructed to, and as I hit the longest three seconds of my life, I felt a sudden jerk, and my body was lifted dozens of feet when my main parachute automatically opened. With that tug, I finally opened my eyes, looked up and, to my relief, saw a perfectly symmetrical and hole-free canopy above me. I felt a cocktail of beautiful emotions coursing through me: peace, love, appreciation. I looked down at the trees waving in the distance, and the gorgeous brown Alabama soil that seemed to be rising to meet me. My equipment was functional, my training was sound, my faith confirmed. I cut through the sky, the wind whipping against my face as I kept my eyes high, staring intently at the horizon.

C heryl, wake up! What the hell is wrong with you?"

Wes took the face of his third and fourth children's mother in his hands and began to shake her. She lay on the couch, saliva dripping out of the corners of her mouth onto her red Gap T-shirt, her pupils dilated and rolling to the back of her head, heroin still flowing through her veins.

Wes ran to the kitchen and rushed back to her with a glass of water, splashing some on her face and pouring some down her throat until she came to. This was not the first time she had gotten high like this, but it was the first time Wes had seen it.

Wes had met Cheryl years before, while he was still living in Dundee Village. She lived down the street from Alicia in a two-bedroom house with her son. She was older than Wes, already twenty-three when they met, but a relationship developed. His two children with Alicia came back-to-back, born in 1992 and 1993; his children with Cheryl came in the same fashion, born in 1995 and 1996.

"Where did you get this from?" Wes asked, but Cheryl just kept repeating the same response, as if they were the only words she knew: "I'm sorry."

Wes cursed himself. He knew he had been turning a blind eye to tell-tale signs that things were moving in this direction. Just a month ago, he'd noticed he was missing money and lectured Cheryl: *Stop bringing your friends into my house if they're going to be stealing my stuff!*

She'd agreed and the conversation had ended, but the problem was not solved. Before that, he'd confronted her after finding a pipe in her closet. "Wes, do you think I would be using while I'm pregnant?" she'd asked. He'd let the matter drop. His love for her and their kids kept him from seeing the truth that now stared him in the face. Cheryl was an addict.

The sight of her coming off her high, stumbling to the bathroom, disgusted Wes. He saw this every day. The people who would line up around the corner for drugs. The people who would do anything to score. He knew these people because he was the one who got them what they needed. It was his job. And it pained him to realize that the mother of his children was just like them. Wes grabbed his keys and walked out the door. He wasn't sure where he was going, but he knew he couldn't stay there.

Wes was tired. Tired of being locked up, tired of watching drugs destroy entire families, entire communities, an entire city. He was tired of being shot at and having to attend the funerals of his friends. He understood that his thoughts contradicted his actions; he had long since accepted that. It was just that his tolerance of his own hypocrisy was wearing thin. He walked down the broken blocks past clusters of abandoned buildings, the glass from shattered windows on the sidewalk, junkies on the steps. He walked for miles through a steady drizzle trying to clear his mind while thirteen-year-olds ran drugs up and down the streets.

Wes turned down Edmondson Avenue, walking toward his friend Levy's house. Levy was a bit younger than Wes but had managed to get out of the hustling game a few months back. At first, Wes had been confused by Levy's decision: why would he give up so much money to go straight? But days like today were making Wes think that maybe Levy was the smart one.

The rain began to subside as Wes approached Levy's house. He walked up the stairs and rang the doorbell.

When Levy saw Wes, his face lit up. "Wes! What's good, yo?" Levy said with his distinctive Baltimore drawl: a trace of a southern twang with words contracted and vowels swallowed. "Come in, come in."

Wes sat on the couch in the middle of the room. His shoulders slumped, his eyes downward. "I'm done, man," he said. "I want to get out. Do something different with my life. But I'm not sure what. I'm not going back to high school. I'm too old for that. But I'm tired of running these streets."

Levy went to the kitchen for a couple of sodas and sat on the couch next to Wes. "Listen, there are definitely some options, but I am telling you, it won't be easy. It will take work, and it will take commitment. Even when the days are tough, you have got to push through. Feel me?"

"Yeah, man, I am ready to try something. Anything."

Levy told Wes about Job Corps, a program he was about to enter. Started in 1964 as a federal initiative, Job Corps was designed to help disadvantaged youth. It was part of Lyndon Johnson's Great Society and was modeled after the Depression era's Civilian Conservation Corps. Levy was hoping to become its newest recruit.

Levy would be entering the Job Corps as a high school dropout but was hoping to leave with a general equivalency diploma (GED) and the skills to help him land a job as a hot-water-boiler repairman. He knew the pay would be lower than what he was making on the streets, but the work was steady and honest, and he would have more time to give his family without injury, death, or incarceration looming.

Wes told him he would think about it. Levy found a piece of paper and wrote down a date and an address. "This is where to go if you are serious about the Job Corps. It doesn't take much, just come through. They'll handle all the rest."

Wes had heard about the Job Corps before. His aunt Virginia had started Job Corps but didn't finish. She said it was too much like jail. What Levy was talking about seemed different, but Wes wasn't sure which version to believe.

As he walked away from Levy's house, Wes pondered other reasons to be doubtful about Job Corps. He had two babies' mothers, four kids, and his own mother to take care of. Wes stepped along beneath streetlights and a quarter moon. The day was coming to an end, but he knew it would be a long night.

Wes looked down at his forearm, at the newest addition to the gallery of images inked on his body. A few weeks back, Wes and three of his friends had gone to a tattoo parlor in Baltimore and all gotten the same design permanently inked on their bodies: a black devil's head with horns and sinister eyes. His skin had almost healed, but the pain behind the tattoo was as fresh as ever.

When the three had arrived at the shop, they'd searched for a symbol that best represented their allegiance to one another and their shared situations. When he was growing up, Wes would occasionally follow his mother to the New Metropolitan Church on Sunday, but even on his sporadic visits, he never felt any connection. He would watch the singing and dancing, cheering and crying, and chalk it all up to theatrics. Wes would wonder if anyone there even knew who or what they were praying to. Where was God when people didn't make enough money to feed their families? Where was God when kids were selling rocks at twelve years old, and their parents encouraged it because the kids were the main breadwinners in the home? Where was God when a young boy came home from a school that was as uninterested in him as he was in it? Where was God when a kid had a question and looked to his friends in the streets for an answer because his father was locked up and his mother strung out?

Wes remembered leaning back in the black, padded parlor chair and taking a puff on his blunt as the tattoo artist sealed the ink into his skin.

"Fuck God," he said, drawing in a lungful of smoke. "If He does exist, He sure doesn't spend any time in West Baltimore."

After agonizing over it, Wes decided to go with Levy to his final Job Corps interview. While there, Wes sat down with a counselor and began a conversation.

"Do you have a high school degree?"

"No," Wes replied.

"Do you have a record?"

"Yes."

"Are you interested in and serious about this program?"

After receiving the same deployment date as Levy, Wes understood that the only question he was asked that mattered was the last one. When the time came, he packed his bags and said goodbye to his family. Where he was going, he had to go on his own.

Two weeks after his conversation with Levy, Wes stood in a parking lot on the corner of Saratoga and Greene streets, waiting for the bus that would take him to the Woodland Job Corps Center in Laurel. The Sunday evening air seemed unusually still as the baby blue school bus rolled. The bus was packed with a motley group of men and women who represented the spectrum of ages, neighborhoods, backstories, and motivations. But they were united in looking for a new chance. They believed the secret to their second lives hid on the sleepy Howard County, Maryland, campus of Job Corps.

Most everyone on the bus slept during the thirty-minute ride, but Wes sat up, staring out the window, wondering about the next few months. He'd been assured during his interview that he would be allowed to return home every weekend if he chose to, and could make a few calls during the week. He was assured he would be able to bring his music and have time to work on his lyrics. He was told that, if he was willing to put in the work, he would leave the program a different person.

The bus finally entered the Job Corps campus. The dark night appeared even darker as they pushed down a long asphalt road. A tree canopy seemed to collapse over the bus as they slowed to a creep. Wes noticed goalposts to his right and, assuming they indicated a football field, he smiled.

The bus stopped at the welcome center and unloaded. The passengers formed a line, awaiting room assignments. When Wes got to the front of the line, an attractive woman in her mid-thirties stood before him with a clipboard and a smile.

"Welcome to Laurel. What's your last name?" she said.

Wes told her his name and she gave him his room assignment.

He stood there smiling at the girl until she nodded at him, as if to say, "Okay, you got your room, now move on." Wes got the hint, grabbed his bags, and carried them along the concrete walkways curving through manicured lawns that led to his dorm. As he walked, his eyes took in the campus. He noticed a beach volleyball court complete with sand. A full basketball court with regulation lines and nets for the rims sat next to a beautiful wooden gazebo. This was exactly what Wes imagined a college campus would look like. He had never seen anything like it before.

When Wes arrived in his room, he found Levy lying back on the bed, his feet crossed and hands behind his head with his fingers interlocked. Smiling. Wes smiled back at him, relieved to see a living piece of home so far away. The spacious room was far from the prisonlike image his aunt Virginia had painted for him.

"So far, so good," Wes said as he dropped his bags and lay on his bed, imitating Levy's leisurely pose.

In the first phase of Job Corps, students are tested to place them at the right level of GED training. One day after they took the test, the results came back: Levy needed to go through the full monthlong pre-GED training. Wes, by contrast, finished near the top of his class. He completed the course work and received his GED a month later. He was already reading at the level of a sophomore in college.

His quick success had Wes thinking differently about his life. He proudly displayed his new diploma at home, excitedly mounting it one weekend in a frame he'd bought the week he received his test scores. The bus would bring him back to Baltimore City every Friday evening, but much of his weekend was spent preparing for the next week in Laurel. Many of the other students were now looking to Wes for help with their GED prep, for assistance with their personal issues, and for friendship. Just as he had on the corners of Baltimore, Wes became a leader.

After completing his academic course work, Wes started on his professional training. He selected carpentry as his vocational specialty. He had always been handy. Years ago, the siding had begun to fall off his mother's house. His brother, Tony, held the siding level as Wes's steady hand nailed the replacement into place. The crack of the hammer as it connected with the head of the nail. The way the body of the nail disappeared into the siding. The joy of admiring a finished product. The quiet thrill of a job well done.

He enjoyed building but was now motivated to learn true skills. After the mandatory training sessions on the use of the equipment and safety precautions, the teacher told the class he wanted them to create something on their own. The teacher made Wes laugh—he was thin and balding, and full of old jokes—but Wes appreciated his skill and his commitment to this group of young men about whom nobody else seemed to care.

As Wes thought about what he wanted to make, the image of his five-year-old daughter came to him. For much of her life, Wes had been gone. Whether at the Job Corps or behind bars, he had missed many of the milestones in her growing up. The situation at home had become even more tenuous. Cheryl's drug problem had become more consuming and overt. The kids were now basically living with Wes's mom. Cheryl complained but never made a real effort to take the kids back. She knew what everyone around her knew: she was in no position to take care of her own children. Wes had to reconsider what it meant to be a father. He wanted to protect his young daughter, shelter her.

One by one, the students declared what they were going to make. The list of objects blurred together—small pieces of furniture and little decorative items—until it was Wes's turn. He had tuned out the conversation around him to become lost in thoughts about his family. The teacher repeated the question to Wes. All Wes could think about was his daughter. Without a thought about what he was taking on, he announced that he wanted to build her a house. The teacher raised his eyebrows and said, "Interesting. A small house?" Wes looked back at the teacher, but in his mind he was looking at the house he wanted to build: "No, a house big enough for her to get in. A house to protect her."

The other people in the room looked at one another and giggled. But Wes did not flinch.

His teacher smiled. "Great, I look forward to seeing it."

He spent the next seven months building his daughter's house from scratch. He sandpapered every board, hammered every nail, leveled every edge. When it was finished, the house stood five feet high and an arm's length across; it included shutters, a door, and windows. It was by far the most complex project in the group. When it was finished, it sat in the display room along with the projects of his classmates, including wooden plaques and a plain box that someone called a telephone base.

To Wes, the house was more than just a project to complete. It was a daily reminder of why he was there. These past months had been the most important and enjoyable in Wes's life. He'd learned skills, gained confidence, and finally felt his life could go in a different direction. He stayed at the Job Corps Center so he could provide a better life for his kids. He stayed for his mother, who sat home watching Tony continue moving in and out of the criminal justice system. He stayed at the Job Corps Center for himself.

After seven months, Wes met his graduation from Job Corps with as much trepidation as excitement. No longer would he have to show up at the large parking lot on Sunday evenings waiting for the blue bus. No longer would he have to share a room with Levy who, after a troubled start, was completing his GED requirements and starting his vocational classes. Wes would now be on his own.

Wes's first job was as a landscaper at a home in Baltimore County. It was a temporary gig, and after five months he moved on to rehabbing homes in the city—another temporary job. After that, he worked as a food preparer at a mall in Baltimore. A year after completing the Job Corps training, Wes realized the only consistency in his employment was inconsistency. That, and the fact that none of these jobs paid over nine dollars an hour.

One day, after completing his shift chopping vegetables, Wes took a detour on the way home. He went by his old West Baltimore neighborhood to pick up a package. He had stayed away from these blocks because he had been so busy since getting back from Laurel. He worked ten hours a day and came home with barely enough energy to play with his kids and barely enough money to feed and clothe them. But the main reason he avoided these streets was that he felt they held nothing for him. He had changed. At least he wanted to believe that, and he continued to tell himself that as he walked through the blocks. He raised his head and acknowledged the many faces he had not seen for over a year.

Wes was amazed as he watched how little the game had changed: the corner boys still pulling lookout, the muscle still looking as intimidating as ever. Wes watched as, across the street, a young man no older than sixteen pulled out a wad of cash, held together by a rubber band, and began showing it off to a friend. Lines of heads circled the block looking for their next hit. Some of the players had changed, but the positions were the same.

Wes in 1990, shortly after he was charged with attempted murder.

Fifteen-year-old Wes (wearing his headset) with family members in Dundee Village.

Tony at sixteen years old.
By then he had gained a fierce
reputation in Baltimore.

Wes and Tony at a
Baltimore club.

Tony with his oldest child.

Wes with his daughter when she visited him in prison.

Woody visiting Wes in prison.

With two other members of my regimental staff during my last year at Valley Forge. That year I was the highest-ranking cadet on campus, with more than eight hundred cadets under my command.

Nikki, Shani, and I after a Johns Hopkins football game.

My host family and I in their home in South Africa.

Preparing to go on a mission with Lieutenant Anthony Delsignore, a good Marine and friend.

Meeting with a group of middle-school kids I worked with in Baltimore.

Moving toward the apex of Mount Kilimanjaro. Unfortunately, altitude sickness kept me from the top.

I proposed!

Cutting the wedding cake with my bride, Dawn. Our wedding day was one of the most amazing days of my life.

Standing under the NASDAQ screen in the heart of Times Square. I rang the closing bell at the New York Stock Exchange with members of the Iraq and Afghanistan Veterans of America.

Speaking in front of tens of thousands at INVESCO Field in Denver. I spoke just hours before Barack Obama accepted the Democratic nomination for president and forty-five years to the day after Dr. Martin Luther King's "I have a dream" speech.

Wes finally got home and went immediately to his kitchen. He was living on his own now, in a small apartment. He placed the package he'd picked up on the table, sat down, and put his head in his hands. The pressure was breaking Wes down. Alicia complained that he was not giving her enough money to provide for the kids they shared. Cheryl was now constantly calling him about wanting more time with the kids—which meant she wanted more money to take care of them. His mother needed more money because she was raising both Wes's and Tony's kids. Wes banged his fists against the top of his head as his elbows rested on the kitchen table. While at the Job Corps Center, Wes had felt his problems floating off in the soft country air of Laurel. A year after graduating, he realized they had not disappeared— they'd simply returned to Baltimore, waiting for him to come back. In his absence, they'd compounded.

Tears welled in Wes's eyes but never fell. He'd realized long ago that crying does no good.

He quickly rose and went to the sink to fill a pot with water. He ignited the flame on the front burner of his stove. While the water was heating, Wes walked to the front of his apartment and turned on 92Q, a popular Baltimore radio station. The last few bars of a Jay-Z song filled the room.

> *When the streets is watching, blocks keep clocking*
> *Waiting for you to break, make your first mistake*

Wes returned to the kitchen. He reached in the refrigerator and pulled out the baking soda. Muscle memory kicked in as he tapped the side of the box and poured three ounces of the baking soda into the black pot, watching the powder swirl and fall to the bottom. He placed the baking soda back in the refrigerator. Taking a deep breath before picking up the package, he took a bound plastic bag out of the brown paper wrapping. He squeezed the package, testing its density. He reached over to the drawer that held his cutlery and pulled out a knife, brought the blade to the corner of the plastic bag. As the baking soda swirled in the rapidly heating pot, Wes held the plastic bag with both hands and poured in nine ounces of cocaine.

EIGHT

Surrounded

The phone had been ringing continuously for three minutes. Mary sat on her sofa, unflinching. She was in no mood to talk, no mood to explain, no mood for consolation. She simply leaned forward, with her elbows resting on her knees, watching the television screen flickering just five feet in front of her. Her hands trembled.

Ten minutes ago, a news report had stopped her cold. Mary didn't watch much television; she felt she never had time, but she just happened to have it on this evening. She saw file footage of a jewelry store she didn't recognize, its redbrick exterior surrounded by police and yellow tape, accompanied by the newscaster's somber narration of events. Mary had been so busy that she was completely unaware this story had gripped the city for days. But as she sat on the sofa, she got caught up on what she had missed.

Three days earlier, in broad daylight, two masked men had run into J. Browns Jewelers waving guns at the customers, ordering them to the ground. Customers screamed in fear and quickly followed the orders as two more masked men entered. These men carried mallets in their gloved hands. The gunmen scanned the room, their weapons trained on the terrified customers and employees, their heads swiveling, looking for any movement. They barked out orders over the screams of their victims. Following the robbers' command, the workers and customers pressed their faces to the ground.

"Keep your hands on the backs of your heads! I ain't playing with you!" yelled one of the armed robbers. "What do you have in your hands?" Another gunman yelled to a woman who had been talking on her cell phone when the four men ran into the store. With her arms outstretched and her torso resting on the ground, she slowly closed her phone, keeping her hands in open sight. The two men with mallets were oblivious to the pandemonium around them. They headed straight to the display cases that housed the watches and necklaces. Their decisive movements showed they knew exactly where to go and what they were looking for.

One of the people being held at gunpoint was Sergeant Bruce Prothero, a thirty-five-year-old, thirteen-year veteran of the Baltimore County police department. Earlier that day, he'd left his wife and five children, ranging in age from two to six, to work his second job as a security guard at the jeweler's. After his wife had triplets, he'd needed to pick up an additional part-time job so she could stay home with the kids. He was supposed to be off that day but was covering for a friend who needed the day off. He was known around the department as a man ferociously devoted to protecting his family and his colleagues. Sergeant Prothero was now being held by the neck, a gun pressed against the back of his head, his hands high in the air. He was unceremoniously forced to the floor with the others.

After grabbing $438,000 worth of watches and jewels from the store, one of the robbers yelled "Let's go," and the four ran out to the adjacent parking lot, where a 1984 Oldsmobile Delta 88 and 1987 Mercury Grand Marquis waited for them. Both cars had been bought a week earlier at an auto auction. Most of the people in the store kept their eyes closed and heads on the ground. A few, including Sergeant Prothero, raised their heads to watch the men leave. Once the thieves cleared the door, these few quickly rose to their feet. Sergeant Prothero followed his instincts and ran out after the robbers. Drawing his weapon from his holster, he sprinted through the entrance. He looked around the parking lot for signs of the four men. He ducked behind cars, carefully peering through glass windows and above hoods. As Sergeant Prothero scampered behind the Delta 88 and began to lift his head, a black-gloved hand reached out the window holding a hand-gun and let off three shots, striking Prothero at point-blank range.

Even after getting shot twice in the chest and once in the head, Sergeant Prothero stumbled off and ran about ten feet, finally falling in the green bushes that surrounded the jewelry store. For the next minutes, he fought a losing battle for his life. The two getaway cars had long since screeched out of the parking lot.

Crime in Baltimore and its suburbs had spiraled out of control, particularly in the city proper. Baltimore City was now averaging over three hundred murders a year, making it one of the per capita deadliest cities in America. Police officers were consistently trying to solve gun crimes, drug-related crimes, domestic abuse crimes, and robberies. But this case was different, more personal to the cops assigned to it. Not only did it take place outside Baltimore City, in the county, an area where vicious murders were less common, but this shooting involved one of their own. All hands would be on deck to make sure that the perpetrators were brought to justice.

The first major lead in the case came a day after the shooting. One of the suspects called a notorious drug dealer to offer him a chance to buy some stolen watches. The drug dealer had an authorized wiretap on his phone and, as a result, the police got a search warrant and went to the house where the call originated. When they found one of the stolen watches under a seat cushion, they suspected they had their man. He later confessed to being in on the robbery but denied that he had pulled the trigger. Through his interviews, the police identified the other three men, where they lived, and more details about the crime.

A day later, another member of the crew was captured. He also confessed to being at the scene but said that he was not the one who pulled the trigger. In fact, he was later quoted as saying, "I was actually unarmed. I was just told I could make fifty thousand dollars to break some glass." This wasn't the first trip through the criminal justice system for either of them. Both men, in their early twenties, had long criminal records that included drug charges, handgun violations, and assault charges. One of them had been charged a year before with two counts of first-degree murder for separate shootings in West Baltimore.

Mary was riveted as she listened to the reporter's dry voice. It was an audacious crime, a troubling sign of the violence that felt like it was closing in on her no matter how far she moved away from the center of the city. Her phone started to ring. Again she ignored it. Then the reporter described the final two suspects. The reporter warned those watching that they should be assumed to be "armed and very dangerous." Mary's large-screen television was now filled with photos of these suspects. Her heart broke when she saw Tony's and Wes's faces staring back at her.

Midnight passed, and one day turned to the next. Mary could not sleep. She felt terrible about the death of the police officer. She prayed her sons were not responsible. As she lay in bed, she realized that, no matter what the outcome, all of their lives had changed forever. Mary knew it was just a matter of time before she would become the target of questioning. She had not spoken to Wes or Tony for days, but after hearing the news, she wanted to speak to them just as much as she was sure the police did.

At 4:00 A.M., Mary heard a loud banging on her metal front door. "Police! Open this door!"

She threw on a blue robe, yelling that she was on her way. She could tell from the increasingly frantic banging that the police were seconds away from coming in—with or without an invitation. She cracked open the door, her right eye peering out to see who was waiting. She looked past the stocky man in plain clothes and saw ten— maybe more—cops lined up behind him. A few wore uniforms. More were wearing plain clothes. All were tense. Some had their weapons raised, some had them holstered, their hands ready to snap the guns loose at a moment's notice. Only a thin, hollow metal door stood between her and them.

The plainclothesman in front of her flashed a badge, showed a search warrant, and brusquely asked Mary for permission to enter. She took a step back and, as soon as she did, the door swung open and the officers flooded into her home.

With weapons drawn, teams split up and searched for Wes, Tony, or any evidence that they'd been there recently. One of the officers escorted Mary out of the house and sat her on the stairs outside. She hugged herself as the cold February air blew through her cotton bathrobe.

Before long an officer appeared before her and unleashed a barrage of sternly delivered questions. But Mary could only keep repeating the truth: she had no idea where the boys were and had not seen them in weeks.

"Did you know that both of your sons are on probation?"

"Yes, I did."

"Tony is supposed to be on home detention for a drug conviction, and Wesley is still on probation for drug charges from a few years ago—"

"I know what they were on probation for, Officer."

"If you knew where they were, would you tell us?"

Mary finally snapped at them. "Look, I just found out that my sons are wanted for killing a police officer. If I find anything out, I will tell you, and I will cooperate however I can, but right now I don't need to be questioned like I did something wrong."

The questions and searching of the house continued for the next hour. The jarring percussion of drawers being opened and closed, dressers being shifted around, and beds being flipped over rattled through the quiet night and shook Mary's nerves. Black, spit-shined police shoes with hard rubber soles cracked down on every inch of hardwood floor. Mary sat on the outdoor concrete steps with the officer standing over her, the two mirroring each other's despair and frustration.

The first rays of morning lit up the still deserted streets of Dundalk, Maryland, where Mary's new home was located, as the cops mounted up to leave her ransacked space. Every crevice had been inspected, every room had been searched, every secret presumably uncovered.

The police departed with a threat: they would be back and would not leave her alone until they found Tony and Wes. To nobody's surprise, they were true to their word.

The search for the Moores had just begun.

Two days after that first early morning visit, Mary's niece, Nicey's daughter, was moments from walking down the aisle for her wedding. As a recording of "Here Comes the Bride" played over the loudspeaker in the Northeast Baltimore church, the rear doors opened and the veiled bride began her slow procession toward the altar. She walked alone down the aisle as the well-wishers in the pews stood and smiled. Tony was supposed to walk arm in arm with his cousin and give her away—her father had never been involved in her life. Her unescorted stroll down the aisle was a subtle reminder that the manhunt for two of Maryland's most wanted was still on, now in day five.

The family had been bombarded with interview requests, police questioning, and neighborhood stares. Both city and county police had been crisscrossing their jurisdictions, looking for any sign of Wes and Tony. The police conducted a raid of the Circle Terrace apartments in Lansdowne, where Tony lived. Acting on a tip, they combed the North Point neighborhood in Baltimore. A team of officers went by Wes's current address, on the 2700 block of Calvert Street in the city—on the outskirts of Johns Hopkins University, close enough that Wes could see and hear the construction slowly creeping in around him. The police plastered the neighborhood with wanted posters, advertising a sizable reward. In the evenings, a police chopper with searchlights flew over the Essex community, where Wes had lived a few years earlier.

The wedding was a reprieve for the family. This celebration was the first time in days that they could simply enjoy one another's company without the events of February seventh dominating the conversation. Today was supposed to be about joy and love.

Following the ceremony, the doors to the church opened to a clear and cool winter day. A hundred or so people slowly filed into the street. The snow that had fallen a few days earlier was now a dark slush shoveled against the sides of the road. All of the attendees loaded into their vehicles, and set off for the reception hall, ten minutes away. Each driver put on hazard lights as the slow convoy snaked its way to Southeast Baltimore.

Two of the vehicles, the ones carrying the eight members of the wedding party, decided to break from the pack and take a quick detour to a 7-Eleven on the Alameda, a main artery in Baltimore City. They wanted to grab a few sodas and some bags of chips before the reception, just in case it took a while for the food to show up after they arrived. A block away from the store, an unmarked police car pulled up behind the vehicles, red and blue lights flashing. The same car had been sitting outside the church, its occupants observing the celebratory congregants as they walked out. The wedding party pulled over.

Doors slammed, and three policemen leaped out of the car and walked up to the wedding party's vehicles. They forced all eight of the passengers from the vehicles and ordered them to sit on the curb of the traffic island that split Alameda. The men, wearing their white tuxedos, and the women, wearing silky silver, spaghetti-strapped dresses, complained about having to sit on the slushy curb in their wedding outfits. They were told that they would have to sit down or be arrested. And then one of the officers addressed the group.

"Y'all know there is a reward for Tony and Wes if you just tell us where they are. It's a lot of money. You sure you don't need that money? This would be much easier on you if you would just say where those two are."

The eight sat silently, shivering in their now soaked clothes, while the police continued to grill them. It had been more than thirty minutes since they were pulled over. No information had been collected, not a single idea about the whereabouts of Wes and Tony had been divulged. The wedding party simply sat on the ground, late for the reception and, by now, tremendously agitated. The police, circling the party, felt much the same way.

Finally, the officers ordered them back into their cars, but not before placing handcuffs on one of the drivers because he didn't have the proper registration for the rental car they were driving. The rest of the wedding party yelled at the officers as they placed their friend in the back of the cruiser. The arresting officer simply looked back at the group and said, "Enjoy the reception. I hope ya'll remember where Tony Moore and Wes Moore are. Quickly."

Wes was walking down a street, a Philly cheesesteak in one hand and a new pair of blue jeans in the other. His brother was by his side. Thirty feet away—at the corner—he noticed a police cruiser. As he got closer, he noticed that the engine was running, and that the two cops inside were murmuring into their walkie-talkies. This was the same squad car Wes had noticed twice earlier in the day, in different parts of the city but always within fifty feet of where he and Tony stood. But no one had made a move for them, so Wes had chalked it up as simple coincidence. He and Tony continued to move through the crowded Germantown streets toward his uncle's house in North Philadelphia. The crime-ridden neighborhood was where Tony and Wes had escaped just days after the murder.

North Philadelphia reminded Wes of the Baltimore neighborhood he had just left. The check-cashing stores instead of banks, the rows of beauty salons, liquor stores, laundromats, funeral homes, and their graffiti-laced walls were the universal streetscape of poverty. The hood was the hood, no matter what city you were in. But just blocks away from their uncle's house, scattered evidence of gentrification— driven by the looming presence of Temple University—had started to manifest. Their uncle's block, where half of the homes sat abandoned and burnt out, represented what the neighborhood had become. Blocks away, where newly built mixed-income homes sat next to pic- turesque buildings like the gothic Church of the Advocate, built in 1887, was the direction the neighborhood wanted to go. But even that dynamic wasn't unique; the same thing was happening in Wes's neigh- borhood, where Hopkins was the driving force of change, aimed at improving the quality of life for students and faculty. Wes wondered where people like him were supposed to go once they'd been priced out of the old neighborhoods, once the land changed hands right under their feet.

When they got back to the house, Wes went upstairs to the room that housed the bunk bed he and Tony shared. Tupac's "Keep Ya

Head Up" was on the radio, and Wes turned it up. It was one of his favorites, Pac's voice defiant over the melancholy chorus sampled from the Five Stairsteps—"Ooh, child, things are gonna get easier." Wes sat down on his bed and opened the plastic bag that held his cheesesteak. The grease leaked from the packaging, and the aroma of the Cheeze Whiz and grilled onions rose from a puncture in the aluminum foil.

Wes had just raised the sandwich to his mouth when Tony walked into the room. "I got to run out for a second, I'll be back."

Wes just nodded, distracted by the cheesesteak. Under the beats from the radio he could hear Tony's white Air Jordans pounding down the stairs. It was midafternoon, so most of the lights in the house were off; the room was filled with shadows and the soft glow of natural sunlight.

Wes heard Tony yell back up the stairs, "I'll be back, yo," and then the sound of the front door creaking open. His uncle was always telling them to close the door behind them to keep the cold air outside and the warm air inside. When Wes didn't hear the door close behind Tony, he took one final bite and ran down the stairs to slam it shut. As Wes hit the final stair, he looked up and saw his brother lying facedown on the floor, a police officer's knee in his back, handcuffs being tightened around his wrists. Before Wes could even react, a half dozen plainclothes officers were on top of him, the barrels of their guns trained on his head and the lights from their flashlights blinding him.

"Don't move! Get your hands in the air!"

The officers were now screaming orders to the Moore brothers, telling them to get on the ground and keep their mouths shut. A task force of over two dozen Philadelphia police officers, Baltimore City and County police officers, and ATF and FBI officials flooded their uncle's narrow three-story row house. Within minutes of receiving word that the Moore brothers were back in the house, police had cordoned off the entire block. Outside the cordon, curious onlookers were kept away by Philadelphia police officers as Wes and Tony were led outside in handcuffs, and thrown into the back of a police wagon. The twelve-day manhunt was over.

Word spread quickly through the Baltimore City and County police departments about the arrest. On the dispatch, a message scrolled across the top of the message board: 02.19/00, DUNDALK DISPATCH ADVISED THAT BOTH OF THE MOORE BROTHERS ARE UNDER ARREST IN PHILADELPHIA!

Cheering responses flowed in. Their colleague had been killed just days earlier. They now believed that the four people responsible were in their custody. The newspapers and television networks ran nonstop coverage of the arrest. Civic leaders held press conferences praising the work of the police officers. The county executive of Baltimore County helped lead a telethon that raised money for the widow of Sergeant Prothero and his children. As word spread, a collective sigh of relief seeped through Baltimore's brisk winter air. At home, Mary wept.

Wes sat still on the ancient wooden chair. His fingers were entwined, resting on the table in front of him. His nervousness had subsided months earlier; he knew he no longer had control over his destiny. A year had passed since the Prothero shooting, and Wes was the fourth and final defendant to find out his verdict. It had also been a year since the governor of Pennsylvania had agreed to extradite Wes to his home state of Maryland to await trial. Wes now sat waiting to find out how the jury of his peers had ruled. The foreman stood up, looked briefly at Wes, and then his eyes darted over to the people in the viewing area of the courtroom. Tony and the other two defendants had all been found guilty and sentenced to life in prison without parole. Tony was charged as the shooter and had avoided a possible death sentence by pleading guilty to felony murder.

Unlike the other three defendants, Wes had decided to take his case to trial. He insisted that he was not there the day of the murder. Twenty-five witnesses were called, sixty exhibits were displayed, store security videotapes were shown, and photos were employed by both sides. Wes's lawyer pleaded that the biggest mistake his client made was going to Philadelphia with his brother. His lawyer argued that when Wes was questioned by Baltimore police the day after the crime, before he was announced as a suspect, he was calm, a clear sign of his innocence. His lawyer claimed the police were harassing people in the neighborhood, trying to drum up shaky evidence and confessions. He also pointed out that Wes had converted to Islam in jail and was a father of four children, whom he talked to almost every day on the telephone from jail.

The prosecution cast suspicions on Wes's argument that he'd taken the trip to Philadelphia without asking his brother what he was on the run for. A saleswoman at the jewelry store testified that she recognized Wes as one of the four men who'd robbed the store. Also, a necklace was found at the scene of the crime that had Wes's DNA on it. The prosecution claimed it was the "calling card" they were looking for to prove Wes was there. Wes's attorney argued that Tony must have borrowed the necklace earlier, and it had accidentally dropped out of his pocket at the store. "There's only one explanation. It came out of a pocket, it came out of the pocket of that jacket," Wes's lawyer proclaimed.

Wes was moments away from finding out which story the jury would believe.

"Please rise," the bailiff requested. Instructions were ordered.

Wes peered over at the jury: six men and six women. They had deliberated for three hours. He looked at each of their faces in turn. No one looked back at him. He felt very alone. He sighed deeply. A sudden apathy sapped him. He knew what the foreman had to say before he even parted his lips. Wes stared straight ahead. He was as still as a soldier on parade awaiting his next command. As he heard the foreman begin, he closed his eyes and leaned his head back.

"On the charge of first-degree felony murder, the jury finds the defendant . . . guilty."

Wes stood quietly, his face set, as the foreman read out ten other charges, all with the same verdict. Wes's consciousness left the scene. He had spent the past year sitting in a cell waiting for this day. With the knowledge of the sentences his brother and the other two defendants had received, he'd known his fate would be the same. He would spend the rest of his life in prison.

The widow of Sergeant Prothero hugged her father and sobbed. She had sat in the pews of different courtrooms for months, and the emotion of watching the sentencing of the final defendant in the slaying of her husband was overwhelming. About ten feet away, Wes's mother, aunt Nicey, and Alicia sat stunned with tears in their eyes as well. A large guard made his way over to Wes, who slowly put his hands behind his back. He kept his head and eyes fixed on the front of the courtroom, never once looking behind him to see the family of the police officer or even his own family. He winced as the cuffs closed around his wrists and the officer began to walk him out of the room. It would be over a month before Wes was in a courtroom again. On that day he would stand before a judge and hear his fate.

"You committed an act like something out of the Wild West, and you didn't even realize how outrageous it was," the judge said. "That makes you a very dangerous person."

The sentence was indeed life in prison without the possibility of parole. The guards placed their hands on Wes and shuffled him away. The hands of the state would stay on him for the rest of his life. Wes had spent much of his adolescence incarcerated, and he knew that occasional bids in the pen were part of the game. But he'd never figured this. Maybe it was because he'd never thought long term about his life at all. Early losses condition you to believe that short-term plans are always smarter. Now Wes's mind wandered to the long term for the first time. Finally, he could see his future.

Wes, the mayor will see you now."

As I began walking toward the mayor's mahogany door, I instinctively stuck my hands in my pockets and pushed down, trying to get the cuffs of my pants lower so my high-waters might brush the tops of my shoes. For close to a decade I'd dressed in a uniform every day. Fashion was not my forte. This was my best blue suit, but because I had owned it since high school, it was no longer much of a fit.

"Hey, General, how's everything going?" Mayor Schmoke said as I cautiously entered and shook his hand. General was his nickname for me, poking fun at the fact that I was a brand-new second lieutenant in the Army Reserve—which, by the way, is as far from a general as an officer can get. Despite my being on my second internship with him and seeing him every day, the mayor still intimidated me. Every time I stepped into his office, I felt the need to genuflect. Even his famously toothy grin failed to put me at ease.

Kurt Schmoke had been the mayor of Baltimore for twelve years. The former boy wonder was now a seasoned and slightly cynical leader of the city he'd called home his entire life. Progress had been made under his leadership; Baltimore had been named an Empowerment Zone by President Clinton in 1994. On his orders, and with the help of 375 pounds of explosives, the buildings of Murphy Homes were brought down in twenty seconds and soon replaced with mixed-income housing. But his frustration at the glacial pace of change in his city had worn on him. He needed to attend fund-raiser after fund-raiser just to remain a viable candidate for public office. The problems he'd warned of—and prioritized—over a decade earlier were persistently difficult to solve. The murder rate had not fallen under three hundred in years. Sexually transmitted diseases throughout Baltimore had risen sharply, alongside the teen pregnancy rate. The young, photogenic Yale-, Oxford-, and Harvard-educated lawyer had learned just how confounding the problems of urban America were.

Of course, to talk about the negative sections and aspects of Baltimore without talking about its strengths, its history, and its opportunities would be inaccurate. Baltimore is the birthplace of Babe Ruth and Thurgood Marshall, Edgar Allan Poe and Billie Holiday. The Battle of Baltimore was one of the deciding battles of the War of 1812 and Francis Scott Key, a lawyer and native Baltimorean, penned "The Star-Spangled Banner" at Fort McHenry while watching soldiers from our new nation fight off the British. Baltimore is home of the B&O Railroad and the best crab cakes anywhere. West Baltimore was one of the intellectual capitals of the East Coast in the early twentieth century.

At the same time, to simply walk along the pristine Inner Harbor or go see the Orioles in action without understanding that all of Baltimore is not downtown would be equally misleading. The truth is that there are two Baltimores. Almost every other major city in this country leads the same double life. Those who brag about Baltimore often ignore these substandard areas. Yet these were the areas Mayor Schmoke knew would determine his legacy of success or failure.

He asked me to take a seat on a couch. I'd found his office imposing when I first saw it, but its quiet elegance had, over time, made the stronger impression. Plaques and awards lined the walls, along with photos of the mayor with presidents, prime ministers, and everyday Baltimoreans. The office reflected the man—hugely impressive and unassuming at once. His waistline had grown slightly over the years; his suspenders now pulled his pants above his belt line. In the final year of his third term and preparing to retire, he was leaving not because of term limits but because of fatigue. He could have easily won a fourth term had he wanted it, but he didn't. What he wanted now was time to spend with his family and for someone else to grab hold of the reins of the city he loved with its daunting array of problems.

Mayor Schmoke eased into a chair across from the couch. He leaned back, rubbing both hands over his thinning hair, now salted with gray, and asked me how I had enjoyed my internship.

I offered a crisp response: "I've loved it, sir." But my glib answer didn't do justice to the impact the time in his office had had on me. I didn't know how to begin to express my gratitude.

I had returned to Baltimore two years earlier, after I'd been accepted at Johns Hopkins University to complete my undergraduate degree, which I'd begun in junior college at Valley Forge. One afternoon at Valley Forge I was talking to my college adviser about what to do after I received my associate's degree. My adviser told me that she knew the assistant director of admissions at Johns Hopkins, whom she wanted me to meet. My mother had been working in Baltimore for the past five years, and I considered Baltimore home, so I knew about Johns Hopkins. I just didn't know anyone who went there. My perception of Hopkins was as a distant force in the neighborhood, a research university responsible for some of the greatest medical gifts the world has ever received, but that had very little to do with the life of the city I knew. Hopkins was also full of kids who did not look or sound like me.

"Ma'am, I do not want to be a doctor," I quickly answered her.

"Wes, it is much more than that. Just have lunch with him. At the very least, I think you'll enjoy each other's company."

A week later, I sat across the table from Paul White, the assistant director of admissions at Johns Hopkins. I was expecting a stodgy, older gentleman who'd offer me canned encomiums about Hopkins and then stiffen and ask for the check when he found out the details of my standardized test scores. What I found was a black man with a warm disposition and a booming voice, who bristled with energy and was constantly in motion, his hands swooping like birds in flight to accentuate his points. I spent much of the lunch telling him my story, and he spent the remaining time selling me on Hopkins. By the end of our meal, I realized that Hopkins represented much more than a chance to attend a great school with a phenomenal reputation. It was also a chance to go home. My relationship with my mother had changed significantly. I'd spent so much of my life running from her, trying to show her I didn't need her as much as she thought. She'd spent much of the same period being an unrelenting disciplinarian. But as I got older, and as she realized her days of hard-core parenting were coming to an end, she became more than a mother, she became a friend.

But there was still the matter of getting in. My SAT scores were hundreds of points below the average for students entering Johns Hopkins, and despite my being a junior college graduate and an Army officer, I knew that landing admission at Hopkins would be a stretch at best. So after filling out the application, I put it out of my mind. But months later, I got the large package in the mail. Not only was I accepted but I would receive scholarship money. I read the letter aloud to my mother over the phone, and she screamed in excitement.

While reading the letter, I thought about Paul White. Having an advocate on the inside—someone who had gotten to know me and understood my story on a personal level—had obviously helped. It made me think deeply about the way privilege and preference work in the world, and how many kids who didn't have "luck" like mine in this instance would find themselves forever outside the ring of power and prestige. So many opportunities in this country are apportioned in this arbitrary and miserly way, distributed to those who already have the benefit of a privileged legacy.

Many of the kids I grew up with in the Bronx—including guys like Shea, who stayed outside the law—never believed that they'd have a shot. Many in the generation before mine believed that maybe they did, but they had the rug pulled out from under them by cuts in programs like the Pell Grants or by the myriad setbacks that came with the age of crack. Reversals spun them right back to the streets and away from their true ambitions. For the rest of us—those who snuck in despite coming from the margins—the mission has to be to pull up others behind us. That's what Paul White did for me, and it changed my life.

I had been talking with Mayor Schmoke for ten minutes when he leaned toward me and asked the dreaded question: "So, Wes, what do you plan on doing after you finish school?" I really had no idea. The words "law school" escaped from my mouth, the fallback answer for many students who have no idea what they want to do with their lives. Mayor Schmoke waved his hand at the idea.

"Have you ever heard of the Rhodes Scholarship?"

I had heard of it—I knew that Mayor Schmoke, President Clinton, and our state's senior senator, Paul Sarbanes, were all Rhodes Scholars, but I didn't know much else about the award.

"Let me show you something," the mayor continued, rising from his wooden seat and moving toward the wall. I followed him. He pulled out a pen and stretched his arm toward a black-and-white framed picture.

"Right there is James Atlas, the writer from *The New Yorker*. Over here, that's Frank Raines. He is the head of the Office of Management and Budget in the Clinton administration." His pen then moved a few inches over on the picture. "And there I am. This is my Rhodes class."

I stared at the photo of eighty young faces smiling into the camera. The plaid suits with large collars, the bushy mustaches and overdue haircuts, and the thick knotted ties were all obviously stylish back when he went to Oxford but looked a little funny through contemporary eyes. Then again, my high-waters and medium-size suit jacket didn't exactly qualify me as a fashion critic. I recognized a few other faces in the crowd and realized that, whether they were household names or not, this was an exclusive group that held a significant amount of influence and power. People who could engineer real change. Mayor Schmoke continued to tell me about his experiences as I listened intently. He reminisced about the stimulating conversations that took place in rustic pubs over warm beer. He told me about living and working in buildings constructed hundreds of years before the United States was even founded. He shared with me some of the trips he took around Europe. And he told me about the odd feeling of being a minority, not because you were African-American but because you were an American in the wider world.

After he completed his anecdotes, Mayor Schmoke ended our meeting. He extended his large, callused hand, and before I could leave the office, he gave me one last order. Mayor Schmoke knew that, weeks after I completed the internship with him, I would be heading to South Africa for a semester abroad. To him this chance to see South Africa less than a decade after the end of apartheid was the perfect preparation for a real understanding of the Rhodes experience and legacy. In his thoughtful, deliberate cadence, he said, "While you are in South Africa, admire the beauty and culture. But make sure you do not leave without understanding the history. Make sure you understand who Cecil Rhodes was and what his legacy is. Know this before you apply for his scholarship." Not sure what to say, I simply said, "Yes, sir," my grip tightening in his hand. I thanked him for the opportunity to serve and began my walk through the archway leading me back into the waiting area.

I found out years later that it was Judge Robert Hammerman and Senator Sarbanes who gave Mayor Schmoke the confidence to apply for the Rhodes Scholarship. I hope that, in some way, Mayor Schmoke felt like he had returned the favor. Of course, he did more than just point me to the Rhodes Scholarship; he instructed me to learn the larger historical context of the award. Although I didn't really understand it at the time, like Colin Powell, he was telling me that our blood-soaked and atrocity-littered past was important but that the future didn't have to be its slave. Even a legacy as ugly as that of Cecil Rhodes—a nineteenth-century imperialist, white supremacist, and rapacious businessman—could be turned around and used by a person like me, someone Cecil Rhodes would've undoubtedly despised, to change the world that Rhodes and people like him had left for us.

I had traveled abroad before. I'd visited Jamaica often to see family when I was growing up. I also went to Cuba with a group of Johns Hopkins students to study the island's arts and culture—a trip I used to try to find my long-lost great-aunt and other family members. But this would be my first long-term trip abroad. The fifteen-hour flight would be just the beginning of a much larger journey.

My January arrival was met with over-eighty-five-degree heat. Because South Africa is below the equator, their seasons are the reverse of ours, so I boarded the plane knowing that I would bypass the winter cold this year. I walked into John F. Kennedy International Airport with my sweater and oversize brown goose-down jacket, and I walked out into the Cape Town heat with just a T-shirt, shorts, and sunglasses shading my eyes.

"Are you Wes?" a strongly accented voice shouted toward me. The pronunciation made my name sound like "Wez." I immediately knew this would take some getting used to. The voice, an unfamiliar mixture of Australian and Dutch inflections, came from the tall and thin but muscular man now walking toward me in khaki shorts and a Bahama shirt. A pair of sunglasses rested on top of his balding head. "I am," I cautiously replied. He smiled and introduced himself as the director of the study abroad program. He said his name was Zed, which, he explained, was a nickname taken from his first initial, Z, which is pronounced "Zed" in much of the English-speaking world. I had never heard that before but took his word for it. I felt a little disoriented by this smiling white Zimbabwean with the odd accent and strange name. I don't know what I was expecting for my introduction to Africa, but it sure wasn't Zed.

I had applied for and received a grant to go to South Africa through the School for International Training, a Vermont-based program that offers the chance to live overseas for a semester or more. That semester, fourteen of us left our respective corners of the United

States and traveled to South Africa. We went to school together at the University of Cape Town and studied culture and reconciliation—a subject for which post-apartheid South Africa had become a living laboratory. Aside from the formal curriculum at the university, we would spend our time learning the language, learning the country, and learning more about ourselves than we ever imagined.

I sat in the back of a spacious van loaded down with bags and a group of confused and overwhelmed American students, staring out the window. I was dumbstruck by the natural beauty of the country. I could see the clouds rolling off Table Mountain and the crowds of wealthy South Africans casually peering into the pristine water at the V & A Waterfront. I was impressed by the natural beauty, but I knew that Africa wasn't just a giant safari. My grandfather, who'd worked throughout Africa as a missionary, would often share the truth with me about the tremendous cultural diversity that lies within the continent. But I was in no way prepared for the massive skyscrapers, gorgeous beachside drives, and awesome monuments I saw on our initial trip in the country. This city could have been dropped onto any American coast and nobody would have batted an eye. Or so it seemed until we moved out of the downtown and into the townships where we would be living. Our van eventually exited the expressway at Langa, the oldest township in South Africa.

The legacy of apartheid was glaringly obvious in South Africa's cities. The institution of a legal, government-sanctioned racial caste system was overturned in 1994 with the first democratic elections, but its effects still haunted the country. Government-supported racial segregation had given way to economically enforced segregation. And, given the significant overlap between race and class in South Africa, whites, coloreds, and blacks all still made their homes in different locations.

Langa was established in 1923 as Cape Town's first black township. Similar to Khayelitsha, Gugulethu, Kopanong, and other historic townships in South Africa, it was created for the sole purpose of isolating black Africans in small, destitute enclaves where laws were instituted to control the residents and police entered to harass, not to protect. When these townships were established, Afrikaners, or whites of Dutch ancestry, made up 9 percent of the population. Black Africans, who generally lived on only 5 percent of the nation's land, made up over 80 percent of the population. These were South Africa's "projects," areas where despair and hopelessness were not accidental products of the environment but rather the whole point. It was obviously a far more egregious situation, but I could sense faint echoes of Baltimore and the Bronx in the story of these townships.

The van bounced steadily up and down as the shocks attempted to adjust to the transition from the paved, multilane highways to the pothole-laden, dirt-covered streets of the township. Kids, dozens of them, lined every street we drove down, staring at the vehicle as we cautiously cruised by them. Their smiles were bright, and they gave us the thumbs-up as we rolled past them, as if they had known us from somewhere else, which just reinforced my disorienting feeling of familiarity.

A few minutes after entering Langa, we stopped in front of an understated white home in the middle of Mshumpela Street. Zed looked over his shoulder from the driver's seat and shared another gigantic smile. "Wez, this is your stop." I stepped out of the van and walked to the back to pull out my one overstuffed bag, my entire wardrobe for half a year crammed into a forty-pound Samsonite. My white Nikes kicked up dust as I made the short walk from the van to the front of the house. This would be my home for the next six months.

A short distance to my left I saw a vertigo-inducing sea of shacks, rolling out as far as the eye could see. The walls of these houses were patchworks of wood or aluminum or metal or whatever scraps were lying around. Spare pieces of metal were propped up as roofs, and pieces of torn cloth were hung as curtains. These shelters were lined up in a sort of organized chaos; they seemed improvised and temporary, but they'd been there for years. Well, some of them at least. I would later find out that, every few months or so, the fires that burned in makeshift stoves would flare out of control, jumping from one tightly packed shack to another and burning out a whole section of the shantytown before they were extinguished. A week later, all the shacks would be rebuilt, and it would be business as usual. As I moved closer to the home where my host family lived, I couldn't stop staring at the shantytown. Living in the Bronx and Baltimore had given me the foolish impression that I knew what poverty looked like. At that moment, I realized I had no idea what poverty was—even in West Baltimore we lived like kings compared with this. An embarrassing sense of pride tentatively bloomed in the middle of the sadness I felt at my surroundings.

I was five feet away from the door covered in peeling white paint when it creaked open. A short, rotund woman with cropped and curled hair, beautifully clear, dark skin, and a radiant smile walked out. She was wearing a dress that reminded me of the West African–inspired kente cloth attire I had seen in the States, but hers was an intricately meshed pattern of black and white, the traditional Xhosa colors. Xhosa was her tribe, and Langa was a mainly Xhosa township. It was also the tribe of Nelson Mandela, Govan Mbeki, and many other heroes of the African National Congress.

I smiled and extended my hand to introduce myself, and was immediately wrapped up in her arms. She hugged me as if I was a family member she had not seen in years. *"Molo!"* she exclaimed into my ear as our cheeks pushed against each other, the Xhosa word for hello.

Her affection was infectious, and I squeezed her right back. Once she let go, I noticed her children standing behind her, a son named Zinzi, who was a few years younger than me, and a daughter named Viwe, who was eight years old, waiting to welcome me to their home. Zinzi moved toward me, his short, dreadlocked hair spiked up on top of his head.

"Hey, *bhuti*, how was the flight?" he said in a deep baritone voice. *Bhuti*, the Xhosa word for brother, was not used loosely. The family went out of their way to make me feel welcomed, at home. Viwe was a sightly but shy girl who stayed close to her mother's hip as she gave me a quick hug. I imagined how odd an experience it must have been for her having this American enter her small home to live. She knew nothing about me. In retrospect, I guess I did know how she felt. I felt much the same way.

The week after I arrived, I walked into the kitchen to find only Mama sitting there. She was making herself some tea and asked me to join her. I sat down at the small wooden table next to the stove, the shaky tabletop stabilized by pieces of cardboard stuck under the legs. This was where most of the family's meals were eaten. She poured the boiling hot water into mugs with tea bags already placed inside and brought our two cups over.

"So tell me more about yourself," she began.

I had been spending so much time with my home-stay brother, Zinzi, his friend Simo, and the other Americans I'd come with, and attending our classes at the university, that I had not had a chance to really speak with her yet. Our tea turned into a three-hour marathon of stories about our lives, fears, and dreams. She explained to me the color dynamic in South Africa, how there I would be considered colored because I was not dark enough to be considered black. Colored was a concept created during the apartheid era to further isolate the races—coloreds received more privileges than blacks did. Not many more, but enough to seed antagonism between the two groups. The lighter your skin was in apartheid South Africa, the better off you were.

I learned about the music of the apartheid era and how it was the musicians and artists, even more than the politicians and activists, who informed the world about the country's injustices. I also learned about *ubuntu*—the Xhosa word for humanity—and the power of authentic leadership as exhibited by giants like Nelson Mandela and a thousand other self-sacrificing visionaries who had managed the unforeseen transition from apartheid to democracy without a bloodbath.

On our third cup of tea, Mama began to tell me about her husband and his role as a freedom fighter during apartheid. She told me about how he and his fellow soldiers were intimidated, arrested, and beaten for failing to comply with government rules about carrying personal identification cards. I listened in amazement and horror as, through trembling lips, she talked about the hopelessness the people felt during this time and the pain of knowing that this level of segregation, this level of poverty, this level of depression was being imposed on a people for things they were in no way responsible for, or should be ashamed of. Finally I had to stop her. "Mama, I am sorry to disturb you, but I am very confused. After all of this pain and heartache, how are you now able to forgive? You seem so at peace with yourself and your life. How are you so able to move on?"

She gave me an easy half smile and took another sip from her mug. "Because Mr. Mandela asked us to."

I'd expected more. I'd expected her to tell me that she was still working on her revenge scheme, or that she was afraid their weapons were too strong so there was no use in fighting. But her simple and profound answer helped me to understand that *ubuntu* was not simply a word. It was a way of life. Her candor and exquisite simplicity framed the rest of my trip and helped me better understand the land I was living in. It also helped me complete a thought that had begun that night with my father and developed through my training and education, and my time with Mayor Schmoke in Baltimore.

The common bond of humanity and decency that we share is stronger than any conflict, any adversity, any challenge. Fighting for your convictions is important. But finding peace is paramount. Knowing when to fight and when to seek peace is wisdom. *Ubuntu* was right. And so was my father. Watende, my middle name, all at once made perfect sense.

A few days later, I finally had a chance to talk to my mother on the phone. I was excited to share all of my experiences. And she, having never been to South Africa, was excited to hear my detailed descriptions. She updated me on how everything was going back home and then shared a piece of strange local news.

"Everything is fine, but I have something crazy to tell you. Did you know the cops are looking for another guy from your neighborhood with your name for killing a cop?"

A few weeks before I was set to leave South Africa and return to the States, I was walking with Zinzi and Simo from the *kumbi,* or bus station, back to the house. The once overwhelming sensory overload of township life now seemed second nature to me. *Kwaito,* a South African mix of hip-hop and house music, blared from cars that passed us. Children kicked soccer balls back and forth on the dirt-covered road, with large rocks serving as goalposts. Women spoke loudly to one another while carrying bags in their arms and on their heads. The sounds of the quick, click-ridden Xhosa language was everywhere. I was beginning to understand the language, and the feel of the street life. My stride through the Langa streets was slower and less frantic than it had been. I was finally feeling at home.

My friendship with Zinzi and Simo had also grown significantly. Every day after class, we would walk around the neighborhoods, talking to girls on the university campus, going to Mama Africa restaurant to grab one of the best steaks I've ever tasted, or watching cricket at a local watering hole. All of this felt particularly sweet in these last days, as the nostalgia that kicks in at the end of any meaningful experience had started to affect us. Simo looked up at us and said, "So both of you all are leaving soon? What am I supposed to do then?" Both Zinzi and I were about to embark on journeys. I would soon be heading back to the United States, where, in a matter of months, I would be accepting my degree from the president of Johns Hopkins, William Brody, who had become a cherished mentor and friend. Despite entering the school with lower scores than the average student, I would walk across the stage as a Phi Beta Kappa graduate who was also the first Rhodes Scholar in thirteen years at Johns Hopkins and the first African-American Rhodes Scholar in school history.

Zinzi, now seventeen years old, was preparing to take the same path as generations of Xhosa boys before him. He would be leaving soon to spend four weeks in the "bush," where he and dozens of other boys would join an aggregate of elders and learn what it means to be a Xhosa man. Within days of arriving, the young men would be circumcised, their foreskins removed like childish cloaks now deemed unnecessary. During the weeks it takes the circumcision to heal, they would learn about the history of the tribe, the battles they'd fought, the land they protected, the leaders they'd created. They would learn about what it means to be a good father and a good husband. The boys would meditate and pray together, eat together, and heal together.

They would return to their homes as heroes. A large feast would be cooked for them. They would wear all white for the month after returning, symbolizing that a boy had left but a man had returned. They would be spoken to differently, viewed differently. I asked Zinzi if he was scared.

"Not really, man, we all have to go through it. Besides, I saw when my older brother went through it and how much respect he got. It will be fine."

"Yeah, but I can't imagine that whole circumcision thing without any drugs, man. Way too painful if you ask me!"

Simo smirked at the thought of it while shaking his head. Zinzi laughed and said, "I hear you, but it's not the process you should focus on; it's the joy you will feel after you go through the process."

We walked through the small alley that separated the main road from Mshumpela Street. Our conversation strayed back to sports and gossip, but as we passed through the alley I was struck by the sight of a young man, splendid in an all-white outfit, from his shoes to his wide-brimmed hat. He appeared barely pubescent but was walking with the dignity of a man double his age. Because of Zinzi, I knew exactly what that man had gone through and the pride and admiration his family now shared about his accomplishment.

My head turned, and I stared at the young man. His bright eyes and straight back demanded attention. The confidence in his stride was something that Zinzi did not yet have, something that Simo did not yet have. Something that I did not yet have.

And again I thought of home. I realized just how similar were the challenges the young boys here and kids like the ones I grew up with faced. In both places, young men go through a daily struggle trying to navigate their way through deadly streets, poverty, and the twin legacies of exclusion and low expectations. But they are not completely unequipped—they also have the history of determined, improvisational survival, a legacy of generations who fought through even more oppressive circumstances. One of the key differences between the two was in the way their communities saw them. Here, burgeoning manhood was guided and celebrated through a rite of passage. At home, burgeoning manhood was a trigger for apprehension. In the United States, we see these same faces, and our reflex is to pick up our pace and cross the street. And in this reflexive gesture, the dimensions of our tragedy are laid bare. Our young men—along with our young women—are our strength and our future. Yet *we fear them*. This tall South African who now captured my attention wore his manhood as a sign of accomplishment, a badge of honor. His process was a journey taken with his peers, guided by his elders, and completed in a celebration. He was now a man. His community welcomed him.

His tribe's influence in making him a man was obvious and indelible. At that moment, I realized the journey I took was never mine alone either. Our eyes met, and he smiled and nodded his head. I nodded my head in return.

Epilogue

Wes has spent every day of his life since 2000 in the Jessup Correctional Institution, a maximum-security facility in Maryland. His day begins at 5:30 A.M. He works as a carpenter, making desks and tables, and sometimes he makes license plates. He gets paid about fifty-three cents a day, which he can use at the prison commissary to buy toothpaste, snacks, stamps, and other miscellaneous items. Lights go out at 10:00 P.M. Guards tell him when to wake up, when to eat, and when to go to the bathroom. He has two hours of free time a day, "outside time" that he can use to play basketball or talk to other inmates.

Wes is now a devout Muslim. Initially, he went to Friday mosque services because they were the only opportunity he had to see his brother, Tony, who was also in Jessup, but eventually he started to pay attention to the message and decided to learn more. He is now a leader in the significant Muslim community in the Jessup prison.

Wes's family still visits him occasionally, but the visits are not easy on Wes. He is exhaustively searched before being let into the visitors' area. The joy he feels when he is sitting across from a loved one quickly dissipates at the end of the visit as he walks back through the gate to his cell. It hurts him that he has no control over what's happening with his family on the outside. He has stopped answering questions like "How are you doing?" His answer doesn't change. His days don't change. When he gets visitors, he mainly sits and listens.

In 2008, Wes and many of his fellow inmates followed the presidential campaign closely, hoping for the election of the first black president in American history. The inmates celebrated when Barack Obama won, but their enthusiasm faded quickly. Wes and the other lifers realized that, no matter who the president was, their fate was sealed.

At the time of this book's writing, Wes has just become a grandfather. He is serving the tenth year of a life sentence. He is thirty-three years old.

Here's what some of the other characters in this story have been up to since 2000:

My mother retired from her job with a foundation for disadvantaged children, where she managed communications for grantees. She is now running her own consultancy focused on helping foundations use film and media to tell their stories. She works in Baltimore and lives just outside the city. She says she enjoys the slower pace and quiet. She remains the rock of our family.

My sisters are both doing very well. Nikki runs her own event-planning business in Virginia. Shani graduated from Princeton University in 2001, after which she attended Stanford Law School on a full scholarship. She and her husband live in Los Angeles.

Uncle Howard has remained a mentor and guide in my life and was the co-best-man (along with Justin) at my wedding. He lives in southern New Jersey with my aunt Pam and their two daughters.

Despite having a difficult time with the death of his mother, Justin managed to finish high school strong and received a scholarship to college. While he was in his senior year of college, his father passed away in a house fire, and Justin himself battled and beat a rare form of cancer. Since graduating from college, he has worked in education and now serves as dean at a prestigious high school outside Philadelphia. He has devoted his professional life to addressing the educational disparities in this country.

Captain Ty Hill graduated from Valley Forge Military College and earned the rank of second lieutenant in the United States Army Reserve. He served in the Army as an officer from 1992 to 1999 and has worked as a corporate lawyer since. He was a groomsman at my wedding and remains a cherished friend and mentor. He lives in New York and still intimidates the hell out of me.

My grandfather passed away from complications of stomach cancer in 2005. Despite the best efforts of my chain of command to get me back to the Bronx from Afghanistan, I could not get there in time to say goodbye. Fortunately, I was able to be home for his funeral and was one of hundreds who were there to pay their respects and let him know how much he meant to us as he was laid to rest.

My grandmother still lives in the same home in the Bronx, presiding as ever as the family matriarch. She is in her eighties and still watches over her family like a lioness protecting her pride. She still makes a mean batch of codfish whenever we come over.

Wes's mother, Mary, works in medical technology, specializing in elder care. She is raising six children: three of Wes's kids, her niece, her nephew, and her youngest son. She lives in Aberdeen, Maryland, a little under an hour away from Baltimore City.

Wes's aunt Nicey has been working for the State of Maryland doing home visits for the elderly, sick, and shut-in for a decade. Her children live in Maryland and Pennsylvania, and her youngest just graduated from high school. All of her children finished high school.

Wes's brother, Tony, was sentenced to life in prison without the possibility of parole after he was convicted as the trigger man in the death of Sergeant Prothero. The death penalty was taken off the table after Tony agreed to cooperate with the state. Sergeant Prothero's sister told Tony as he was leaving the courthouse after sentencing that "Bruce stood for everything that was good in society, and you stand for everything that is evil." Never remorseful, Tony coolly replied, "Same to you." In March 2008, Tony died in prison from kidney failure. He was thirty-eight years old.

Wes's best friend, Woody, spent many of his years after high school going in and out of prison. When the second of his three children was born, his sister had a stern talk with him about getting a legitimate job so he could watch his kids grow up. She helped him get work as a truck driver in Baltimore, a job he holds to this day. Now in his mid-thirties, Woody lives in West Baltimore and has three children.

White Boy dropped out of high school to be a waiter. He lives just outside Atlanta, where he works for a magazine, running the printing press. Woody was the best man at his wedding.

Alicia is currently raising only one of her two children with Wes. She works security for the Transportation Security Administration at a Maryland airport and lives in Aberdeen, close to Wes's mother.

Cheryl battled drug addiction for years and eventually lost custody of her two children with Wes. In 2002, she fell down a flight of stairs and was paralyzed. She died soon after from complications of the injuries. She was twenty-four years old.

As for me, after receiving the Rhodes Scholarship, I spent two and a half years completing my master's in international relations at Oxford. It was as revelatory, exciting, intense, and surreal as Mayor Schmoke promised. My time at Oxford began immediately after the attacks of September 11, 2001, which further heightened my sensitivity to being an American abroad but also helped me get a better understanding of the international reaction to those searing events.

When I returned to the States, I interned in Washington, D.C., focusing on homeland security issues. But many of my mentors told me that if I really wanted to understand the changes going on in American and international policy, I needed to understand the global economic system. So, after completing my graduate degree, I joined the world of high finance on Wall Street.

While I was working there, two American wars raged on. The young men and women who were heading to Iraq and Afghanistan to serve and fight weren't just anonymous recruits but friends of mine, brothers and sisters in arms. I spoke with a mentor and great friend, Lieutenant Colonel Michael Fenzel, who had just been named deputy brigade commander of the hallowed 1st Brigade of the 82nd Airborne Division. The 82nd was preparing to depart for Afghanistan for a yearlong tour, and he told me he would love for me to join them. After weeks of prayer, I decided to take a leave of absence from my career and join the fight overseas. I became a member of the 82nd Airborne and headed to Afghanistan.

For the next several months—from the summer of 2005 to the spring of 2006—I was deployed in the town of Khost, on the border of Afghanistan and Pakistan. Spending so much time with my fellow soldiers reminded me why I'd joined the military. The camaraderie, intensity, and passion for the job, and the sense of duty to something larger than myself, was something I had missed desperately. Our unit conducted lethal operations under the star-filled night sky. We maneuvered through snowcapped mountain ranges and simmering valleys. We felt the joy of a mission accomplished and the heartache of a lost comrade. To serve with young people and the young at heart alike, who live without a fear of dying and who talk about commitment, integrity, and sacrifice without a hint of sarcasm, was refreshing. I could not be more proud of my brothers and sisters in battle. That pride is a badge of honor emblazoned on my heart and will be until my last breath.

Upon my return to U.S. soil, I was accepted in the White House Fellow program. I had the honor of spending a year as a special assistant to the secretary of state, Condoleezza Rice. It was a fascinating experience to follow a year spent executing American policies as a soldier overseas with one watching how those policies are formulated. The nonpartisan fellowship also gave me the chance to learn from the other fellows, an impressively diverse and talented group from all over the country. And the most important occasion of that eventful year was getting married to Dawn, the most remarkable woman I know and the best friend I have.

I've climbed Mount Kilimanjaro and felt how quickly the dense Kenyan heat at the base of the mountain transforms into the chill of its snowcapped peak, where deep breaths are hard to find. I've worshiped with thousands of other Christians in the Yoido Full Gospel Church, the world's largest Christian congregation, in Seoul, Korea. And I've stood in awe as dusk settled on the blue-tiled Sultan Ahmed Mosque in Istanbul. I stood in the cell that held Nelson Mandela for eighteen years on Robben Island, and I searched for family in a small

Cuban town outside Havana. I have danced all night in Haarlem, Amsterdam, and in Harlem, USA. I have climbed through the Pyramid of Khufu in Giza with nothing but a flashlight to show the way and kissed my wife for the first time in St. Mark's Square in Venice on a cold New Year's Eve. I have sung in Carnegie Hall, chanting with a group of choir cadets acting as a jubilant Army preparing for war, and I've stood in humbled silence at the Memorial to the Murdered Jews of Europe in Berlin. I have sat with the former president of Brazil, Fernando Cardoso, and listened intently as he argued the virtues of cane-based ethanol, and I've worked with a small-farm owner in Brazil as we both chewed the honeyed liquid from freshly cut cane stalks. And I proudly spoke in front of tens of thousands of people at INVESCO Field in Denver on a balmy August evening forty-five years to the day after Dr. Martin Luther King gave his "I Have a Dream" speech at the historic March on Washington and just hours before President Barack Obama would take the same stage and at the same microphone proudly accept the Democratic nomination for President of the United States. And, sometime in 2007, I began working on this book.

This book is the product of hundreds of hours of interviews, some with people I have known for years and others with people I met minutes before I interviewed them about the most intimate details of their lives. The process of tracking down these people and listening to their stories has been one of the most interesting experiences of my life. These folks have told me some of the funniest, saddest, and most thought-provoking stories I've ever heard. I have no journalistic experience or training, but I attacked this project with a fervor and excitement that I didn't know I had. For over two years, my days would begin at 5:30 in the morning, and a cup of tea later, I was in front of my computer, taking my notes and research and trying to piece them into a coherent story about these two very real lives. My father was a journalist, and I hope that, in some way, this journey has proven that, as my mother says, I honestly inherited his passion for getting the story right.

I have also enjoyed going around the country and globe speaking to people about these stories—and then hearing back from all kinds of audiences about the Weses they've known, or even been themselves. And when I finish my story, the question that comes up the most is the one that initiated this quest: "What made the difference?"

And the truth is that I don't know. The answer is elusive. People are so wildly different, and it's hard to know when genetics or environment or just bad luck is decisive. As I've puzzled over the issue, I've become convinced that there are some clear and powerful measures that can be taken during this crucial time in a young person's life. Some of the ones that helped me come to mind, from finding strong mentors to being entrusted with responsibilities that forced me to get serious about my behavior. There is no one thing that leads people to move in one direction or another. I think the best we can do is give our young people a chance to make the best decisions possible by providing them with the information and the tools and the support they need.

Things have not been perfect for me in the years since this book's story ended. Like many boys who grow up without a father in the home, I searched for ways to fill that hole, sometimes in places I shouldn't have looked. I made some tremendous mistakes along the way. I have done things I deeply regret, said things I wish I could take back, and disappointed people in ways that still embarrass me. I have fought battles I should not have engaged in, and walked away from causes that needed and deserved a champion. But I've had the freedom to make those mistakes, and the freedom to seek redemption for them.

When we're young, it sometimes seems as if the world doesn't exist outside our city, our block, our house, our room. We make decisions based on what we see in that limited world and follow the only models available. The most important thing that happened to me was not being physically transported—the moves from Baltimore to the Bronx to Valley Forge didn't change my way of thinking. What changed was that I found myself surrounded by people—starting with my mom, grandparents, uncles, and aunts, and leading to a string of wonderful role models and mentors—who kept pushing me to see more than what was directly in front of me, to see the boundless possibilities of the wider world and the unexplored possibilities within myself. People who taught me that no accident of birth—not being black or relatively poor, being from Baltimore or the Bronx or fatherless—would ever define or limit me. In other words, they helped me to discover what it means to be free. As I wrote at the outset of this book: The chilling truth is that Wes's story could have been mine; the tragedy is that my story could have been his. My only wish—and I know Wes feels the same—is that the boys (and girls) who come after us will know this freedom. It's up to us, all of us, to make a way for them.

Afterword

After the hardcover edition of this book came out, the most common question I got at events and interviews was the question I'd explicitly avoided answering in the book itself: what made the difference between you and the other Wes Moore? I'd avoided answering the question in part because I found it difficult to put my finger on the exact moment or opportunity—or missed opportunity—that made the difference in my life. I'm not sure that I'll ever know for certain, but the past year spent traveling all over our wonderful country and talking with parents, teachers, students, community activists, and religious leaders has helped me clarify my thinking on the subject. The first thing that became clear is that I was thinking about this question the wrong way.

Many readers came up with their own answers to the question of what made the difference. Some said the mentors we encountered were the key. Others pointed to the different levels of cultural capital and social resources our mothers possessed: my parents were college graduates, as were my grandparents, and my mother was able to tap into a wide network of supportive friends, family, and professional contacts when she needed help. Some said Wes's true downfall was his apparent indifference to birth control—having kids at an early age strained him to the breaking point. I suspect all these things were important, but I'm not sure any of them singlehandedly determined our fates. Very few lives hinge on any single moment or decision or circumstance.

But what all these responses have in common is that they point to the decisive power of *information* and *stories*—the kind provided and modeled by friends, family, mentors, or even books—which has only reinforced my initial decision to write this story in the first place. It was reading Colin Powell's *My American Journey* as a young man that made me realize the incredible power of stories to change people's lives. By establishing himself as the protagonist of his own story, he inspired me and countless other young people to see ourselves as capable of taking control of our own destinies, and to realize how each decision we make determines the course of our life stories. I hope the story of my life and Wes's will serve a similar function in the lives of readers.

I will never forget the letter I received from a fifteen-year-old young man from Baltimore who has already spent part of his young life in juvenile detention. He said this was the first book he had ever read cover to cover, and after reading it he was forced to think about the type of man he wants to be, for himself and his family. I've heard from teachers who tell me that the book is sparking conversations in their classrooms about personal responsibility, and from a fifteen-year Michigan police veteran who recommended the book to young officers on his team to help them better understand the kids they might encounter in the streets, so they can not just arrest juvenile offenders when they've gone wrong, but stop them before they do.

I've heard from parents who feel overwhelmed by the challenges of raising their children in hostile environments and who are taking advantage of the resources in the guide. I've heard from military school graduates who have been inspired to share their own stories about how the military taught them the value of service and being a part of something larger than themselves. And more than anything else, people have told me how my mother's example of fortitude and her refusal to let anything get in the way of her kids' success have given them the strength to do the same.

What I found most striking about the response to the book was the ease with which people were able to share *their* stories with *me*. They felt as if they could trust me with the intimate details of their own lives because Wes and I were willing to share ours with them. I'll carry this new collection of stories with me for the rest of my life.

Above all, I hope that this book can provide young people with a way to identify with success as a possibility, and a reason to believe that a story that begins with struggle, apathy, and the pain of loss can still have a happy ending. I am eternally grateful to these new friends, and countless others who have read the book and answered the call. Thank you for being the champions for those who need champions the most.

In the eternal words of Sir William Ernest Henley:

> *Beyond this place of wrath and tears*
> *Looms but the Horror of the shade,*
> *And yet the menace of the years*
> *Finds, and shall find, me unafraid.*
>
> *It matters not how strait the gate,*
> *How charged with punishments the scroll,*
> *I am the master of my fate:*
> *I am the captain of my soul.*

A Call to Action

I originally agreed to write the Call to Action for this book because of my high regard for Wes's beloved mother, Joy. But as busy as I was when I started to read Wes's manuscript, I could not set it down. The intriguing narrative of Wes and Wes urged me to consider more deeply the wisdom of my dear brother Dr. Cornel West, who steadfastly contends that "our roots help to determine our routes." The choices we make about the lives we live determine the kinds of legacies we leave.

The truth is, some of us have been blessed beyond measure. What some call "the favor of God" I call "unmerited favor," that is, grace and mercy. The parallels and trajectories of the two Weses' lives remind me to count my many blessings every day and to pray that when the evening comes and the night falls, I will have done something during the day for others that I can present to the Lord so that I might not feel so ashamed.

The words of the author Samuel Beckett summarize the central message of this text: "Try again. Fail again. Fail better." In fact, I believe that this describes the ebb and flow of life itself—try again, fail again, fail better. Failing doesn't make us a failure. But not trying to do better, to be better, does make us fools.

In the spirit of the Covenant series, *The Other Wes Moore* is a welcome component of a larger conversation in this nation about the decisions we make and the people we have in our lives who help us to make these decisions. My call to action, our call to action, is this: read these words but, more important, absorb their meanings and create your own plan to act and leave a legacy.

Fundamentally, this story is about two boys, each of whom was going through his own personal journey and searching for help. One of them received it; the other didn't. And now the world stands witness to the results. Small interactions and effortless acts of kindness can mean the difference between failure and success, pain and pleasure—or becoming the people we loathe or love to become. We are more powerful than we realize, and I urge you to internalize the meanings of this remarkable story and unleash your own power.

There are organizations around the country that are helping to do just that every day, and in many different ways. At the back of this book, Wes has compiled an impressive list of more than two hundred youth-serving organizations that open their doors to help young people walk through to brighter tomorrows. I implore you to reach out to them and others in your communities for help, whether you are a young person in search of direction, an adult in need of support for the young people in your life, or a philanthropist or community servant who is looking to help.

Wes Moore has written a most engaging polemic that is enlightening, encouraging, and empowering. *The Other Wes Moore* serves as a reminder that ultimately the battle of life is won in the trying, and in the serving. God will take care of the rest.

Tavis Smiley
Los Angeles, California
October 2009

Resource Guide

Here is a list of organizations that are helping youth across the country live up to their greatest potential. For an up-to-date list, visit www.theotherwesmoore.com.

ADVOCACY

ORGANIZATION	SERVICES PROVIDED TARGETING YOUTH	GEOGRAPHY/ SCOPE	CONTACT INFORMATION
Congressional Black Caucus Foundation (CBCF)	The CBCF determines policy initiatives that facilitate the economic and social well-being of black men.	National	1720 Massachusetts Ave., NW Washington, DC 20036
Gay, Lesbian and Straight Education Network (GLSEN)	The GLSEN strives to ensure that each member of every school community is valued and respected regardless of sexual orientation or gender identity/ expression.	National	GLSEN 90 Broad St., 2nd Floor New York, NY 10004 Phone: (212) 727-0135 Fax: (212) 727-0254 www.glsen.org

ORGANIZATION	SERVICES PROVIDED TARGETING YOUTH	GEOGRAPHY/ SCOPE	CONTACT INFORMATION
Generations United (GU)	GU is focused on improving the lives of children and older people through intergenerational programs.	National	1331 H St., NW, #900 Washington, DC 20005-4739 Phone: (202) 289-3979 Fax: (202) 289-3952 www.gu.org
NAACP	The mission of the NAACP is to ensure the political, educational, social, and economic equality of rights of all persons.	National	4805 Mt. Hope Dr. Baltimore, MD 21215 Phone: (410) 580-5777 Toll Free: (877) NAACP-98 www.naacp.org
National CASA	Court Appointed Special Advocates work with the court system to help vulnerable children find the services and permanent, caring homes they need.	National	100 West Harrison St. North Tower, Suite 500 Seattle, WA 98119 www.nationalcasa.org
National Council of La Raza (NCLR)	The largest national Hispanic civil rights and advocacy organization in the United States.	National	Raul Yzaguirre Building 1126 16th St., NW Washington, DC 20036 Phone: (202) 785-1670 Fax: (202) 776-1792 www.nclr.org
Stand for Children	Stand for Children seeks to make children and their needs a higher political priority.	National	516 SE Morrison St., Suite 410 Portland, OR 97214 Toll Free: (800) 663-4032 Fax: (503) 963-9517 www.stand.org

ORGANIZATION	SERVICES PROVIDED TARGETING YOUTH	GEOGRAPHY/ SCOPE	CONTACT INFORMATION
Twenty-First Century Foundation	The Twenty-First Century Foundation works to advance the welfare of the black community through research, donor education, and donor services.	National	132 West 112th St. Lower Level, #1 New York, NY 10026 Phone: (212) 662-3700 Fax: (212) 662-6690
United Nations Association of the United States of America	The UNA operates Model United Nations, an authentic simulation of the UN General Assembly and other multilateral bodies, which catapults students into the world of diplomacy and negotiation.	National	801 2nd Ave., 2nd Floor New York, NY 10017 unahq@unausa.org Phone: (212) 907-1300 Fax: (212) 682-9185 www.unausa.org
Gay-Straight Alliance (GSA) Network	Gay-Straight Alliance Network is a youth leadership organization that connects school-based GSAs to one another and to community resources.	California	1550 Bryant St., Suite 800 San Francisco, CA 94103 Phone: (415) 552-4229 Fax: (415) 552-4729 www.gsanetwork.org
Bay Area Youth Agency Consortium (BAYAC)	BAYAC AmeriCorps is a collaborative of community service organizations that provide tutoring, after-school activities, and volunteer coordination.	San Francisco, CA	3219 Pierce St. Richmond, CA 94804 Phone: (510) 525-9980 Fax: (510) 525-9981 www.bayac.org
LA's BEST	LA's BEST provides a safe and supervised after-school education, enrichment, and recreation program for children ages five through twelve.	Los Angeles, CA	Los Angeles Unified School District 711 East 14th Pl. Los Angeles, CA 90021 Phone: (213) 745-1900 Fax: (800) 267-0342 www.lasbest.org

AFTER-SCHOOL PROGRAMS

ORGANIZATION	SERVICES PROVIDED TARGETING YOUTH	GEOGRAPHY/ SCOPE	CONTACT INFORMATION
African American Golf Foundation, Inc. (AAGF)	The AAGF's mission is to provide Atlanta's underprivileged and minority K–12 students with after-school and summer enrichment programs.	Atlanta, GA	PO Box 2217 Smyrna, GA 30081-2217 Phone: (770) 431-4865 Fax: (770) 431-4915 www.aagf.org
STAIR (Start the Adventure in Reading)	STAIR provides literacy tutoring to children who are reading below their grade level.	New Orleans, LA	1545 State St. New Orleans, LA 70118 Phone: (504) 899-0820 Fax: (504) 895-2668 www.stairnola.org
Chesapeake Center for Youth Development	The CCYD's after-school program strives to help youths achieve educational milestones.	Baltimore, MD	301 East Patapsco Ave. Baltimore, MD 21225 Phone: (410) 355-4698 Fax: (410) 354-8160 www.ccyd.org
The Osborne Association	The Osborne Association works to raise awareness and reform policy around the impact of incarceration and criminal justice policies on children.	New York, NY	Brooklyn Site 175 Remsen St., 8th Floor Brooklyn, NY 11201 Phone: (718) 637-6560 Fax: (718) 237-0686
Fund for the City of New York	The Fund has developed policies to advance the functioning of government and nonprofit organizations in New York City.	New York, NY	121 Ave. of the Americas, 6th Floor New York, NY 10013-1590 Phone: (212) 925-6675 Fax: (212) 925-5675

ORGANIZATION	SERVICES PROVIDED TARGETING YOUTH	GEOGRAPHY/ SCOPE	CONTACT INFORMATION
Heart House (Austin)	At Heart House, children have access to mentors, homework assistance, art enrichment, computer learning, health and safety education, and literacy programs.	Austin, TX	Heart House North Trails at Vintage Creek Apts. 7224 Northeast Dr. Austin, TX 78723 Phone: (512) 929-8187 Heart House South Learning Center 815 West Slaughter Lane Austin, TX 78748
Heart House Dallas	Heart House Dallas is a free after-school program dedicated to providing a safe haven and academic support to children of low-income families.	Dallas, TX	PO Box 823162 Dallas, TX 75382-3162 Phone: (214) 750-7637 Fax: (214) 750-1843 www.hearthousedallas .org

ARTS EDUCATION

ORGANIZATION	SERVICES PROVIDED TARGETING YOUTH	GEOGRAPHY/ SCOPE	CONTACT INFORMATION
Kanye West Foundation	The Kanye West Foundation provides underserved youths access to music production programs that will enable them to unleash their creative ability and reach their full potential.	National	Kanye West Foundation 8560 West Sunset Blvd., Suite #210 West Hollywood, CA 90069 www.kanyewest foundation.org

ORGANIZATION	SERVICES PROVIDED TARGETING YOUTH	GEOGRAPHY/ SCOPE	CONTACT INFORMATION
Forwardever Media Center	The FMC provides writing workshops and media literacy training to at-risk black youths.	Oakland, CA	PO Box 24662 Oakland, CA 96623 www.forwardevermedia .com
Fuqua Film Program	The Fuqua Film Program is a twelve-week summer film intensive in Brownsville, Brooklyn.	New York, NY	Fuqua Film Program Inc. 511 6th Ave., Suite #35 New York, NY 10011 Phone: (917) 494-7209 fuquafilmprogram.org
Ghetto Film School, Inc. (GFS)	GFS connects talented young people to artistic, educational, and career opportunities in the world of film and video.	New York, NY	PO Box 1580 Blvd. Station Bronx, NY 10459 Phone: (718) 589-5470 Fax: (718) 589-2204 www.ghettofilm.org
Manchester Craftsmen's Guild (MCG)	The MCG offers programs in ceramics, photography, digital arts, and painting to more than 4,000 young people each year.	Pittsburgh, PA	1815 Metropolitan St. Pittsburgh, PA 15233 Phone: (412) 322-1773, ext. 301 www.manchesterguild .org/youth

EDUCATION

ORGANIZATION	SERVICES PROVIDED TARGETING YOUTH	GEOGRAPHY/ SCOPE	CONTACT INFORMATION
ACE Mentor Program of America	ACE's mission is to inform high school students of career opportunities in architecture, construction, and engineering, and to provide scholarship opportunities.	National	400 Main St., Suite 600 Stamford, CT 06901 Phone: (203) 323-0020 Fax: (203) 323-0032 www.acementor.org

ORGANIZATION	SERVICES PROVIDED TARGETING YOUTH	GEOGRAPHY/ SCOPE	CONTACT INFORMATION
Action for Healthy Kids	Action for Healthy Kids is committed to engaging diverse organizations, leaders, and volunteers in actions that foster sound nutrition and physical activity in schools.	National	4711 Golf Rd., Suite 625 Skokie, IL 60076 Toll Free: (800) 416-5136 Fax: (847) 329-1849 www.ActionforHealthy Kids.org
Alpha Phi Alpha Fraternity	This fraternity is committed to the development and mentoring of youths and providing service and advocacy for the African-American community.	National	2313 Saint Paul St. Baltimore, MD 21218 Phone: (410) 554-0040 Fax: (410) 554-0054 www.alpha-phi-alpha .com
ATLAS Communities	ATLAS Communities is dedicated to improving student learning by combining innovative learning experiences with state and local standards.	National	249 Glenbrook Rd., Unit 2224 Storrs, CT 06269-2224 Toll Free: (888) 577-8585 Fax: (860) 486-6348 www.atlas communities.org
Banking on Our Future (BOOF)	Operation HOPE, Inc.'s, BOOF provides on-the-ground and online financial literacy programs that teach children basic money skills.	National	HOPE Global Headquarters 707 Wilshire Blvd., 30th Floor Los Angeles, CA 90017 Phone: (213) 891-2900 Fax: (213) 489-7511 Toll Free: (877) 592-HOPE (4673) www.bankingonour future.org

ORGANIZATION	SERVICES PROVIDED TARGETING YOUTH	GEOGRAPHY/ SCOPE	CONTACT INFORMATION
Boys Hope Girls Hope	Boys Hope Girls Hope helps academically capable and motivated children-in-need to meet their full potential by providing value-centered, familylike homes, opportunities, and education through college.	National	12120 Bridgeton Square Drive Bridgeton, MO 63044 Phone: (314) 298-1250 Toll Free: (877) 878-HOPE hope@bhgh.org www.boyshope girlshope.org
The Coalition of Schools Educating Boys of Color (COSEBOC)	COSEBOC promotes and supports schools determined to make success an attainable goal for all of their male students of color.	National	14 Priscilla Way Lynn, MA 01904 Phone: (781) 775-9461 Fax: (781) 593-8961 www.coseboc.org
East River Development Alliance (ERDA)	ERDA's youth development programs focus on improving and expanding educational and extracurricular opportunities to prepare young people and their families to go to and succeed in college.	National	12–11 40th Ave. Long Island City, NY 11101 Phone: (718) 784-0877 www.erdalliance.org/ site/index.php?section _name=Youth+ Development
Institute for Responsible Citizenship	The IRC prepares high-achieving African-American men for successful careers in business, law, government, public service, education, journalism, the sciences, medicine, ministry, and the arts.	National	1227 25th St., NW, 6th Floor Washington, DC 20037 Phone: (202) 659-2831 Fax: (202) 659-0582 www.i4rc.org
Jackie Robinson Foundation	The Jackie Robinson Foundation serves as an advocate for young people with the greatest need and offers an extensive mentoring program and summer internships.	National	1 Hudson Square 75 Varick St., 2nd Floor New York, NY 10013-1917 Phone: (212) 290-8600 Fax: (212) 290-8081 www.jackierobinson .org

ORGANIZATION	SERVICES PROVIDED TARGETING YOUTH	GEOGRAPHY/ SCOPE	CONTACT INFORMATION
KIPP Schools	KIPP is a national network of free, open-enrollment, college-prep public schools with a track record of preparing students in underserved communities for success in college and in life.	National	135 Main St., Suite 1700 San Francisco, CA 94105 Toll Free: (866) 345-KIPP Fax: (415) 348-0588 www.kipp.org
National Alliance for Public Charter Schools	Public charter schools foster an environment in which parents can be more involved, teachers are given the freedom to innovate, and students are provided the structure they need to learn.	National	1101 15th St., NW, Suite 1010 Washington, DC 20005 Phone: (202) 289-2700 Fax: 202-289-4009 www.publiccharters .org
National Alliance of African American Athletes	The goal of the National Alliance of African American Athletes is to empower young men through athletics, education, and public programs.	National	PO Box 60743 Harrisburg, PA 17106-0743 Phone: (717) 234-6352 Fax: (717) 652-3207
National Association of Charter School Authorizers (NACSA)	NACSA is an association of educational agencies that authorize and oversee charter public schools.	National	105 West Adams St., Suite 1430 Chicago, IL 60603-6253 Phone: (312) 376-2300 Fax: (312) 376-2400 www.qualitycharters .org
National Institute for Literacy	The National Institute for Literacy aims to improve opportunities for adults, youths, and children to thrive in a progressively literate world.	National	1775 I St., NW, Suite 730 Washington, DC 20006 Phone: (202) 233-2025 Fax: (202) 233-2050 www.nifl.gov

ORGANIZATION	SERVICES PROVIDED TARGETING YOUTH	GEOGRAPHY/ SCOPE	CONTACT INFORMATION
National Urban Technology Center, Inc. (Urban Tech)	Urban Tech aims to provide access to technology and training to address the widening computer literacy and achievement gap in inner-city communities through its two flagship programs, SeedTech and the Youth Leadership Academy (YLA).	National	80 Maiden Lane, Suite 606 New York, NY 10038 Toll Free: (800) 998-3212 Fax: (212) 528-7355 www.urbantech.org
The Panasonic Foundation	The Panasonic Foundation aims to improve public education in the United States.	National	3 Panasonic Way, 2I-1 Secaucus, NJ 07094 Phone: (201) 392-4132 Fax: (201) 392-4126 www.panasonic.com/ meca/foundation
TERC	TERC is an education research and development organization dedicated to improving mathematics, science, and technology teaching and learning.	National	2067 Massachusetts Ave. Cambridge, MA 02140 Phone: (617) 547-0430 Fax: (617) 349-3535 www.terc.edu
The Tom Joyner Foundation	The Tom Joyner Foundation helps students continue their education at black colleges.	National	www.blackamericaweb .com
United Negro College Fund (UNCF)	UNCF is the nation's most comprehensive higher-education assistance organization for students of color. UNCF provides scholarships and internships for students, as well as faculty and administrative professional training.	National	8260 Willow Oaks Corporate Dr. PO Box 10444 Fairfax, VA 22031-8044 www.uncf.org

ORGANIZATION	SERVICES PROVIDED TARGETING YOUTH	GEOGRAPHY/ SCOPE	CONTACT INFORMATION
WorldofMoney .org (WoM)	WoM is focused on improving the financial literacy of underserved youths ages twelve through eighteen through workshops designed to help students become financially responsible.	National	Phone: (212) 969-0339 www.worldofmoney .org
Young People's Project (YPP)	The mission of YPP is to use math literacy as a tool to encourage young leaders to radically change the quality of education and life in their communities.	National	YPP Chicago 3424 South State, Suite IC3-2 Chicago, IL 60616 Phone: (773) 407-4732 www.typp.org
ZipRoad.org	ZipRoad.org helps parents find, rate, and comment on education-related resources in their communities.	National	1220 19th St., NW, Suite 610 Washington, DC 20036 Phone: (202) 393-0051 Fax: (202) 393-7260 www.ziproad.org
Operation HOPE	Operation HOPE is America's first nonprofit social investment bank and a national provider of financial literacy and economic empowerment programs free of charge.	International	707 Wilshire Blvd., 30th Floor Los Angeles, CA 90017 Phone: (213) 891-2900 Fax: (213) 489-7511 Toll Free: (877) 592-HOPE (4673) www.operationhope .org

ORGANIZATION	SERVICES PROVIDED TARGETING YOUTH	GEOGRAPHY/ SCOPE	CONTACT INFORMATION
Arizona Quest For Kids (AQFK)	AQFK is a mentoring program for high-potential students from low-income families to provide support and guidance for college enrollment and graduation.	Phoenix, AZ	1430 East Missouri Ave., Suite B-205 Phoenix, AZ 85014 Phone: (602) 636-1860 Fax: (602) 636-1857 www.azquestforkids .org
Fulfillment Fund	The Fulfillment Fund's purpose is to mentor, counsel, and guide disadvantaged high school students to achieve a college education.	Los Angeles, CA	6100 Wilshire Blvd., Suite 600 Los Angeles, CA 90048 Phone: (323) 939-9707 Fax: (323) 525-3095 www.fulfillment.org
Huckleberry Youth Programs (HYP)	HYP provides San Francisco and Marin youths and their families with a network of services and opportunities from caring peers and adults.	San Francisco, CA	3310 Geary Blvd. San Francisco, CA 94118 Phone: (415) 668-2622 TTY: (800) 735-2929 Fax (415) 668-0631 www.huckleberryyouth .org
The Stuart Foundation	The Stuart Foundation is dedicated to the protection, education, and development of children and youth.	California and Washington	500 Washington Street, 8th Floor San Francisco, CA 94111 Phone: (415) 393-1551 www.stuartfoundation .org
African American Leadership Institute	The AALI sponsors a statewide program for African-American male students to promote interest in post-high-school education and career planning.	Denver, CO	700 East 24th Ave., Suite 8 Denver, CO 80205 Phone: (303) 299-9055; (303) 299-9035 Fax: (303) 299-9064 www.aali-rockymtn .org

ORGANIZATION	SERVICES PROVIDED TARGETING YOUTH	GEOGRAPHY/ SCOPE	CONTACT INFORMATION
Capital Preparatory Magnet School	The Capital Preparatory Magnet School is a year-round college-prep school with a social justice theme.	Hartford, CT	950 Main St. Hartford, CT 06103 Phone: (860) 695-9800 Fax: (860) 722-8520 www.capitalprep.org
Bridges Public Charter School	The school's mission is to provide free early-childhood education.	Washington, DC	1250 Taylor St., NW Washington, DC 20011 Phone: (202) 545-0515 Fax: (202) 545-0517 www.bridgespcs.org
College Bound, Inc.	The mission of College Bound, Inc., is to prepare public and public charter school students in the metropolitan D.C. area to enter college, earn a degree, and achieve their personal and professional goals.	Washington, DC	128 M Street, NW, Suite 220 Washington, DC 20001 Phone: (202) 842-0858 Fax: (202) 842-1926 info@collegebound .org www.collegebound .org
DC Children's Investment Trust	The trust's Cross-Cities Learning Circle aims to improve graduation rates by examining relevant social systems and establishing key partnerships within the community.	Washington, DC; Philadelphia, PA; Baltimore, MD	1400 16th St., NW, Suite 500 Washington, DC 20036 Phone: (202) 347-4441
District of Columbia College Success Foundation	The DCCSF seeks to provide students the educational and financial incentives, mentoring, and other supports necessary to gain admission to college.	Washington, DC	1220 12th St., SE, Suite 110 Washington, DC 20003-3722 Phone: (202) 207-1800 Toll Free: (866) 240-3567 www.dccollegesuccess foundation.org

ORGANIZATION	SERVICES PROVIDED TARGETING YOUTH	GEOGRAPHY/ SCOPE	CONTACT INFORMATION
Latin American Youth Center (LAYC)	LAYC serves low-income youths and families across the District of Columbia and in Maryland's Prince George's and Montgomery counties. LAYC provides multilingual, culturally sensitive programs in five areas: educational enhancement, workforce investment, social services, art and media, and advocacy.	Washington, DC	1419 Columbia Rd., NW Washington, DC 20009 Phone: (202) 319-2225 Fax: (202) 462-5696 www.layc-dc.org
Septima Clark Public Charter School	At the Septima Clark Public Charter School, preschool through eighth-grade boys master advanced academic skills.	Washington, DC	425 Chesapeake St., SE Washington, DC 20032 Phone: (202) 563-6556 Fax: (202) 563-6550 www.scpcs.org
Edward Waters College (EWC)	EWC's Black Male College Explorers Program is a pre-college intervention program for black males in seventh through eleventh grades who are at risk or likely to drop out of high school.	Jacksonville, FL	College Explorers Program 1658 Kings Rd. Jacksonville, FL 32209 Phone: (904) 470-8001 www.ewc.edu
B.E.S.T. Academy at Benjamin S. Carson	The B.E.S.T. Academy at Benjamin S. Carson is one of twenty-eight middle schools among the Atlanta public schools.	Atlanta, GA	1890 Donald Lee Hollowell Pkwy. Atlanta, GA 30318 Phone: (404) 802-4944 srt4.atlantapublic schools.us/best/site/ default.asp

ORGANIZATION	SERVICES PROVIDED TARGETING YOUTH	GEOGRAPHY/ SCOPE	CONTACT INFORMATION
The Morehouse Male Initiative	Morehouse College plays an active role in conducting and disseminating research and best practices regarding the affirmative development of African-American males.	Atlanta, GA	www.morehousemale initiative.com
Ron Clark School in Atlanta	The Ron Clark School aims to empower youth to take charge of their own destinies.	Atlanta, GA	228 Margaret St., SE Atlanta, GA 30315-4105 Phone: (678) 651-2100 www.ronclarkacademy .com
Chicago Urban League	The Urban League in Chicago's Boys Leadership Institute (BLI) operates as a Saturday school for African-American males K–12 at the University of Chicago's Donoghue Charter School.	Chicago, IL	4510 South Michigan Ave. Chicago, IL 60653 Phone: (773) 285-5800 Fax: (773) 285-7772
Hales Franciscan High School	The goal of Hales is to provide a competitive college-prep education.	Chicago, IL	4930 South Cottage Grove Ave. Chicago, IL 60615 Phone: (773) 285-8400 www.halesfranciscan .org
Providence St. Mel School	Providence St. Mel School in grades K–12 is committed to preparing students to be admitted to and succeed in some of this country's best colleges and universities.	Chicago, IL	119 South Central Park Blvd. Chicago, IL 60624 Main Office: (773) 722-4600 Fax: (773) 722-6032 www.psm.k12.il.us

ORGANIZATION	SERVICES PROVIDED TARGETING YOUTH	GEOGRAPHY/ SCOPE	CONTACT INFORMATION
Urban Prep Charter Academy for Young Men	Urban Prep is Chicago's only all-male academy that has a faculty consisting of 70 percent black males.	Chicago, IL	Urban Prep Academies 420 North Wabash, Suite 203 Chicago, IL 60611 Phone: (312) 276-0259 Fax: (312) 755-1050 www.urbanprep.org
Dr. Bernard C. Watson Academy for Boys	The Dr. Bernard C. Watson Academy for Boys is committed to challenging each child to develop his maximum potential in all social, academic, and cultural endeavors.	Gary, IN	2065 Mississippi St. Gary, IN 46407-1665 Phone: (219) 886-6568 Fax: (219) 881-4100 www.garycsc.k12.in.us/ Watson/index.html
Young Leaders' Academy	The Young Leaders' Academy of Baton Rouge, Inc., provides at-risk African-American boys with Saturday classes in math, English, and public speaking skills.	Baton Rouge, LA	PO Box 16165 Baton Rouge, LA 70893 Phone: (225) 346-1583 Fax: (225) 346-4753 www.youngleaders .org
U.S. Dream Academy	The U.S. Dream Academy focuses on three pillars— skill building, character building, and dream building. The overall goal is to nurture the whole child while changing attitudes about education.	Maryland	10400 Little Patuxent Pkwy., Suite 300 Columbia, MD 21044 Phone: (410) 772-7143 Fax: (410) 772-7146 www.usdreamacademy .org

ORGANIZATION	SERVICES PROVIDED TARGETING YOUTH	GEOGRAPHY/ SCOPE	CONTACT INFORMATION
Schott Foundation for Public Education	The Schott Foundation's goal is to create a movement to improve the educational experiences of black boys to ensure that they graduate from high school with the confidence to become successful members of society.	Massachusetts	678 Massachusetts Ave., Suite 301 Cambridge, MA 02139 Phone: (617) 876-7700 Fax: (617) 876-7702 www.schottfoundation .org
Wheelock College	Wheelock strives to educate people to create a safe, caring, and just world for children and families.	Boston, MA	200 The Riverway Boston, MA 02215 Phone: (617) 879-2000 www.wheelock.edu
Barringer's Ninth Grade Success Academy	Barringer's Ninth Grade Success Academy helps students adjust academically and socially to the rigors of high school.	Newark, NJ	Barringer Success Academy 24 Crane St. Newark, NJ 07104 Phone: (973) 268-5100
St. Benedict's Preparatory School	The St. Benedict's Preparatory School community meets each morning for song, readings, and prayer, and to discuss common problems and opportunities.	Newark, NJ	520 Martin Luther King Blvd. Newark, NJ 07102 Phone: (973) 792-5746
The Academy of Business and Community Development (ABCD)	ABCD is the first public all-boy school whose mission is to provide a challenging academic program that includes business education in every grade.	New York, NY	141 Macon St. Brooklyn, NY 11216 Phone: (718) 783-4842 Fax: (718) 783-4869 www.abcd612.org

ORGANIZATION	SERVICES PROVIDED TARGETING YOUTH	GEOGRAPHY/ SCOPE	CONTACT INFORMATION
Brotherhood/ Sister Sol	Brotherhood/Sister Sol is a Harlem-based organization with a mission to empower black and Latino young women and men to think critically and become leaders in their communities.	New York, NY	512 West 143rd St. New York, NY 10031 Phone: (212) 283-7044 www.brother hood-sistersol.org
The Children's Aid Society/The African American Male Initiative	The African American Male Initiative works to gain an understanding of the issues facing young black males.	New York, NY	105 East 22nd St. New York, NY 10010 Phone: (212) 949-4800; (212) 949-4969 www.stepstosuccess .org
Eagle Academy for Young Men	Eagle Academy offers a one-on-one mentoring program that matches up students, based on their career interests and/or social needs, with a member of 100 Black Men for the duration of high school.	New York, NY	244 East 163rd St. Bronx, NY 10451 Phone: (718) 410-3952 www.eagleny.org
The Eagle Academy Foundation	The Eagle Academy Foundation is committed to developing a network of all-male college-prep public schools committed to excellence in character, scholastic achievement, and community service.	New York, NY	105 East 22nd St., Suite 911 New York, NY 10010 Phone: (212) 777-7070 Fax: (212) 995-5145 www.eagleacademy foundation.com
Enterprise Charter School	The mission of the Enterprise Charter School is to provide students with the resources to lead and succeed in the school and the community.	Buffalo, NY	275 Oak St. Buffalo, NY 14203 Phone: (716) 855-2114 Fax: (716) 855-2967 www.enterprisecharter .org

ORGANIZATION	SERVICES PROVIDED TARGETING YOUTH	GEOGRAPHY/ SCOPE	CONTACT INFORMATION
Excellence Boys Charter School of Bedford Stuyvesant	Excellence Boys Charter School of Bedford Stuyvesant prepares students to enter, succeed in, and graduate from outstanding college-prep high schools.	New York, NY	225 Patchen Ave. Brooklyn, NY 11233 Phone: (718) 638-1830 Fax: (718) 638-2548 www.uncommon schools.org
Let's Get Ready	The mission of Let's Get Ready is to expand college access for motivated, low-income high school students by providing free SAT preparation and college admission counseling.	New York and Boston	New York Office: 50 Broadway, Suite 806 New York, NY 10004 Phone: (646) 808-2760 Fax: (646) 808-2770 Boston Office: 89 South Street Boston, MA 02111 Phone: (617) 345-0080 Fax: (617) 439-0701 information@ letsgetready.org www.letsgetready.org
Cornel West Academy of Excellence (CWAE)	The Cornel West Academy of Excellence (CWAE) is a nonprofit organization started to address many of the needs of minority at-risk male students in the second to sixth grade. The academy currently provides its services to thirty-five minority male students ranging from the second to sixth grade from Wake County, North Carolina. The program is open to young men from surrounding counties.	North Carolina	info@ cornelwestacademy .org

ORGANIZATION	SERVICES PROVIDED TARGETING YOUTH	GEOGRAPHY/ SCOPE	CONTACT INFORMATION
Durham Nativity School (DNS)	The mission of DNS is to help break the cycle of poverty through a quality middle school education that will help empower each child.	Durham, NC	1004 North Mangum St. Durham, NC 27701 Phone: (919) 680-3790 Fax: (919) 680-3976 www.durhamnativity .org
Holton Career & Resource Center	The career center offers programs that provide training in traditional and emerging industries.	Durham, NC	Durham Public Schools 511 Cleveland St. PO Box 30002 Durham, NC 27702 Phone: (919) 560-2000 www.dpsnc.net
Dayton Boys Prep Academy	Teachers at the Dayton Boys Prep Academy use the Effective Teacher Training model to implement the curriculum.	Dayton, OH	2400 Hoover Ave. Dayton, OH 45402 www.dps.k12.oh.us/cms/ schools/elementary/ dbpa.html
Alpha: School of Excellence	The Youngstown City School District is determined to develop lifelong learners and productive citizens by respecting individuality.	Youngstown, OH	2546 Hillman Ave. Youngstown, OH 44507 Phone: (330) 744-7535 Fax: (330) 480-1906 www.ycsd.k12.oh.us
"I Have a Dream" Foundation— Oregon	The "I Have a Dream" Foundation provides a long-term program of mentoring, tutoring, and enrichment with a partial college scholarship available to all Dreamers (students) who graduate from high school.	Portland, OR	1478 NE Killingsworth St., 1st Floor Portland, OR 97211 Phone: (503) 287-7203 Fax: (503) 287-0539 Toll Free: (800) 762-4920 www.ihavedream foundation.org

ORGANIZATION	SERVICES PROVIDED TARGETING YOUTH	GEOGRAPHY/ SCOPE	CONTACT INFORMATION
Boys' Latin of Philadelphia Charter School	Boys' Latin offers its students a rigorous contemporary/classical education that prepares them for college.	Philadelphia, PA	5501 Cedar Ave. Philadelphia, PA 19143 Phone: (215) 387-5149 Fax: (215) 387-5159 www.boyslatin.org
Valley Forge Military Academy & College	Valley Forge Military Academy is an all-male college-prep school that enrolls cadets from grade seven through postgraduate. Students benefit from a comprehensive education, leadership opportunities, athletic competition and social interaction with a diverse group of peers.	Wayne, PA	1001 Eagle Rd. Wayne, PA 19087-3695 Phone: (610) 687-8003 www.vfmac.edu
Houston A+ Challenge	Houston A+ Challenge's mission is to promote an academically rich and purposeful education and to demonstrate the skills that students need to succeed academically, professionally, and socially.	Houston, TX	2700 Southwest Freeway, Suite B Houston, TX 77098–4607 Phone: (713) 658-1881 Fax: (713) 739-0166 www.houstonaplus.org
IDEA Public Schools	IDEA Public Schools prepares students from underserved communities for success in college and citizenship.	Texas	505 Angelita Dr., Suite 9 Weslaco, TX 78596 Phone: (956) 377-8000 Fax: (956) 447-3796 www.ideapublicschools .org

ORGANIZATION	SERVICES PROVIDED TARGETING YOUTH	GEOGRAPHY/ SCOPE	CONTACT INFORMATION
King Street Center	King Street Center is a preschool that also hosts a large and diverse after-school program for children in kindergarten through the fifth grade. The center also offers an innovative after-school program for middle and high school youths.	Burlington, VT	87 King St. Burlington, VT 05401 Phone: (802) 862-6736 Fax: (802) 658-5328 www.kingstreetcenter .org
Thurgood Marshall Elementary School	The Thurgood Marshall Elementary School community celebrates diversity, compassion, and global citizenship.	Seattle, WA	2401 South Irving St. Seattle, WA 98144 Phone: (206) 252-2800

ENTREPRENEURSHIP

ORGANIZATION	SERVICES PROVIDED TARGETING YOUTH	GEOGRAPHY/ SCOPE	CONTACT INFORMATION
Management Leadership for Tomorrow (MLT)	MLT has made groundbreaking progress in developing the next generation of African-American, Hispanic, and Native American leaders in major corporations and nonprofit organizations.	National	15 Maiden Lane, Suite 900 New York, NY 10038 Phone: (212) 736-3411 Fax: (212) 629-9737 Toll Free: (888) 686-1993 www.ml4t.org
National Foundation for Teaching Entrepreneurship (NFTE)	NFTE provides entrepreneurship education programs to young people from low-income communities.	National	120 Wall St., 29th Floor New York, NY 10005 Phone: (212) 232-3333 Toll Free: (800) FOR-NFTE (367-6383) www.nfte.com

FAMILY STRENGTHENING AND MENTORING

ORGANIZATION	SERVICES PROVIDED TARGETING YOUTH	GEOGRAPHY/ SCOPE	CONTACT INFORMATION
The Black Star Project	The Black Star Project seeks to increase the involvement of fathers and other positive male role models of color in the educational lives of children.	National	3473 South King Dr. Chicago, IL 60605 Phone: (773) 285-9600 www.blackstarproject .org
Concerned Black Men (CBM)	CBM provides youth development services to children from disadvantaged communities.	National	The Thurgood Marshall Center 1816 12th St., NW, Suite 204 Washington, DC 20009 Phone: (202) 783-6119 Fax: (202) 783-2480 Toll Free: (888) 395-7816 www.cbmnational.org
Daddy's Promise	Daddy's Promise is designed to focus the attention of the African-American community on the positive relationship that can and should exist between fathers and daughters.	National	www.daddyspromise .com
Raising Him Alone	The Raising Him Alone Campaign is committed to increasing advocacy for single mothers raising boys.	National	Raising Him Alone/ Urban Leadership Institute 2437 Maryland Ave. Baltimore, MD 21218 Toll Free: (877) 339-4300 Raising Him Alone (New Jersey Office) 403 Alpine Trail Neptune, NJ 07753 www.raisinghimalone .com

ORGANIZATION	SERVICES PROVIDED TARGETING YOUTH	GEOGRAPHY/ SCOPE	CONTACT INFORMATION
A Home Within	A Home Within seeks to heal the chronic loss experienced by foster children by promoting relationships with other current and former foster youths.	National	2500 18th St. San Francisco, CA 94110 Toll Free: (888) 898-2AHW (2249) Fax: (415) 621-6548 www.ahomewithin.org
4-H	4-H empowers youths to reach their full potential, working and learning in partnership with caring adults.	National	7100 Connecticut Ave. Chevy Chase, MD 20815 Phone: (301) 961-2800 www.nifa.usda.gov/ Extension/index.html
Amachi	Amachi is a unique partnership of secular and faith-based organizations working together to provide mentoring to children of incarcerated parents.	National	www.amachimentoring .org
Big Brothers Big Sisters of America	Big Brothers Big Sisters of America helps men have positive mentoring experiences with children, while at the same time giving back to the community.	National	230 North 13th St. Philadelphia, PA 19107 Phone: (215) 567-7000 Fax: (215) 567-0394
BOOST Youth Enhancement Service	BOOST's mission is to provide programs that enhance and enrich the quality of life for each participant.	National	www.boostfoundation inc.org
Boy Scouts of America National Council	The BSA provides a program for young people that builds character, trains them in the responsibilities of citizenship, and develops their personal fitness.	National	www.scouting.org

ORGANIZATION	SERVICES PROVIDED TARGETING YOUTH	GEOGRAPHY/ SCOPE	CONTACT INFORMATION
Boys and Girls Clubs of America	This organization seeks to inspire and enable all young people to realize their full potential as productive, responsible, and caring citizens.	National	1275 Peachtree St., NE Atlanta, GA 30309-3506 Phone: (404) 487-5700 www.bgca.org
Institute for Responsible Citizenship	The IRC is an intensive leadership program for America's best and brightest African-American male college students.	National	1227 25th St., NW, 6th Floor Washington, DC 20037 Phone: (202) 659-0581 Fax: (202) 659-0582 wkeyes@i4rc.org
Jumpstart	Jumpstart brings college students and community volunteers together with preschool children in low-income communities for individualized mentoring and tutoring.	National	Jumpstart National Office 308 Congress St., 6th Floor Boston, MA 02210 Phone: (617) 542-5867 Fax: (617) 542-2557 www.readfortherecord.org
Junior Achievement	JA teaches children how they can impact the world around them as individuals, workers, and consumers.	National	JA Worldwide 1 Education Way Colorado Springs, CO 80906 Phone: (719) 540-8000 Fax: (719) 540-6299 www.ja.org
Kappa Alpha Psi	Guide Write, KAP's national service program, provides programming, role models, mentors, and financial assistance for young men between the ages of five and twenty-five.	National	8332 Stoneshire Dr. Baton Rouge, LA 70818 Phone: (225) 261-6416 www.kappaalphapsi1911.com/committees/guideright.asp

ORGANIZATION	SERVICES PROVIDED TARGETING YOUTH	GEOGRAPHY/ SCOPE	CONTACT INFORMATION
The Links, Incorporated	The Links, Incorporated, has a six-decade tradition of mentoring and preparing black children for a bright future.	National	1200 Massachusetts Ave., NW Washington, DC 20005 Phone: (202) 842-8686 Fax: (202) 842-4020 www.linksinc.org
MAD DADS	MAD DADS walk city streets to identify unsupervised youths and draw them into program activities.	National	5732 Normandy Blvd. Jacksonville, FL 32205 Phone: (904) 781-0905 www.maddads.com
MENTOR/ National Mentoring Partnership	MENTOR believes that, with the help and guidance of an adult mentor, each child can discover how to unlock his or her potential.	National	1600 Duke St., Suite 300 Alexandria, VA 22314 Phone: (703) 224-2200 www.mentoring.org
National CARES Mentoring Movement	This organization promotes the mobilization of African Americans to take the lead in fulfilling society's spiritual and social responsibility to children.	National	230 Peachtree St., Suite 530 Atlanta, GA 30303 Phone: (404) 584-2744 Fax: (404) 525-6226 www.caresmentoring .com
National Center for Global Engagement	The NCGE is a nonprofit social venture established to create international study, service, and work opportunities for promising American students of color by providing scholarships for study abroad, foreign language training, and meaningful professional development and civic engagement experiences.	National	Phone: (404) 585-4205 info@nc4ge.org www.nc4ge.org

ORGANIZATION	SERVICES PROVIDED TARGETING YOUTH	GEOGRAPHY/ SCOPE	CONTACT INFORMATION
National Urban League (NUL)	NUL serves as a convening and national partner with the National CARES Mentoring Movement in its attempt to galvanize millions of committed, conscientious, and capable mentors to support today's youths.	National	120 Wall St., 8th Floor New York, NY 10005 Phone: (212) 558-5300 www.nul.org
Police Athletic League	The Police Athletic League is a program in which members of the law enforcement community initiate prevention services.	National	34½ East 12th St. New York, NY 10003 Phone: (212) 477-9450 Fax: (212) 477-4792 Toll Free: (800) PAL-4KIDS (725-4543) www.palnyc.org
Steve Harvey Foundation	The mission of the Steve Harvey Foundation is to improve public schools in urban areas by upgrading facilities and providing educational and mentoring opportunities that enable students to realize their dreams.	National	3495 Piedmont Rd., Building 11, Suite 560 Atlanta, GA 30305 www.steveharvey foundation.com
Tavis Smiley Foundation	The Tavis Smiley Foundation aims to develop a cadre of young leaders with critical-thinking skills who will share their knowledge and abilities and make a positive impact on the world.	National	4434 Crenshaw Blvd. Los Angeles, CA 90043 Phone: (323) 290-1888 Fax: (323) 290-1988 www.youthtoleaders .org

ORGANIZATION	SERVICES PROVIDED TARGETING YOUTH	GEOGRAPHY/ SCOPE	CONTACT INFORMATION
United Way Worldwide	The United Way movement mobilizes millions to action—to give, advocate, and volunteer—to improve the conditions in which they live.	International	1725 I St., NW, Suite 200 Washington, DC 20006 Phone: (202) 488-2000 www.unitedway.org
Ready for College, Inc.	The mission of Ready for College, Inc., is to prepare students to communicate clearly, analyze data, and think creatively at a college level.	Tallassee, AL	PO Box 780537 Tallassee, AL 36078 Phone: (334) 283-2115 www.ready4college .com
Future for Kids	Future for Kids is dedicated to providing at-risk children education through mentorship and sports programs.	Scottsdale, AZ	6991 East Camelback Rd., Suite D301 Scottsdale, AZ 85251 Phone: (480) 947-8131 www.futureforkids.org
Phoenix Youth at Risk	Phoenix Youth at Risk has three comprehensive mentoring programs, all of which are free to participating youths and their families.	Phoenix, AZ	1001 East Pierce St. Phoenix, AZ 85006 Phone: (602) 258-1012 Fax: (602) 258-6840 www.phoenixyouthat risk.org
A Father Forever	A Father Forever is dedicated to educating, motivating, and inspiring men of all ages to be productive and responsible fathers.	Los Angeles, CA	PO Box 470143 Los Angeles, CA 90047 Phone: (323) 810-1952 www.afatherforever .org
Children's Institute	Project Fatherhood aims to give fathers the tools to participate actively in the rearing and well-being of their children.	Los Angeles, CA	711 South New Hampshire Ave. Los Angeles, CA 90005 Phone: (213) 385-5100 Fax: (213) 383-1820·

ORGANIZATION	SERVICES PROVIDED TARGETING YOUTH	GEOGRAPHY/ SCOPE	CONTACT INFORMATION
Barrios Unidos	Barrios Unidos was created to prevent and curtail violence among youths within Santa Cruz County by providing them with life-enhancing alternatives.	Santa Cruz, CA	1817 Soquel Ave. Santa Cruz, CA 95062 Phone: (831) 457-8208 Fax: (831) 457-0389 www.barriosunidos.net
Boys to Men Mentoring Network	The Boys to Men model is based on a proven and successful program that sets out to develop the skills mentors need to address the needs of the boys they intend to help.	California	9587 Tropico Dr. La Mesa, CA 91941 Phone: (619) 469-9599 Fax: (954) 301-8115 www.boystomen.org
Endowment for Youth Committee	The committee's scholarship and mentoring program provides students with tutorial services, college field trips, mentoring, educational conferences, and ultimately scholarship funding for college or vocational school.	Santa Barbara, CA	1136 East Montecito St., Suite 2 Santa Barbara, CA 93103 Phone: (805) 730-3347 Fax: (805) 730-3349 www.eyc4kids.org
Leadership Excellence	Leadership Excellence provides an African-centered learning curriculum, racism and sexism awareness camps, and a community development trip to Ghana for Oakland-area youths.	Oakland, CA	1924 Franklin St., #201 Oakland, CA 94612 Phone: (510) 267-9770 www.leadership excellence.org
M.A.L.E. INSTITUTE	The M.A.L.E. INSTITUTE's goal is to positively impact lives by helping males strengthen themselves, their families, and their communities by becoming responsible men.	California	Walker & Associates 281 East Colorado Blvd., Suite #701 Pasadena, CA 91102 Phone: (626) 396-9593 www.maleinstitute .com

ORGANIZATION	SERVICES PROVIDED TARGETING YOUTH	GEOGRAPHY/ SCOPE	CONTACT INFORMATION
Omega Boys Club/Street Soldiers	The Omega Boys Club/ Street Soldiers' mission is to keep young people unharmed by violence and free from incarceration.	San Francisco, CA	1060 Tennessee St. San Francisco, CA 94107 Phone: (415) 826-8664 Fax: (415) 826-8673 www.street-soldiers .org
Volunteers of America, Bay Area	Volunteers of America, Bay Area, seeks to reduce recidivism among parolees by providing intensive case management services for young adults both before and after their release from San Quentin State Prison.	Bay Area, CA	www.voaba.org
Asian Youth Mentorship Program (AYMP)	AYMP at the Asian Pacific Development Center is an at-risk prevention program designed to work with youths in the Denver metropolitan area.	Denver, CO	1544 Elmira St. Aurora, CO 80010 Phone: (303) 365-2959 www.apdc.org
Colorado Youth at Risk	Colorado Youth at Risk aims to reduce the number of high school dropouts by matching students with adult mentors.	Colorado	1700 East 28th Ave. Denver, CO 80205 Mailing Address: PO Box 13410 Denver, CO 80201 Phone: (303) 623-9140 Fax: (303) 623-9139 www.coyar.org
Denver Kids, Inc. (DKI)	DKI provides long-term preventive counseling to students in Denver public schools.	Denver, CO	1330 Fox St. Denver, CO 80204 Phone: (720) 423-8266 www.denverkidsinc.org

ORGANIZATION	SERVICES PROVIDED TARGETING YOUTH	GEOGRAPHY/ SCOPE	CONTACT INFORMATION
Friends for Youth (FFY)	FFY reaches out to homeless and displaced youths by providing caring adult mentors, safe gathering places, a caring faith community, and challenging experiences to assist them in reaching their full potential.	Denver, CO	5500 East Yale Ave. Denver, CO 80222 Phone: (303) 756-9285 Fax: (303) 300-7990 www.friendsforyouth .com
Horton's Kids, Inc.	Horton's Kids provides comprehensive services to children, ages four through eighteen, from Washington, DC's Wellington Park neighborhood in Ward 8, improving the quality of their daily lives.	Washington, DC	110 Maryland Ave., NE, Suite 207 Washington, DC 20002 Phone: (202) 544-5033 Fax: (202) 544-5811 www.hortonskids.org
CityTeenz	CityTeenz is designed to enhance the overall well-being of Orlando's youths (ages twelve through nineteen) through tutoring, mentoring, sports, after-school and summer activities, health initiatives, and specialty camps.	Orlando, FL	CityTeenz 649 West Livingston St. Orlando, FL 32801 Phone: (407) 292-6500 Fax: (407) 292-6599 www.cityteenz.org
Florida Council on the Social Status of Black Men and Boys	The Florida Council on the Social Status of Black Men and Boys provides an environment conducive to productivity, success, and excellence for black men and boys.	Florida	Florida Council on the Social Status of Black Men and Boys Office of the Attorney General The Capitol, PL-01 Tallahassee, FL 32399-1050 Phone: (850) 414-3369 Fax: (850) 413-0633 www.cssbmb.com

ORGANIZATION	SERVICES PROVIDED TARGETING YOUTH	GEOGRAPHY/ SCOPE	CONTACT INFORMATION
Another Way Out, Inc.	Another Way Out matches mentors with mentees to help youths broaden their perception of the opportunities life has to offer.	Atlanta, GA	1180 Utoy Springs Rd. Atlanta, GA 30331 Phone: (404) 349-4712 Fax: (404) 349-4848 www.awoinc.com
Future Foundation, Inc.	Future Foundation, Inc., offers a safe haven to thousands of youths at risk in grades five through twelve—providing innovative programs for long-term empowerment.	Atlanta, GA	1892 Washington Rd. East Point, GA 30344 Phone: (404) 766-0510 Fax: (404) 766-0736 www.future -foundation.com
Men Building Men and Women Building Women (MBM & WBW)	MBM & WBW provides families of DeKalb County with assistance in the form of a mentoring program to help youths make positive choices.	Atlanta, GA	PO Box 1604 Lithonia, GA 30058 Phone: (404) 557-4966
Safe Haven/ Mentoring Project	Safe Haven is committed to a comprehensive risk-avoidance message with an emphasis on building assets and skills in youths in addition to preventing common negative outcomes. The goal of this approach is to develop multifaceted programs that help youths grow into mature and successful adults.	Atlanta, GA	778 Rays Rd., Suite 105 Stone Mountain, GA 30083 Phone: (404) 292-2366 Fax: (404) 292-2367 www.thesafehaven.com info@thesafehaven.com
Centers for New Horizons	Centers for New Horizons provides a holistic approach to community development centered on the strengthening of families.	Chicago, IL	4150 South King Dr. Chicago, IL 60653 Phone: (773) 373-5700 www.cnh.org

ORGANIZATION	SERVICES PROVIDED TARGETING YOUTH	GEOGRAPHY/ SCOPE	CONTACT INFORMATION
Mercy Home for Boys & Girls	Mercy Home for Boys & Girls is a Catholic organization answering the Gospel call by ministering to children and families in need.	Chicago, IL	1140 West Jackson Boulevard Chicago, IL 60607 Phone: (312) 738-7560 www.mercyhome.org
TeamMates	TeamMates intends to positively impact the world by inspiring youths to reach their full potential through mentoring.	Iowa; Nebraska	6801 O St. Lincoln, NE 68510 Phone: (402) 323-6252 Fax: (402) 323-6255 Toll Free: (877) 531-TEAM (8326) www.teammates.org
Gulfsouth Youth Action Corps	The corps's mission is to engage, inspire, and empower youth leaders to become responsible for making their communities more vibrant places to live.	New Orleans, LA	201 St. Charles Ave., Suite 2560 New Orleans, LA 70170 Phone: (504) 529-1922 Fax: (504) 265-0507 www.thegyac.org
Center for Urban Families— Responsible Fatherhood	The Baltimore Responsible Fatherhood Project assists low-income Baltimore fathers in becoming actively and positively engaged in their children's lives.	Baltimore, MD	2200 North Monroe St. Baltimore, MD 21217-1320 Phone: (410) 383-1240 www.cfuf.org
Identity, Inc.	Identity works with Latino youths to empower them to reach their full potential.	Montgomery County, MD	414 East Diamond Ave. Gaithersburg, MD 20877 Phone: (301) 963-5900 Fax: (301) 963-3621 www.identity.ws

ORGANIZATION	SERVICES PROVIDED TARGETING YOUTH	GEOGRAPHY/ SCOPE	CONTACT INFORMATION
Mayor's Workplace Mentoring Program (MWPMP)	MWPMP matches eighth-through twelfth-grade youths from Baltimore's middle and high schools with Baltimore city employees/mentors.	Baltimore, MD	517 North Charles St., Suite 200 Baltimore, MD 21201 Phone: (410) 685-8316 Fax: (410) 752-5016 Toll Free: (800) 741-2687 www.marylandmentors .org
Mentoring Children of Incarcerated Parents Program (MCIP)	The mission of MCIP is to create one-on-one relationships that provide young people with caring role models for future success.	Baltimore, MD	Phone: (443) 984-1013
Mentoring Male Teens in the Hood	The mission of Mentoring Male Teens in the Hood is to provide guidance to young men who lack for positive male role models.	Maryland	Phone: (410) 852-8013 info@ mentoring maleteens.org www.mentoring maleteens.org
Urban Leadership Institute (Center for Male Development— CMD)	CMD specializes in developing customized training programs, workbooks/curriculum materials, and professional development opportunities for organizations that work with young males.	Baltimore, MD	2437 Maryland Ave. Baltimore, MD 21218 Phone: (410) 467-1605 Fax: (410) 467-1607 Toll Free: (877) 339-4300 www.urbanleadership institute.com
DREAM (Directing Through Recreation, Education, Adventure, and Mentoring)	DREAM combines best practices from both mentoring and community development programs to create a unique mentoring experience for college students and children.	Massachusetts; Vermont	87 Elm St., Family Center Winooski, VT 05404 Phone: (802) 655-9015 Fax: (802) 654-8598 www.dreamprogram .org

ORGANIZATION	SERVICES PROVIDED TARGETING YOUTH	GEOGRAPHY/ SCOPE	CONTACT INFORMATION
Winning Futures	The goal of Winning Futures is for students to create a positive relationship with an adult mentor, and learn skills that will last a lifetime.	Michigan	27500 Cosgrove Warren, MI 48092 Phone: (586) 294-8449 Fax: (586) 698-4532 www.winningfutures .org
Metro Youth Partnership (MYP)	The mission of MYP is to mobilize the community to provide developmental assets for area youths.	Moorhead, MN	810 4th Ave. South, Suite 147 Moorhead, MN 56560 Phone: (218) 299-KIDS (5437) Fax: (218) 299-5336 www.metroyouth partnership.org
Healthy Families Counseling & Support	Healthy Families' mission is to strengthen families through in-home and community-based parenting education and mental health treatment services designed to prevent abuse, ensure healthy physical and emotional development, and keep families intact.	Kansas City, MO	Northland Human Services Building 3100 NE 83rd St., Suite 1401 Kansas City, MO 64119 Phone: (816) 468-6336 Fax: (816) 468-0289 www.healthyfamilieskc .org
Nevada Youth Alliance (NYA)	NYA provides youth- and family-related programs that fulfill the diverse needs of communities, businesses, and organizations.	Las Vegas, NV	70 East Horizon Ridge Pkwy., Suite 124 Henderson, NV 89015 Phone: (702) 566-4662 Fax: (702) 656-4910 www.nevadayouth alliance.org

ORGANIZATION	SERVICES PROVIDED TARGETING YOUTH	GEOGRAPHY/ SCOPE	CONTACT INFORMATION
The Boys' Club of New York	The Boys' Club of New York strives to sustain an environment that nurtures individual talent, strengthens families, and promotes strong citizenship while fostering a passion for learning.	New York	287 East Tenth Street New York, NY 10009 Phone: (212) 677-1102 Fax: (212) 353-0016 www.bcny.org
The Charles Hayden Foundation	The Charles Hayden Foundation seeks to promote the mental, moral, and physical development of youths ages five through eighteen in metropolitan New York and Boston.	New York, NY; Boston, MA	140 Broadway, 51st Floor New York, NY 10005 Phone: (212) 785-3677 Fax: (212) 785-3689 www.charleshayden foundation.org
Harlem Children's Zone	The Harlem Children's Zone Project is a unique, holistic approach to rebuilding a community so that its children can stay on track through college and go on to the job market.	New York, NY	35 East 125th St. New York, NY 10035 Phone: (212) 360-3255 Fax: (212) 289-0661 www.hcz.org
iMentor	iMentor's mission is to improve the lives of young people from underserved communities in New York City through innovative, technology-based approaches to youth mentoring and education.	New York, NY	iMentor Office 30 Broad St., 9th Floor New York, NY 10004 Phone: (212) 461-4330 Fax: (212) 461-4331 www.imentor.org

ORGANIZATION	SERVICES PROVIDED TARGETING YOUTH	GEOGRAPHY/ SCOPE	CONTACT INFORMATION
Future Black Men of America, Inc. (FBMA)	FBMA's Project Brotherhood offers black males ages seven through seventeen life skill sessions, group mentoring, and educational field trips; teens learn to develop discipline and career plans.	Raleigh, NC; Washington, DC	9660 Falls of Neuse Rd., Suite 138, #336 Raleigh, NC 27615 Phone: (919) 210-3516 www.futureblackmen.org
Giving U Inspirational Lives Through our Youth (GUILTY)	GUILTY is a youth development organization that works to better the lives, build the confidence, and create a positive future for at-risk youths.	Charlotte, NC	1001 East W. T. Harris Blvd., Suite P75 Charlotte, NC 28213 Phone: (704) 598-8169 Fax: (866) 545-0311 www.imguilty.org
Omega CHAMPS Youth Mentoring Program	The mission of the Omega CHAMPS Youth Mentoring Program is to expose young African-American men to positive role models and experiences and provide primary prevention and early-intervention efforts to facilitate the positive development of the community's youths.	Raleigh, NC	PO Box 14112 Raleigh, NC 27620 Phone: (919) 743-5433 Fax: (919) 743-5434
Right Moves for Youth	Right Moves for Youth works to reduce student dropouts by providing the motivation and resources for students in grades four through twelve to succeed in school.	Charlotte, NC	2211 West Morehead St. Charlotte, NC 28208 Phone: (704) 377-4425 Fax: (704) 377-3196 www.rightmovesforyouth.org
Tulsa Boys' Home	Tulsa Boys' Home provides the highest-quality residential care for young boys needing placement outside their homes.	Tulsa, OK	PO Box 1101 Tulsa, OK 74101-1101 www.tulsaboyshome.org

ORGANIZATION	SERVICES PROVIDED TARGETING YOUTH	GEOGRAPHY/ SCOPE	CONTACT INFORMATION
Step It Up, Inc.	Step It Up, Inc., is an organization that connects career-oriented high school students with professional career internships during the summer and pays them a stipend/scholarship.	Portland, OR	The Lloyd Center Mall Suite 2218 Portland, OR 97232-1311 Phone: (503) 284-1640 www.step-it-up.org
Reach to Your Youth Mentor Project	The Reach to Your Youth Mentor Project was established to teach the importance of education, character building, skills enhancement, and self-empowerment.	Philadelphia, PA	PO Box 5726 Philadelphia, PA 19120 Phone: (610) 931-8672; (215) 849-6650 www.rtyymp.org
South Kingstown CARES	South Kingstown CARES's mentoring program involves teachers, principals, and parents who recommend to the program students who could benefit from having a caring adult in their lives.	Rhode Island	307 Curtis Corner Rd. Wakefield, RI 02879 Phone: (401) 360-1304 Fax: (401) 360-1330 www.skcares.org
Real Connections	The goal of the Real Connections program is to ensure that all youths leave state care with positive, permanent adult connections and options for a successful future.	Providence, RI	55 South Brow St. East Providence, RI 02914 Phone: (401) 438-3900 Fax: (401) 438-3901 Foster Parent Help Line: (401) 438-3916 24-Hour Help Line: (800) 655-7787

ORGANIZATION	SERVICES PROVIDED TARGETING YOUTH	GEOGRAPHY/ SCOPE	CONTACT INFORMATION
The Met Center	The Met Center is a system of six small public high schools in Rhode Island in which each student's curriculum is determined by his or her unique interests, background, and learning style.	Providence, RI	325 Public St. Providence, RI 02907 Phone: (401) 752-2624 www.metcenter.org
Boys-to-Men	This organization seeks to build youths into spiritually vital, physically well, educationally motivated adults who can positively impact their communities.	Tennessee	PO Box 4426 Johnson City, TN 37602 Phone: (423) 610-1242 Fax: (423) 610-1244 www.boys-to-men.org
PENCIL Foundation	PENCIL administers educational programs that involve the community as volunteers and mentors, provide academic enrichment opportunities, prepare students for graduation, and get school supplies into the hands of children who need them.	Nashville, TN	421 Great Circle Rd. Nashville, TN 37228 Phone: (615) 242-3167 Fax: (615) 254-6478 www.pencilfd.org
Boysville	Boysville is a residential facility designed to help children in crisis who cannot remain in their own homes, and to work toward ending cycles of abuse and poverty.	Texas	PO Box 369 8555 East Loop 1604 North Converse, TX 78109-0369 Phone: (210) 659-1901 Fax: (210) 659-6527 www.boysvilletexas .org

ORGANIZATION	SERVICES PROVIDED TARGETING YOUTH	GEOGRAPHY/ SCOPE	CONTACT INFORMATION
Dallas Community Lighthouse	This organization assists at-risk youths in discovering pathways to success by concentrating on their social, educational, personal, and environmental issues.	Dallas, TX	PO Box 495787 Garland, TX 75049-5787 Phone: (972) 682-5455 www.communitylighthouse.org
Junior Achievement of South Texas	Junior Achievement uses hands-on experiences to help young people understand the economics of life.	Texas	403 East Ramsey, Suite 201 San Antonio, TX 78216 Phone: (210) 490-2007 Fax: (210) 490-1548 www.jast.org
Mentoring Brother 2 Brother, Inc.	Mentoring Brother 2 Brother is designed to support the social, emotional, and cultural well-being of youths and to empower both single parents and young men to new levels of responsibility.	Texas	PO Box 2702 Cedar Hill, TX 75106 Phone: (972) 345-9194 Fax: (928) 496-3771 www.mb2b.org
Utah Youth Mentor Project	The Utah Youth Mentor Project's mission is to help youths transition from foster care to independent living.	Salt Lake City, UT	699 East South Temple, Suite 320 Salt Lake City, UT 84102 Phone: (801) 755-3735 Fax: (801) 657-4671 www.youthmentorproject.org
Linking Learning to Life	Linking Learning to Life aims to engage youths in diverse community-based learning opportunities that improve their educational performance and career prospects.	Burlington, VT	52 Institute Rd. Burlington, VT 05401 Phone: (802) 951-8848 Fax: (802) 951-8851 www.linkinglearningtolife.org

ORGANIZATION	SERVICES PROVIDED TARGETING YOUTH	GEOGRAPHY/ SCOPE	CONTACT INFORMATION
Northern Virginia Therapeutic Riding Program	The Northern Virginia Therapeutic Riding Program provides equine-assisted activities for children and adults with disabilities, youth-at-risk, veterans, and their families in an inclusive community setting. Our program was originally chartered, in 1980, as Fairfax 4-H Therapeutic Riding Program, under the Virginia 4-H extension program.	Virginia	P.O. Box 184 Clifton, VA 20124 Phone: (703) 764-0269 info@nvtrp.org www.nvtrp.org
Links	Links encourages teenagers to make positive life choices by providing mentoring and guidance through wholesome recreational and personal development programs.	Waukesha, WI	212 Wisconsin Ave. Waukesha, WI 53186 Phone: (262) 408-2951 www.one2oneteen center.org
Mentoring Connections	Mentoring Connections provides mentoring services to children who have an incarcerated parent.	Madison, WI	Madison-Area Urban Ministry 2300 South Park St., Suite #5 Madison, WI 53713 Phone: (608) 256-0906 www.emum.org
My Brothers Keeper (MBK)	MBK is a program for adult males who want to have a positive effect on the youths in their communities.	Green Bay, WI	1039 West Mason St. Green Bay, WI 54303 Phone: (920) 884-1150 www.mybrotherskeeper inc.net

REENTRY

ORGANIZATION	SERVICES PROVIDED TARGETING YOUTH	GEOGRAPHY/ SCOPE	CONTACT INFORMATION
Project Choice	Project Choice provides intensive coaching and case management, as well as wraparound support services, to youths and young adults paroling to Oakland.	Oakland, CA	Department of Human Services 150 Frank H. Ogawa Plaza, 4th Floor Oakland, CA 94612 www.oaklandhuman services.com
The Fortune Society	The Fortune Society is a nonprofit organization dedicated to strengthening the fabric of our communities by promoting successful prisoner reentry.	New York, NY	29-76 Northern Blvd. Long Island City, NY 11101 Phone: (212) 691-7554 Fax: (347) 510-3451 www.fortunesociety.org

SOCIAL SERVICES

ORGANIZATION	SERVICES PROVIDED TARGETING YOUTH	GEOGRAPHY/ SCOPE	CONTACT INFORMATION
100 Black Men of America, Inc.	The mission of the 100 Black Men of America, Inc., is to improve the quality of life within the black community and enhance educational and economic opportunities for all African-Americans.	National	141 Auburn Ave. Atlanta, GA 30303 Phone: (404) 688-5100 Fax: (404) 688-1028 www.100blackmen.org

ORGANIZATION	SERVICES PROVIDED TARGETING YOUTH	GEOGRAPHY/ SCOPE	CONTACT INFORMATION
Boys Town	Boys Town is a beacon of hope for America's children and families through its life-changing youth care and health care programs across the United States.	National	Boys Town National Hotline Toll Free: (800) 448-3000 www.boystown.org Boys Town National Research Hospital Phone: (402) 498-6749 www.boystownhospital .org
Children's Defense Fund (CDF) Freedom Schools	The CDF Freedom Schools program partners with community-based organizations to provide free summer and after-school care that helps children and youths better fulfill their potential.	National	25 E St., NW Washington, DC 20001 Toll Free: (800) CDF-1200 www.childrensdefense .org
Children's Health Fund	Children's Health Fund is committed to providing health care to the nation's most medically underserved children.	National	215 West 125th St., Suite 301 New York, NY 10027 Phone: (212) 535-9400 www.childrenshealth fund.org
Hip Hop 4 Life	Hip Hop 4 Life is dedicated to empowering young people to adopt a healthy lifestyle. Hip Hop 4 Life serves young people ages ten through eighteen, with a special emphasis on at-risk and low-income youths.	National	511 Ave. of the Americas New York, NY 10011 Phone: (646) 706-7370 Fax: (646) 706-7377

ORGANIZATION	SERVICES PROVIDED TARGETING YOUTH	GEOGRAPHY/ SCOPE	CONTACT INFORMATION
National Safe Place	National Safe Place provides access to immediate help for young people in crisis through a network of sites sustained by qualified agencies, trained volunteers, and businesses.	National	2411 Bowman Ave. Louisville, KY 40217 Phone: (502) 635-3660 Toll Free: (888) 290-7233 www.nationalsafeplace .org
YMCA	The YMCA's 2,686 facilities across the nation respond to critical social needs by drawing on collective strength.	National	YMCA of the USA 101 North Wacker Dr. Chicago, IL 60606 Toll Free: (800) 872-9622 www.ymca.net
Our House, Inc.	Our House provides the working homeless (families and individuals) with safe, clean, comfortable housing; food; free child care; education; and job training in order that they may return to independence.	Little Rock, AR	PO Box 34155 Little Rock, AR 72203 Phone: (501) 374-7383 Fax: (501) 374-9611 www.ourhouseshelter .org
The Mentoring Center	The Mentoring Center serves as a technical assistance and training provider for Bay Area mentoring programs and provides intensive case management services for juveniles both before and after release from incarceration.	Oakland, CA	1221 Preservation Pkwy., Suite 200 Oakland, CA 94612 Phone: (510) 891-0427 Fax: (510) 891-0492 www.mentor.org

ORGANIZATION	SERVICES PROVIDED TARGETING YOUTH	GEOGRAPHY/ SCOPE	CONTACT INFORMATION
Alliance of Concerned Men (ACM)	ACM is an organization with the goal of saving lives of at-risk youths residing in high-crime areas of the Washington, DC, metropolitan community.	Washington, DC	2905 11th St., NW Washington, DC 20001 Phone: (202) 986-6200 Fax: (202) 986-6588 www.allianceof concernedmen.com
Orchard Place	Orchard Place provides mental health and juvenile justice services to children from birth through age twenty-two.	Des Moines, IA	925 SW Porter Ave. Des Moines, IA 50315-7267 Phone: (515) 285-6781 www.orchardplace.org
Vietnamese American Young Leaders Association of New Orleans (VAYLA-NO)	VAYLA-NO is dedicated to the empowerment of Vietnamese-American and underrepresented youths.	New Orleans, LA	4646 Michoud Blvd., Suite 2 New Orleans, LA 70129-1800 Phone: (504) 253-6000 Fax: (504) 754-7762 www.vayla-no.org
Family Strengthening Training Institute	The institute impacts children and families by providing skill development for those who are offering direct services.	Baltimore, MD	Phone: (410) 396-4274
Urban Leadership Institute (ULI)	ULI, based in Baltimore, focuses on leadership development by providing management, consultation, program development, research, and market analysis services.	Baltimore, MD	2437 Maryland Ave. Baltimore, MD 21218 Phone: (410) 467-1605 Fax: (410) 467-1607 Toll Free: (877) 339-4300 www.urbanyouth.org

ORGANIZATION	SERVICES PROVIDED TARGETING YOUTH	GEOGRAPHY/ SCOPE	CONTACT INFORMATION
Barr Foundation	The Barr Foundation is committed to enhancing the quality of life for all of Boston's residents.	Boston, MA	The Pilot House Lewis Wharf Boston, MA 02110 Phone: (617) 854-3500 Fax: (617) 854-3501 www.barrfoundation .org
Tumbleweed Runaway Program, Inc.	Tumbleweed's mission and goals are all directed toward the prevention of homelessness, running away, and delinquency.	Billings, MT	505 North 24th St. Billings, MT 59101 Phone: (406) 259-2558 Toll Free: (888) 816-4702 www.tumbleweed program.org
Renaissance Church of Newark— Community Center	The community center's goal is to return at-risk individuals and families to society with the skills and knowledge necessary to support a rewarding and productive lifestyle.	Newark, NJ	400 7th Ave. Newark, NJ 07107 Phone: (973) 481-3431 Fax: (973) 481-4142 www.rcdcc.org
Lighthouse Youth Services, Inc.	Lighthouse Youth Services is a multiservice agency providing social services to children, youths, and families in southeastern Ohio.	Ohio	401 East McMillan Cincinnati, OH 45206 Phone: (513) 221-3350 Fax: (513) 221-3665 Toll Free: (800) 474-4138 www.lys.org

ORGANIZATION	SERVICES PROVIDED TARGETING YOUTH	GEOGRAPHY/ SCOPE	CONTACT INFORMATION
Congreso de Latinos Unidos	Congreso offers a wide range of adult and youth services, including truancy intervention, workforce development, drug and alcohol counseling, housing counseling, health education, teen pregnancy prevention and intervention, maternal and child health programs, and HIV/AIDS services.	Philadelphia, PA	216 West Somerset St. Philadelphia, PA 19133 Phone: (215) 763-8870 www.congreso.net
Child & Family	Child & Family is a place where people come together to give help, to receive help, and to support the work of others.	Rhode Island	31 John Clarke Rd. Middletown, RI 02842 Phone: (401) 849-2300 Fax: (401) 841-8841 www.cfsnewport.org
Out Youth	Out Youth is an organization providing services to gay, lesbian, bisexual, and transgender youths ages twelve through nineteen in Austin and central Texas.	Austin, TX	909 East 49½ St. Austin, TX 78751 Phone: (512) 419-1233 Fax: (512) 419-1232 www.outyouth.org
River City Youth Foundation	The foundation's Leaders In Waiting program provides access to educational support and positive lifestyle examples, and its Successful Families program celebrates fathers, mothers, and role models.	Austin, TX	5209 South Pleasant Valley Rd. Austin, TX 78744 Phone: (512) 440-1111 Fax: (512) 220-6646 www.rivercityyouth.org

ORGANIZATION	SERVICES PROVIDED TARGETING YOUTH	GEOGRAPHY/ SCOPE	CONTACT INFORMATION
STARRY	STARRY's goal is to support children, youths, and parents in crisis through services that protect, educate, and promote strong families.	Round Rock, TX	1300 North Mays Round Rock, TX 78664 Emergency Shelter: (512) 246-4276 Counseling: (512) 388-8290 Foster Care: (512) 246-4229 S.A.F.E. Program: (512) 246-4301
Youth First Texas	Youth First Texas is committed to providing social services, education opportunities, and recreational activities to GLBTQ youths through age twenty-two.	Dallas, TX	3918 Harry Hines Blvd. Dallas, TX 75219 Phone: (214) 879-0400 www.youthfirsttexas .org

TUTORING

ORGANIZATION	SERVICES PROVIDED TARGETING YOUTH	GEOGRAPHY/ SCOPE	CONTACT INFORMATION
Bertie County Family Resource Center's Community Technology Hub (The Hive)	During school hours, the Hive operates as the Hive Academy, providing at-risk students a second chance and preparing them for the workforce by teaching them technical proficiency and life skills.	Lewiston and Windsor, NC	PO Box 598 Lewiston, NC 27849 Phone: (252) 348-2010
Everybody Wins! Vermont	Through Power Breakfast and Power Lunch programs, adult volunteers are paired with students at local elementary schools to promote reading for pleasure.	Vermont	25 School St. PO Box 34 Montpelier, VT 05601 Phone: (802) 229- BOOK (2665) Fax: (802) 229-1010 www.ewvt.org

Acknowledgments

This book is a culmination of support from friends, family, and mentors from all aspects of my life, and for all of them I am eternally thankful.

But, most important, my first acknowledgment goes to my God and Creator. To Him goes all the glory.

Micha Bar-Am once said, "If you're too close [to events], you lose perspective. It is not easy to be fair with the facts and keep your own convictions out of the picture. It is almost impossible to be both a participant in events and their observer, witness, interpreter." Therefore, I went into this process with a tremendous amount of humility and uncertainty—both about whether or not to take on the endeavor and how the final product would ring true to its intent.

There were countless people in my life who helped me make this decision and transition to the literary world. To Terrie Williams: before anyone else, you believed in my ability to develop a story that is transcending. You are an angel and a guide. To my book agent, Linda Loewenthal, thank you—you helped me shape this project from a reluctant idea to a proud reality. To Cindy Spiegel and Julie Grau, whose reputation in this industry truly precedes them, you took a big bet on an unproven entity and threw your overwhelming support behind it. Sally Marvin, Barbara Fillon, Karen Fink, Avideh Bashirrad,

Tom Perry, Debbie Aroff, Carol Schneider, and the entire Spiegel & Grau team, from editing to production to marketing—I could not have aligned myself with a better shop and a more committed and talented group of literary activists. Mya Spalter, you have helped guide this process from jump and I am sincerely grateful. And to my editor, Chris Jackson, you are part genius editor, part psychiatrist! I am thankful for your God-given skill, your diligent eye, and your belief in this project's purpose. To you all, thank you.

To my researchers, William Davis, Nikki Moore, Ginger Wilmot, Yetsa Tuakli-Wosornu, and Patricia Nelson, your diligence made this project more than simply a story—it added the context to the anecdotes. To my "ghostreaders," Ian Klaus, Randy Baron, Mustafa Riffat, Taiye Tuakli-Wosornu, and Shani Moore Weatherby, you never hesitated in reading and rereading my drafts and keeping me focused. Your fingerprints are all over this, and I am honored to have such talented friends and family. And to my "author friends," Craig Mullaney, Alex Kotlowitz, Jared Cohen, Nate Fick, Paul Rieckhoff, Steve Mariotti, Bill Rhoden, Khephra Burns, Susan Taylor, Reverend Dr. Suzan Johnson Cook, Hsu-Ming Teo, Angela Giltrap, and Mirta Ojito, thanks for the help and warm embrace into the club.

I am thankful for the transparency and honesty of Wes, his family, and his friends. Mary, Nicey, Woody, Coach, Alicia, and all the others, you gave me hours of your time and, most important, your trust. This project was not an easy one to navigate, but your openness helped ease the process. To the family of Bruce Prothero, your strength and the memory of Bruce sat with me every day, and always will.

There are a handful of people who, very early on, believed in this project and lent their voices and influence to make it happen: Juan Williams, Armstrong Williams, Dr. Ben Carson, Dr. Sampson Davis, Mayor Cory Booker, Geoffrey Canada, Stephen A. Smith, Judge Gerald Lee, Tavis Smiley, Reverend Dr. Brad Braxton, Dr. Freeman Hrabowski, the Honorable William Cohen and his wonderful wife, Janet Langhart Cohen, Ambassador James Joseph, and Dr. Na'im Akbar. Thank you for your early and stalwart support.

Very special thanks and a debt of gratitude go to my maternal and paternal family. You have been the roots that have allowed me to grow, and I know that without you there could be no me. There are countless people who grace this group, but to every Moore, Thomas, Flythe, Anglin, Avant, Banks, Blue, Boyd, Broadnax, Cannon, Carolina, Clarke, Coleman, Crawford, Drayton, Duncan, Dwyer, Hackett, Jarvis, Moyston, Simmons, Traylor, and Weatherby, thank you. Special acknowledgment goes to Mama Win, whose love and example are extraordinary and overwhelming. Have faith, not fear! My mother, words can hardly express what you mean to me; you are the epitome of love and compassion, and the kind of parent and friend I hope to be. You wore sweaters so we could wear coats. Dawn, my soul mate and battle buddy, years after marrying you I still get butterflies when I am around you! "Even when the skies are gray, you will rub me on my back and say, 'Baby it will be okay.'" To my sisters, Nikki and Shani, and Rita and brothers Jamaar and Earl, you have always kept me grounded and I am eternally grateful to be your brother. To Mama Gwen; Pandora Flythe; my aunts Pam, BB, Donna, Dawn, Evelyn, Toni, Tawana, Michelle, Valerie, Thea, Camille, Karen, Cheryl, Ellen, Iris, Carol, Connie, Cookie, Osie, Angie, Mira, Linda, Pam, Mary, Helen, Edna, Vicki, Gail, Alexis, Debbie, Thursa, and Lark; to my uncles Howard, Ralph, Ty, Gerald, Bernie, Bobby, Sonny, Cecil, Derek, Garrick, Harold, Donyell, Milton, Robert, David, and Kermit; to my cousins Denise, Phil, Marcus, Tenai, Elijah, Adrian, Aaron, Erroll, Lamar, La-Toshia, Ciara, Christian, Julisa, Tamara, Mimi, Michael, Paul, Ryan, Wayne, Carlton, Maurice, Taira, Nikki, Craig, Terrell, Guy, Phillip, Fred, Roland, Patty, Linette, Annette, Lisa, Karen, Blossom, Dorice, Ladrice, and Naquan—your gentle love and generosity helped fuel my journey. I have hundreds of family members, from Washington State to Washington, D.C., and in dozens of nations around the world, and I am thankful for all of you.

Papa Jim and Daddy, no acknowledgment list would be complete without you. Your soul, spirit, and love live on. I am who I am because you were who you were. I am also so thankful because I know, and can feel, even from your new perch, your love and guidance. I love you, I love you, I love you.

Along the way, there have been people who have touched my life in special ways and been so helpful through various phases of this process—Justin Brandon and Angela Miklavcic, John and Marcy McCall-MacBain, Tod Lending, Kathryn Shagas and Tony Machowski, Kris Coffey, Billo Harper, Karen Thomas, Linda Duggins, Dia Simms, Ericka Pittman, Toni Bias, Tanya Carr, Lois Vann, Denise Pines, Derick, Kendra, and Wynter Ausby, Nikki and Jeff Harris, Mike Fenzel, Tom and Stephanie Pellathy, Donald and Godly Davis, Jeshahnton Essex, Tommy and Christy Ransom, Lev Smirdov, David and Debbie Roberts, Howie Mandel, Lee Hendler, Chris, Jean, and Margaret Angell, Tom and Andi Bernstein, Loida Lewis, Don and Katrina Peebles, Ty Hill, RADM and "Mom" Hill, LTC Murnane, Barney and Carl Smith, Ken and Judy Ravitz, Nikki and Jeff Harris, Bill and Sue Floyd, Mike and Lisa Fenzel, Alonzo Fulgham, Darrell and Felice Friedman, Tracey Alexander, William and Wendy Brody, Jarvis and Stacey Stewart, Faye Charles, Doris Atkins, LaRian Finney, Robert Reffkin, Howard Buffett, Zach Druker, Coach Ogs and Spring, Dan and Avery Rosenthal, Adrian Talbot, Tahir and Priti Radhakrishnan, Jan and Larry Rivitz, Eddie and Sylvia Brown, the entire Lunn family, Sharon Lopez and Raisa Lopez-Rhoden, David Lasky, Tricia and Ken Eisner, Ralph Smith, Doug Nelson and the entire Annie E. Casey family, Julian Harris, Esther Tang, Vic Carter, Kai Jackson, Lawrence Penn, and Khalil Byrd. Thank you all for being there at every step of this book process.

To my Valley Forge and Army brethren, you are my role models and friends. I pray that this book illustrates, in some way, how much your example, love, patriotism, and professionalism have meant to me. Tim, Sean, and Josh, five-year family forever! And to the leadership of Phi Theta Kappa, I continue to be in awe of your commitment to scholarship and excellence.

Johns Hopkins will always hold a special place in my heart, not simply for the education I received, but for the friendships I treasure. To the graduating group of 2001, and to the board members I now share that title with, thank you. You are the model of commitment to and concern for our nation's future.

My Citi team could not have been more supportive of this book process as well as of my career development. Pam Flaherty, your support and belief in me brought me into Citi, and your support and that of so many others have kept me there. Ray McGuire, you inspire me to be a better financier and, more important, a better man. "Eagles do not fly in flocks." Special thanks to Liz Fogarty, who has been a third eye throughout this process. Your support has been invaluable.

Bobby and Dawn Wylie, not only did you make our transition at Oxford easy, but our friendship has lasted. My entire Rhodes class, Rochelle Aucheim and the Rhodes Trust, and the alumni of the Scholarship have been nothing but encouraging.

To Daniel Pellathy, Michael, Holley, and Noelle Thomas, Mark Vann II, and Earl Flythe IV, I could not be more proud of you. I will always be there for you.

And to other young people who will read this book, understand this: you have never been, and will never be, alone. We have all walked our own personal journeys—flawed and all—but our goal is the same: to ensure that we end up closer to a more beautiful and God-honoring destiny.

There are so many others I am indebted to who have also stood by me and loved me throughout this journey of life. I have the most extraordinary set of friends and mentors a person could ask for, so if I have not named you specifically, please know that I hold you in my heart and I hope and pray you understand just what you mean to me.

God bless you all and thank you. . . .

Elevate. . . .

Wes

The Other Wes Moore

Wes Moore

A Reader's Guide

A Conversation with Wes Moore

By Farai Chideya

New York-based journalist, author, and novelist Farai Chideya spoke by telephone with Wes Moore about his story, the other Wes Moore's story, and what we can all do to help bridge the opportunity gap that plagues our society. Their conversation was originally published in SMITH *Magazine on June 22, 2010.*

Farai Chideya: You talk about the South Bronx so beautifully in your book and how it has changed between the time your grandparents bought a house there in the fifties and when you moved there in the eighties. How did you first come to understand place?

Wes Moore: I think the first time I really understood place was actually when I first started to understand my need to be a part of one, and I felt myself having difficulty finding that. As I was in the Bronx and started getting older and going through that burgeoning process of manhood, and tried to get that understanding of what that felt like and what that was—and my mother was working multiple jobs to send me to the school across town—I increasingly found myself "too rich" for the kids in my neighborhood. I was one of the only kids in my class that didn't go to school in the area. But as I went across town for this other school, I found myself being "too poor" for the kids in my school because they didn't understand anything about my background or why I was one of the only kids in the school who had to travel an hour-plus to get to school. That's the first time I started to understand place and my role and my footing because I found myself searching for it—I found myself searching for that comfort, that support, that acceptance that seemed so elusive at every turn. I just found myself increasingly more uncomfortable everywhere I went.

FC: One of the moments in your book that had me cracking up was that, because your family was financially strapped, you actually sometimes wore your older sister's pants to school. You say that you thought you could pull it off, but in retrospect people were probably rolling their eyes. You have a lot of moments like that in your book, lightness and humor in a book that has a lot of tough moments, starting with the death of your father prematurely on.

WM: That definitely came through in the first draft. One thing I realized throughout this process very early was that if I was going to do any justice to this process, I needed to be transparent, I needed to be honest about it. As I was going on thinking about my life there were a lot of lighthearted, humorous moments and I wanted to make sure that my story highlighted that—and Wes's story also. This wasn't just some purely macabre story about how bad things are, but about reality and about the reality of all of our lives. And the fact is there were, even in the midst of chaos, a lot of lighthearted moments that not only are important to remember, but also helped you kinda get by, particularly as you think back in retrospect and you can look at them from a different place. There were things that really came out in the first draft and ended up making it to the final cut.

FC: Let's talk about the other Wes Moore. You have spent hundreds of hours with him at this point, but you didn't grow up with him. You write about his interior narrative very convincingly. Did you ever think you crossed the line and took too many liberties with how you constructed his life on paper? How did you hit the right tone?

WM: My talks with the other Wes Moore were free-ranging conversations where you'd be asking one question and the next thing you know it's an hour later and you've got all these amazing anecdotes, and these amazing facts, and these amazing stories that you're going to have to go back and make sense of and let them process once you've done your transcription. It wasn't about me coming up with a framework and having him fill in the colors in between the lines. It was more taking what he was giving me and then processing it, and I think a lot of that came from Wes. The format of the book wasn't something I came into the process with. It wasn't like I came in and said, "Okay, we're going to go over these couple of years: tell me about 1982, tell me about 1984." It really was about hearing these different stories, and that was when I started noticing a pattern and noticing a trend. Some of the years where Wes had some of the most influential and important factors in his life ironically took place in my life [as well]. It was really taking what he gave me and being able to process it from there.

FC: Do you think you ever overstepped the line in turning his life into prose?

WM: No, not at all. It's interesting because Wes was one of the people who really pushed me to write this book when I was first approached by author and publicist Terrie Williams. She knew that I had reached out to Wes and I had gotten to know him. She said, "I think this is something bigger, I think this could be a book." I was at first very reluctant, and told her, "I don't know, Terrie."

There were two things that pushed me over. One was that I thought about the tragic death of the police officer, and I thought if I could do something that would help keep these tragedies from happening again, I think it's necessary and could be useful. And then I thought about something that Wes told me. He told me, "I've wasted every opportunity in my life and I'm going to die in here, and if you can do something that can help people better understand the ramifications of their decisions and also understand the neighborhoods these decisions are being made in, then I think you should do it."

FC: My mother was a Baltimore City school teacher; the other Wes Moore is from Baltimore and you really paint a picture of his struggles as a smart kid in tough schools. When I read your book I thought of my mother. Some of the kids she taught sixth grade science to went on to get MDs and PhDs. Others were in the drug game and shot dead on the street. Their potential was wasted.

WM:　*Wasted* is really the best word to use. One of the things I want to show is: this is not a dumb guy. This book is not a celebration of the exception, this is a book that questions why we even have exceptions in our society in the first place. There's very little [that] separates us and someone else altogether. That's one of the things I wanted to show with Wes—had that intervention been there, had those supports been there, had there been a certain level of attention instead of a certain level of apathy about his final destiny, I can't help but think that things would be different.

FC:　You mentioned your book was originally supposed to be more prescriptive. What do you hope this book can do for readers, for kids, for society?

WM:　I wanted people to understand their potency and I wanted people to actually do something about it. In addition to the call to action, I wanted to add all of these organizations where people could get involved, and all of them are vetted organizations that would love to hear from you, either if you're looking for help or you're looking to help. That was genuinely important to me, because one thing the book helps to show is that if we're willing to get engaged, if we're willing to get involved, then we can really make a substantial and permanent impact, not just in the life of someone else, but in the life of our entire society.

FC:　How does being an author and the process of writing compare to being a paratrooper or a Rhodes Scholar or a White House Fellow—some of the other roles you've played?

WM:　I think some of the things I had done before really prepared me to be a writer in some ways. First of all, writing takes a real level of discipline. For example, with my schedule I would wake up at

5:15 A.M. and write for a couple of hours before getting ready to go to work, and then go work my day job for the rest of the day. There were some mornings I would literally sit in front of the computer for an hour with nothing to say, but I forced myself to go through this process because I knew that was the only time I could really efficiently get it out. When you wake up reading articles about a father of five, a police officer that went to work one day and will never come home, and then you read letters from someone who will spend the rest of their life in prison, it adds a certain level of humility to your day and a certain level of clarity in a certain context. Everything I did before helped me respect the discipline of writing.

FC: Your life has intersected in different ways with different types of African diasporic histories. Your family has roots in Jamaica and Cuba as well as the U.S. I'm wondering how you think of blackness in the twenty-first century, since we are so much more diverse in terms of immigrant groups influencing American blackness and we're also at a critical point in history.

WM: One thing that I have always been taught and believed in is understanding our past and our history and our roots. Not just for where you're going—understand where you come from. There's a certain pride in that. When you think about not just my family but the larger diasporic movements, and the evolutions and the successes and the victories that have taken place, it has really been pretty extraordinary. It's something that gives me a great sense of pride, it's something that gives me a really strong foundation in terms of where we can go, because I really do appreciate where we've come from.

FC: One of the pivotal moments in your book is when your family sends you to military school in order to get you off the streets of the South Bronx. You went on to train as a paratrooper and serve in Afghanistan. How can veterans get what they need from our nation?

WM: One of the partner nonprofits we have throughout the book tour is Iraq and Afghanistan Veterans of America, the first and largest organization that supports younger veterans, particularly from the Iraq and Afghanistan wars. We'll spend so much time giving soldiers, sailors, airmen, and marines support when they are overseas, and then when they come home it stops. Something that was really important to me—this is personal—I saw the challenges that so many families, including my own, had to deal with having someone deployed and not knowing who is coming home to you. If we are going to send people overseas to fight, then we need to support them [when they come home] as much as we did overseas.

FC: It seems like today, versus when I was growing up, there is more of a disconnect between the role[s] of servicemen and women and other citizens. Right now, maybe people are fatigued from the war, but it doesn't seem as if we are having a dialogue.

WM: We've been in Afghanistan for close to a decade, and you think about the amount of casualties we've had in Afghanistan and the casualties we've had in Iraq. But if you ask people what the biggest issue in the country is, I don't know where the fact that we have more than a hundred thousand troops serving fits in their consciousness. Less than 1 percent of the population has served. Less than 1 percent really knows from a firsthand experience what it's really like over there. In terms of what can be done, a lot of it will be up to not only the citizenry and population, but also up to the policy makers to make sure that this is a group on Americans' minds.

FC: And finally, Wes Moore, what's your Six-Word Memoir?

WM: Grandma said have faith not fear.

Questions for Discussion

1. The author says to the other Wes, "I guess it's hard sometimes to distinguish between second chances and last chances." What do you think he means? What is each Wes's "last chance"? Discuss the differences in how each one uses that chance and why they make the decisions they do.

2. During their youth, Wes and Wes spend most of their time in crime-ridden Baltimore and the Bronx. How important was that environment in shaping their stories and personalities?

3. Why do you think the incarcerated Wes continues to proclaim his innocence regarding his role in the crime for which he was convicted?

4. The book begins with Wes and Wes's discussion of their fathers. What role do you think fatherhood plays in the lives of these men? How do the absence of their fathers and the differences in the reasons for their absences affect them?

5. Wes dedicates the book to "the women who helped shape [his] journey to manhood." Discuss the way women are seen in Wes's community. What impact do they have on their sons?

6. The author says "the chilling truth is that [Wes's] story could have been mine. The tragedy is that my story could have been

his." To what extent do you think that's true? What, ultimately, prevented their stories from being interchangeable?

7. Throughout the book, the author sometimes expresses confusion at his own motivations. Why do you think he is so driven to understand the other Wes's life?

8. The author attributes Wes's eventual incarceration to shortsightedness, an inability to critically think about the future. Do you agree?

9. Wes states that people often live up to the expectations projected on them. Is that true? If someone you care for expects you to succeed—or fail—will you? Where does personal accountability come into play?

10. Discuss the relationship between education and poverty. In your discussion, consider the education levels of both Weses' mothers, how far each man got in his education, the opportunities they gained or lost as a result of their education, and their reasons for continuing or discontinuing their studies.

11. The book begins with a scene in which the author is reprimanded for hitting his sister. Why is it important for conflicts to be solved through means other than violence? In what way do the Weses differ in their approaches to physical confrontations, and why?

12. Why is the idea of "going straight" so unappealing to the incarcerated Wes and his peers? What does it mean for our culture to have such a large population living and working outside the boundaries of the law?

About the Author

WES MOORE is a Rhodes Scholar and a combat veteran of Afghanistan. As a White House Fellow, he worked as a special assistant to Secretary Condoleezza Rice at the State Department. He was a featured speaker at the 2008 Democratic National Convention, was named one of *Ebony* magazine's Top 30 Leaders Under 30 (2007), and, most recently, was dubbed one of the top young business leaders in New York by *Crain's New York Business*. He works in New York City.